The Curious Perspective

The Curious Perspective

Literary and Pictorial Wit
in the Seventeenth Century

ERNEST B. GILMAN

New Haven and London, Yale University Press, 1978

Designed by Sally Harris
and set in IBM Aldine Roman type.
Printed in the United States of America by
The Vail-Ballou Press, Inc., Binghamton, N.Y.

Published in Great Britian, Europe, Africa, and
Asia (except Japan) by Yale University Press,
Ltd., London. Distributed in Australia and
New Zealand by Book & Film Services, Artarmon,
N.S.W., Australia; and in Japan by Harper & Row,
Publishers, Tokyo Office.

Library of Congress Cataloging in Publication Data

Gilman, Ernest B., 1946–
    The curious perspective.

    Based on the author's thesis, Columbia University.
    Includes bibliographical references and index.
    1. English literature—Early modern, 1500–1700—History and criticism. 2.
Perspective. 3. Wit and humor—History and criticism. 4. Painting, Modern—
17th and 18th centuries. 5. Arts, Renaissance. I. Title.
PR438.P47G5   820'.9'004   78-6075
ISBN 0–300–02222–0

To my parents,
Jack and Dorothy Gilman
and to my wife,
Lois

Contents

Figures

Acknowledgments

It is a pleasure to record my gratitude to Edward W. Tayler and James V. Mirollo, who planted the seeds of fresh invention when this book first took root as a doctoral dissertation at Columbia University. They chiefly, but also other teachers and friends at Columbia, including Karl L. Selig, Robert Egan, and Martin Elsky, read earlier drafts and gave freely of their criticism and concern. I am grateful to Columbia for its steady intellectual and financial support, culminating in the Whiting Fellowship for 1974–75 that assured the time to write.

The labor of revision was eased in important ways by the insights of my students and by the generous help of my colleagues at the University of Virginia, especially Paul Barolsky, William Kerrigan, Arthur Kirsch, and Kenny Marotta. I wish to thank the University of Virginia for two Faculty Summer Grants, in 1975 and 1976, that made it possible for me to complete the present version. Patricia Richards, Vera Camden, and Judith White were invaluable in the preparation of the final manuscript.

I should like to express my appreciation to the considerate reference staffs at the Columbia University Libraries, the New York Public Library, and the Folger Shakespeare Library for making my spadework more efficient and productive; to the editors of the *Journal of General Education* and *Renaissance Drama* for their permission to include here revised versions of material that originally appeared in their pages; and to the museums and individuals who have granted me the right to reproduce photographs of works of art in their collections. Ellen Graham and Lynn Walterick of the Yale University Press expertly led this book and its author through the process of publication.

Finally, I have been fortunate at every stage of this project to enjoy the support of my family and friends. To more than the few I can list here I owe a debt of time and kindness easier to acknowledge than to repay: Lotte Prager, Brian and Susan Wong, Neil and Katherine Foran, Eleanor Prescott, and David Heim, to whom I owe a note of special thanks for drafting the drawings in this book. My wife, Lois Gilman, has given me the best perspective I could bring to this work: for love, all love of other sights controls.

Introduction: "I Have Been Studying How I Might Compare"

I intend to propose that displays of metaphysical wit in poetry are like displays of visual wit in what the seventeenth century called the "curious perspective," pictures or devices which manipulate the conventions of linear perspective to achieve ingenious effects. Poets recognized the kinship between verbal and visual wit and knew that their readers would also, for the seventeenth century marveled at optical ingenuity of all kinds—in anamorphic images, perspective boxes, mirrors and lenses, telescopes and prisms—and at the tricks of perspective possible in such diverse fields as landscape gardening and theatrical design. This fascination finds its way into verse not only through the importation of optical imagery but through a deeply-felt concern with the ways we look at the world. Unfortunately one century's fascination is another's footnote: we have grown nearly blind to a vital aspect of the European rage for wit, perhaps from the habit of too much close reading without the light of the visual arts. I believe that some understanding of wittiness in the sister arts will illuminate witty poetry, since both ask us to exercise a double vision that defeats and transcends single-minded comprehension.

But before suggesting any such "interdisciplinary" comparisons I must take up several preliminary issues to protect my argument, summarized in this way, from appearing overly blunt and suspiciously broad. First, none of the comparisons between artists and poets will depend upon, or argue for, an influence in either direction. My assumption will be that, within limits I hope to stake out, Europeans of the late Renaissance stood on a common imaginative and intellectual ground and shared ways of looking at the world which took shape in a variety of media. Second, I am not out to build a pigeon-hole labeled "metaphysical wit" or "conceit" in which all available seventeenth-century pigeons can be housed. These terms have little categorical meaning and often produce more heat than light in critical writing—especially when they begin to collide with other terms imported from the continent.

Certainly seventeenth-century English poets, to the extent that their work seems attuned to wider European concerns, create their own insular versions of the Mannerist and the Baroque. If Richard Crashaw's Teresian ecstacies are colored and perfumed with the spirit of the High Baroque, George Herbert's "Death" may illustrate the style of a less sensual Protestant Baroque, while Donne may appear exuberantly Baroque in one place (the second "Anniversarie"), tortuously Mannered in another ("Twickenham Garden"). These grand terms encourage an equally lofty strain of critical discourse which unfurls and salutes its own banners perhaps more reverently than it studies the features of a poem, or a painting. For the same reason I do not deal systematically with the paintings I discuss from an art historian's point of view. After isolating some elements from the visual tradition that I believe bear on witty poetry, I intend to focus on a few difficult texts that may be illuminated by comparison. These texts invite, and in fact expect, a reading against a pictorial background. The goal will be to show how language works in a given instance, not to juggle critical terms.

Third, the problems raised by a comparative method must be dealt with explicitly. Despite Simonides' pronouncement that "Painting is a dumme Poesie, and Poesie a speaking picture,"[1] we still cannot avoid asking: just how is a poem *like* a painting? Indeed the very possibility of a relationship suggested by the word *like* cannot be taken for granted. There may be, in the nature of things, an impassable chasm between the two objects that is treacherously camouflaged by *like*. The comparatist's dilemma is itself like King Richard's in the keep of Pomfret Castle:

> I have been studying how I might compare
> This prison where I live unto the world.
> And, for because the world is populous,
> And here is not a creature but myself,
> I cannot do it. Yet I'll hammer it out.[2]
>
> [5.5.1–5]

We are all imprisoned within the walls of our academic discipline, and though no one would deny that there are fundamental connections between literature and the other arts, no literary critic has produced a methodological key (or, at least, a key that can be duplicated successfully) to that populous world outside. It seems that we are stymied by the fear of an irreducible, essential difference between the two worlds that makes comparison meaningless—the difference between a word and a splotch of pigment.

In Lessing's classic statement of the problem, poetry exists in time, the visual arts in space, and there is no intersection between either the media or the subject matter of the sister arts:

> . . . if it is true that in its imitations painting uses completely different means or signs than does poetry, namely figures and colors in space rather than articulated sounds in time, and if these signs must indisputably bear a suitable relation to the thing signified, then signs existing in space can express only objects whose wholes or parts coexist, while signs that follow one another can express only objects whose wholes or parts are consecutive.
>
> Objects or parts of objects which exist in space are called bodies. Accordingly, bodies with their visible properties are the true subjects of painting.
>
> Objects or parts of objects which follow one another are called actions. Accordingly, actions are the true subjects of poetry.[3]

Despite its narrow stipulation of the "true subjects" of the arts, Lessing's argument has a core of common sense that refuses to crack. It makes us uneasy about the terms we normally, and loosely, use to conceal the differences between pictures and words. When, for example, we speak of the poet's "texture" or of the painter's "vocabulary" we have already fallen into the gulf against which G. Giovannini warns us:

> What is described as a common element in two art objects is likely to be an element actually given (i.e., perceptible to sense) in one object and objectively analyzable in it, and not given in the other but merely suggested in the affective response and applicable to the object only by way of metaphor.[4]

The search for such a "common element," a convincing link between the arts, has occupied the opening chapters of much recent comparative criticism. Jean Hagstrum believes he has forged such a link in what he calls "literary pictorialism," that is, in the study of images "capable of translation into painting or some other visual art," whose "leading details and their manner of presentation must be imaginable as a painting or sculpture."[5] But the precision such a statement leads us to expect grows fuzzy by the middle of the book when we are told, for example, that the "second and fourth stanzas" of Marvell's "The Gallery" give off an "obscure and brooding light that one finds in Rembrandt."[6] Nowhere does Hagstrum distinguish a poetic "image," itself a metaphorical term in a literary context, from an image proper on canvas.

Robert Petersson, in his book on Bernini and Crashaw, shares the belief of some artists that

> there exists an invisible center from which all the arts arise. Like Baudelaire, Wallace Stevens talks about "an unascertained and fundamental aesthetic," or order, of which poetry and painting are manifestations, but of which, for that matter, sculpture or music or

any other aesthetic realization would equally be a manifestation.[7]

He points out that comparative studies should be particularly helpful in the Renaissance and seventeenth century, which perceived and created connections among the arts in such forms as the painted ceiling, the opera, and the masque. Thus Crashaw's "poetry of music" and Bernini's feeling for the *bel composto* in sculpture are both part of a "unitive vision" that comparative criticism can reclaim.[8]

John Steadman develops the idea of a unitive vision more fully in his study "Iconography and Renaissance Drama." In the Renaissance the poetic tradition could not be rigidly separated from the pictorial tradition, and indeed they continued to borrow from each other as they had from antiquity. They shared the same mythological and ethical motifs collected in treatises like those of Horapollo and Conti, Cartari and Ripa, as well as, to varying degrees, the same esthetic principles: the end of both arts was to teach and delight, and if painters were urged to adopt such poetic concepts as imitation, the unities, and distinction in genre and levels of style, poets were advised to strive for *enargeia* or pictorial vividness. Steadman also notes—and this has special importance for an interdisciplinary study of wit—that both arts could make use of the same technical devices: "personification and allegory, enigma and metaphor—or forms of word play such as *notitia* and paranomasia. . . . As the seventeenth century progresses, painters and poets alike exploited the conceit as an instrument of maraviglia."[9]

Within the context Steadman suggests, the most provocative recent treatment of the comparative problem is Mario Praz's *Mnemosyne*. In his earlier book, *The Flaming Heart,*

Praz's interest in the emblem as a joint literary and pictorial form, and in the various aspects of the Baroque, frequently led him to graceful comparative gestures:

> Lines 54–104 and 112–26 of [Crashaw's] "Musicks Duell" may be said to create in verse an effect similar to that of many a baroque building, and to illustrate the fundamental baroque tendency to avoid a closed composition, to develop single parts irrespective of the ensemble, to emphasize the picturesque and the spectacular to the detriment of design and balance.[10]

In *Mnemosyne* Praz develops the comparative theory that underlies such observations: for him, the arts exist in a "family relationship" like that among the Indo-European languages.[11] All the artistic productions of a historical period exhibit the same characteristic *ductus,* or handwriting, which is susceptible to analysis. Wellek and Warren are wrong to think that differences in media are so critical that, in the extreme case, even when the same man writes and draws, the products will be radically different. Quite the contrary, Praz argues,

> there is a general likeness among all works of art of a period, which later imitations confirm by betraying heterogeneous elements; . . . there is either a latent or manifest unity in the productions of the same artist in whatever field he tries his hand.[12]

That "likeness"—as the term *ductus,* borrowed from calligraphy, suggests—is primarily stylistic, or, as Praz would have it, structural. The imaginative structures typical of an age (at least up to the nineteenth century) are most clearly expressed in its architecture because buildings are closest to people's lives, basic and widespread in a way that music and literature are not. Working within traditional architectural periodizations, Praz sees, for example, the Baroque *ductus* in the figure of the curve, with its suggestion of infinity or sublimity finding expression as well in Crashaw's "sweet inebriated ecstasy" and Dryden's description of Cleopatra as in the "magic of a baroque ceiling."[13]

Praz insists that these likenesses are not merely loose metaphors but the concrete form of beliefs and assumptions in which the arts of a period are rooted. Behind the Renaissance *ductus* of proportion, harmony, and symmetry, summarized in Leonardo's "l'uomo è misura del mondo,"

> there lies a trend of philosophic thought, the complex Pythagorean-Platonic theory . . . , whose chief manifestation was in architecture, though all the other arts, including literature, were permeated by it. Here is to be found the main structure, the ductus of the age.[14]

Such formulations contain an appeal to the *zeitgeist* to supply the metal for forging links among the media, if not the links themselves. A common cultural seedbed for the various arts, a ground for comparability, is indispensible to the whole notion of comparison. What the *zeitgeist* does not provide is a language for talking about links that will not do violence to the integrity of any one medium in the process of connecting it to others. Praz's characterization of the *ductus* of Mannerism as the "serpentine line" is useful insofar as it isolates that "tortuous, unstable pattern" common to the arts of that period.[15] But lest we get our critical lines crossed, we should be mindful that the "line" in an El Greco painting (that squiggle of color) and the "line" in a Donne poem only intersect at the point of metaphor.

Any account of a poem or a picture in discursive prose is at best an approximation, a re-creation in a foreign medium, though the critical vocabularies of the separate disciplines are sometimes capable of shaping the account into a tolerable fit with the original. I think we must admit that any links we construct in comparative ventures are even more tenuous. Like Praz's "serpentine line" they are all analogical, based on the unspoken proportion: as "blank" is to literature, so "blank" is to painting (or architecture, or whatever). We are limited to indirections. Yet an analogical relation is not in itself invalid or misleading unless we try to pass it off as an identity. The question is not which analogies are true according to some absolute, panartistic canon, but rather, of all possible analogies, which are the most fruitful for our understanding of the arts involved?

We have in the *zeitgeist* one proving ground for the relevance of analogies. If the different arts proceed from a single culture, the philosophical or religious or esthetic values of that culture will define large areas of comparability, as they do for Praz, and endow the particular elements of the comparison with meaning. I would like to propose an additional proving ground located where the two sides of the analogy meet again and the differences imposed by material media no longer matter: in the experience of the reader of literature or the viewer of a painting (let us call him the "witness" to a work of art). By experience I do not mean the kind of "affective response" Giovannini dismisses—that is, an emotional quivering in the presence of art, or a revery of free association from books to ballerinas or from paintings to childhood memories. The experience of a witness to a literary text (here including the viewer of a play) and to a painting are comparable in a way the objects themselves are not. Both experiences consist in two phases that might be called "reading" and "seeing'—a processional and an integrative, or reflective, phase which together generate understanding.

The witness reads a literary text from page to page over time. But his understanding is ideally not complete until he "sees" the work as a whole, as if spatialized in his mind as a simultaneous pattern of significance—what Northrop Frye, using the Aristotelian term, calls the *dianoia* of a work of literature.[16] This pattern may be thematic, formal, psychological, or a combination of these or other elements; it may take shape before he has finished the book, or perhaps not before he has read it many times; it will certainly grow richer and more clearly defined through rereading. People usually think that the experience of a book lies in the enjoyment of reading it, after which there is only discussion and opinion. When they take classes in literature they often move up to the view that the act of reading is a burdensome preparation for "getting the picture," for "seeing what the author is trying to say." In fact, both the reading and the "seeing" are necessary to the experience of literature. Although Aristotle is rightly concerned as much with the effect of drama on an audience as with the formal properties of a play, we in our more objective age are cautioned not to rely on the response of the reader; the "average" reader, we hear, is not to be trusted, while the "ideal" (Renaissance or other) reader is a flimsy critical fiction. Yet much is lost if we refuse on principle to consider the activity of reading, the process of our interacting with a book.[17]

The experience of a painting is in an important sense the same. The witness sees the painting as a pattern, but does not understand it fully until he "reads" it. The "reading" is not primarily the interpretation of iconic imagery, though that act is often part of the experience of Renaissance painting, but rather the more general process of moving from one detail to another over time—of perceiving the interrelationships of light, color, form, gesture, surface, space, point of view, and so on. The order of experience in painting (seeing first, then "reading") is superficially the reverse of the literary experience, except that the final painting which, having been seen and "read" is finally known, is no longer identical with the square of canvas we happened to notice when we first walked into the room. It is seen again, inwardly re-vised. Like the literary *dianoia,* this painting occupies a portion of our mental space and contains not only a visual memory of the canvas but an understanding of its significance. That understanding will be formed in part by each person's needs and desires, rechanneled through the convolutions of an individual consciousness that (as Norman Holland tells us) projects its own identity into a work of art and extracts from it its own psychic urgencies and comforts.[18] Yet if discussion is to proceed, our assumption must be that the main outlines of the work survive such distortions.

There are, as Kenneth Burke points out, distinctions between literature and the visual arts that influence the nature of our involvement. A painting, like a concert, is a "finished performance" requiring trained appreciation and "empathy." A book, like a musical score, contains only a "set of instructions" for performance and demands the more active collaboration of the reader, first to decode the orthographic signs on the page into their significations, and then to speak them (or imagine them spoken) with the proper sense and feeling. So also a play on the boards (whether well or poorly done) is the finished performance, a script the set of instructions.[19] We may object, along E. H. Gombrich, that our full participation in a painting is more strenuous than is suggested by a word like *empathy:*

> The very process of perception [in the visual arts] is based on the same rhythm . . . [as] representation: the rhythm of scheme and correction . . . a constant activity on our part in making guesses and modifying them in light of our experience.[20]

In any case the distinctions Burke makes refer to the ontological status of a work of art, to the conditions of its medium, rather than to our unmediated understanding of it. The experience that interests us lies in conception, not perception. It may be instructive to know whether a patch of color triggers different electro-chemical reactions than a written word, but the experience of art involves the conception of "significant form" in Susanne Langer's phrase, and only instrumentally the perception of sensory stimuli. The work of art, in whatever medium,

is designed to abstract and present forms for perception—forms of life, feeling, activity, suffering, self-hood—whereby we can conceive these realities, which otherwise we can but blindly undergo.[21]

From a conceptual point of view we could just as well eliminate the quotation marks from the phrases "seeing" a book and "reading" a painting, since both activities take place in a proper sense in the experience of the witness, where painting has a temporal dimension and literature a spatial one. Focusing in this way on the experience of the work of art has the virtue of taking us beyond, or around, Lessing's forbidding categories. By suggesting this model of the complementary modes in which we possess a work of art, I am proposing a marriage (or at least a temporary alliance) between two methods that have seemed to me unnecessarily antagonistic: on the one hand the various reader-response criticisms of Holland, Stanley Fish, and William Spanos, which notate our existential engagement with the movement of the work in time, and on the other, the more detached, patterned overview afforded us in Joseph Frank's conception of "spatial form."[22] Since to a greater or lesser extent we combine both activities in our experience of art, we should try to accommodate both in our practical criticism.

These observations may be sufficient to sketch out three areas of discourse that together form a workable comparative method: the study of cultural concerns that influence expression in the various artistic media; the construction of likely analogies (with proper regard for the limitations of the analogical relationship); and the testing of the fruitfulness of such analogies in the experience of the witness. If the analogy is work making, the sister arts should strike sparks whose light is only visible from an interdisciplinary point of view.

This is the procedure I would like to follow with the analogy suggested at the beginning between manipulations of perspective and poetic wit. A survey of art treatises and witty art from Alberti to the seventeenth century will show that linear perspective, which begins in the earlier Renaissance as an expression of confidence in the certainty of human knowledge, gradually comes to reflect a more complex and ambiguous relationship between the knower and the knowable. Perspective theory in the seventeenth century is analogous to contemporary theoretical state-ments (such as they are) on poetic wit—a connection which the Italian critic Tesauro makes explicit by sub-suming visual and verbal manifestations of *ingegno* under an "interdisciplinary" notion of metaphor.

After exploring these analogies I shall discuss a series of literary examples against the background of visual wit. Two chapters on Shakespeare—one on a history play, one on comedy—will take as their point of departure the tan-gled conceit on "perspectives" in act 2 of *Richard II,* a witty knot that our experience of Hans Holbein's *The Am-bassadors* will help us to untangle. The dramatist's gesture toward the curious perspective may be read as an implicit stage direction for the role a Shakespearean audience must play.

Two chapters on lyric poetry will follow. The first fo-cuses on a strain of "metaphysical" religious verse con-cerned (in matter and manner) with the difficulties of seeing, darkly, through Saint Paul's glass. Since mirrors in the seventeenth century were preeminently witty, associated both with anamorphic "perspectives" and with telescopic "perspective glasses," poets could find a model for Pauline vision in the curious perspective. The final chapter, on Andrew Marvell by way of Diego Velázquez, considers the problem of a quiet country estate suddenly transformed in the reader's experience into a witty visual spectacle.

I The Albertian Perspective and the Curious Perspective

The invention of a systematic linear perspective in the fifteenth century transformed not only the look of European painting but the very notion of what a painting is and does.[1] Previously the term *perspectiva,* or *prospectiva,* had been used to translate the Greek ὀπτική, the mathematical study of vision formulated by Euclid, preserved in Arabic texts, and revived for the Western Middle Ages in the writings of Roger Bacon, John Peckham, and others. Euclidean optics constructed a geometry of sight on the assumption that our field of vision takes the form of a pyramid or cone with its base in the thing seen and its apex in the eye. The concept of a "visual pyramid," diagrammed in cross-section as a triangle, made it possible to use the ordinary rules of plane geometry to calculate the relationships among distance, height, and the angle of vision. It was the genius of Alberti and his successors to apply the Euclidean *prospectiva*—which in itself has nothing to do with art—to the problems of graphic representation: they created the *prospectiva pingendi,* as Piero called it, or the *prospectiva artificialis* as opposed to the *prospectiva naturalis* of the Euclidean theory.*

Alberti's aim in the *Della pittura* is to devise a method for drawing a mathematically (and therefore, he thought, optically) correct representation of space in which the relative size of objects at different distances and the apparent convergence of parallel lines will be as convincing to the eye in art as they are in nature. Painters had been working toward this goal since the time of Giotto, whose advances in suggesting corporeality and depth were a challenge for others to struggle with the problems of three-dimensional space. In both Italy and the north there were such workshop procedures as the one, preserved in a fourteenth-century treatise, of painting buildings so that "the moulding of the base . . . runs upward from below, in the opposite way to the upper cornices which hang down."[2] Although these rules of thumb anticipated the *prospectiva artificialis,* Alberti regards them as makeshift conveniences which his new method will supersede.[3] This method soon came to be known as the *costruzione legittima.* We do not know how Alberti devised it, or whether he did so singlehandedly, but his account of it, reproduced and elaborated by later writers, remains the central document of Renaissance perspective theory.[4]

---

*The meaning of the English "perspective" expanded as well to accommodate the new connection between optics and the visual arts. By the seventeenth century it could refer to the theory of linear perspective; to a telescope (perspective glass) in particular, but also to a microscope or other refracting lens; to an expansive view in nature or to the representation of such a view in a painting that made conspicuous use of linear perspective; or to a perspective device such as those described below.

Although the *costruzione legittima* occupies only a few pages in a more general treatise, Alberti's modesty does not prevent him from enjoying "the glory of being the first to write of this most subtle art."[5] His other comments on painting and the role of the painter flow directly from his sense of the power of the new perspective. To share that sense, we will find it helpful to pause briefly over the details of Alberti's construction. The problem Alberti sets himself is to draw a checkerboard floor with the orthogonal lines in the pattern (those perpendicular to the plane of the picture) converging toward a "centric point," and the transversal lines (those parallel to the picture plane) receding into the distance at correctly diminishing intervals. This checkerboard is intended to serve as a standard for determining the apparent size and spatial relationships of objects in the painting, as well as to suggest the illusion of depth. Alberti first defines the painter's surface as an intersection of the visual pyramid between the observer's eye and the object to be depicted. This surface is to be imagined as a transparent plane, an "open window," through which the painter sees what he wishes to portray. As he works the artist should "seek to present the forms of things seen on this plane as if it were of transparent glass." The act of painting thus becomes a process of recording precisely the images projected (to put it anachronistically) from the rear onto the screen of the artist's canvas.[6]

The actual instructions for drawing the floor are cryptic and incomplete in Alberti's text—he himself hopes they are "not completely obscure"[7] —and have had to be recon-structured with some guesswork. Nevertheless they were clear enough to Alberti's contemporaries, who presumably had the benefit of additional explanation. The method can be illustrated in a few steps. After inscribing the "open window," the quadrangle in which the picture is to be painted, the artist decides on the height of a man who would stand at the front of the scene, in the picture plane itself. He divides this height into three equal parts, which would be "proportional to that measure called a braccio, for in measuring the average man it is seen that he is about three braccia." Then he marks off the baseline of his quadrangle into braccio-units (diagram 1a).

In the quadrangle he now plots a "centric point"—the vanishing point—"no higher from the baseline than the height of the man I have to paint there," and connects it with each of the braccio-marks on the baseline to construct the converging orthogonals of the checkerboard pattern (diagram 1b).

The next step determines the intervals between the other set of parallel lines that will complete the pattern. On a separate diagram the artist copies the baseline from the first; to this second baseline he draws a perpendicular (AB) at one end, and a parallel (CD) at the same height as the centric point was from the baseline in the original picture (diagram 1c).

Starting from A, the artist marks off a point (E) along AC at the (arbitrarily chosen) distance of the observer's eye from the painting. He then connects this distance point E with each of the braccio-marks on the baseline (diagram 1d).

The points at which these lines cross AB determine a se-

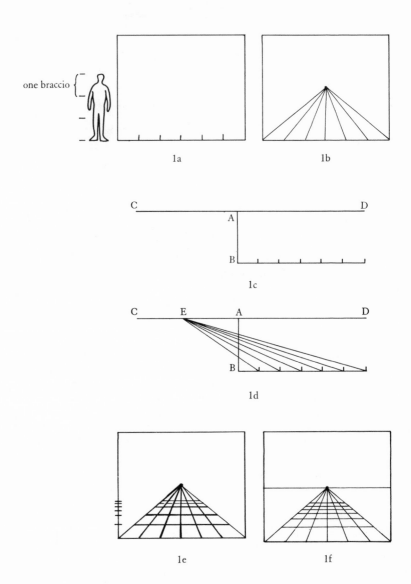

one braccio

1a

1b

C   D

A

B

1c

C   E   A   D

B

1d

1e

1f

Diagram 1

ries of diminishing values which, transferred to the original drawing, give the intervals between the transversal lines (diagram 1e).

To understand Alberti's procedure here, we must imagine the second drawing as a side view in which AB indicates the edge of the picture plane, now perpendicular to us. The points marked off on AB thus represent the points at which the visual rays cut the picture plane on their path between the squares "inside" the frame and the eyes "outside."

As a final help, the artist draws a "centric line"—a horizon—through the "centric point" and parallel to the baseline: "For me this line is a limit above which no visible quantity is allowed unless it is higher than the eye of the beholder"[8] (diagram 1f).

Alberti's construction defines a unified volume of space within the painting by giving a system of coordinates that govern the whole composition. Since the width of a checkerboard square anywhere in the painting is proportional to one braccio, the apparent height of a man standing on that square, namely three braccia, is automatically determined. All lines perpendicular to the picture plane converge in the centric point. The centric line provides an exact gauge of the eye level both of the painted figures on the checkerboard and of the observer. In this way Alberti's method forged a powerful tool for the rationalization of space. An important question, which was to occupy Leonardo in theory and other painters in practice, was whether it also produced an optically correct space. In fact it did not in all cases, but minor imperfections in the system hardly dampened the enthusiasm of Alberti and his followers. At the

end of the treatise Alberti seems confident that if he only
has a successor more studious than himself in the art of
perspective, painting can be made "absolute and perfect."[9]

One reason for Alberti's confidence is that perspective
had now elevated painting from a craft to a discipline with
its own *ratio*. The painter, no longer a shop worker, should
now be "as learned as possible in all the liberal arts, but
first of all . . . [in] geometry."[10] Indeed perspective appeared as the tenth liberal art on the tomb of Pope Sixtus
IV by Antonio Pollaiuolo (1484), qualifying along with
the seven classical arts, Philosophy, and Theology as a
theoretical pursuit. Perspective, like music and mathematics, was seen to be based on a satisfying system of
proportions—between the objects to be painted and their
images, between the braccio and every figure in the painting, and between the distance of the observer's eye and the
entire construction. It embodied and revealed the sub-
stratum of the harmonious order of nature, and put the
painter, no less than the philosopher, in touch with the
intelligible world.

At the center of this order is man. The proportions of
the human body provide the basic unit of perspective
measurement, and the painting is organized around the
viewpoint of the individual spectator. The popular Renaissance diagram, taken out of Vitruvius, of a man cirum-
scribed in a circle and a square—as it were the pattern for
the two most perfect geometric forms—is methodically
enacted in the making of a perspective picture (figure 1).
Alberti emphasizes the point:

> Since man is the thing best known to man, perhaps
> Protagoras, by saying that man is the mode and mea-

sure of all things, meant that all the accidents of things
are known through comparison to the accidents of
man. In what I say here, I am trying to make it understood that no matter how well small bodies are painted
in the picture they will appear large and small by comparison with whatever man is painted there. It seems to
me that the antique painter, Timantes, understood this
force of comparison, for in painting a small panel of a
gigantic sleeping Cyclops he put there several satyrs
who were measuring the giant's thumb; by comparison
with them the sleeper seemed immense.[11]

Man is the measure of painting: with the invention of perspective, as students of Burckhardt have argued,[12] the new
Renaissance notion of individualism found its artistic
counterpart.

The individual's point of view, together with the definition of a painting as an open window instead of an opaque
surface for decoration, distinguish the "illusionistic" art
of perspective from earlier "conceptual" styles. An Egyp-
tian figure represented with the face in profile and the
body in a frontal pose hardly creates the optical *illusion* of
a man, but presenting as it does all the human features in
their fullest detail, such a pictogram is perfectly adequate
to convey the *concept* of man. In the conceptual art of the
Middle Ages Christ may well be drawn twice the height of
a disciple as a symbol of his greater spiritual stature, with
no regard for the optical inconsistency. The conceptual
artist, in Gombrich's terms, "makes" formally independent
images whose only allegiance is to the interior conventions
of his art, whereas the illusionist artist "matches" his
forms to the appearances of the visual world.[13] A concep-

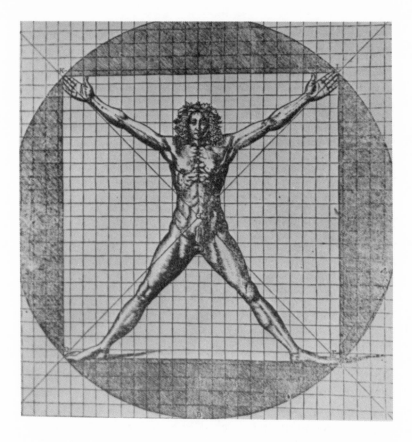

Figure 1. Man inscribed in a circle and square, from Cesare Cesariano's edition of Vitruvius (1521).

tual painting establishes no relationship with the actual space surrounding it except as a decorative addition to that reality. It makes no effort to disguise its material nature as a board, a section of wall, or a tessallated mosaic surface. A perspective painting, however, assumes a viewer at a definite position—and Alberti stresses the precision with which this relationship must be calculated: the plane of the picture intersects the visual pyramid "at a definite distance with definite lights and a definite position of centre in space and in a definite place in respect to the observer." A painted object "can never appear truthful where there is not a definite distance for seeing it." The viewer's position is specified, as we have seen, by the placement of the centric point and the distance point. Since the centric point locates the viewer's eye level as well as that of the figures on the checkerboard floor, "the beholder and the painted things he sees will appear to be on the same plane."[14] Thus the floor in effect extends through the open window and unites the world of the painting with our own in an unambiguous, geometrically exact fit.

Equipped with the perspective method, the artist can aspire to the goal of creating an illusion that may be taken (or mistaken) for reality. The Renaissance never tired of repeating Pliny's anecdote about the competition between Zeuxis and Parhassius: Zeuxis's painted grapes fooled the birds, but Parhassius was proclaimed the better artist because his painted curtain fooled Zeuxis himself. Alberti adds the fanciful claim that Narcissus must have been the inventor of painting, "for what else can you call painting but a similar embracing with art of what is presented on the surface of the water in the fountain?" Behind this

goal lies the assumption that the world *can* be comprehended by a rational method. Alberti recommends that
the artist look at his subject through a "velo"—a net or
grid—as an aid to composition.[15] This device, often illustrated in later treatises (figure 2), imposes a rule on nature
and brings it under the artist's control. In the seventeenth
century Donne would use the lattice as a metaphor of the
"fallacies" of human understanding: in heaven, he assures
us, "Thous shalt not peepe through lattices of eyes."[16]
But what Donne sees as an impediment to true knowledge,
the earlier Renaissance regards as evidence of the power of
the artist's *ratio* to frame the world in rectangles. The
spectator has an equally privileged position from his own
firm point of view. He is the ideal observer of a scene organized for his sake, tailored to his measure, and fully revealed to his gaze.

Whatever the subject matter of a perspective painting,
the viewer sees an infinite and homogeneous volume of
space successfully recreated on a two-dimensional surface.
As the idea of space becomes more prominent for the
Renaissance—whether in the philosophy of Cusanus,
the expanded vistas opened by explorers, or the specula-
tions of astronomers—perspective contributes a method
for representing it concretely. Indeed, in his studies of
Renaissance logic, Walter Ong emphasizes the "role which
spatially oriented conceptualizations begin to play in
the notion of knowledge itself."[17] The growth of print
culture increasingly embodies knowledge in visual rather
than oral forms. The force of the new topical logics of
Peter Ramus and Rudolph Agricola lay in their claim to
be able to tabulate, that is, spatialize or picture, the

Figure 2. The "velo" as an aid to perspective composition. From Hieronymus Rödler, *Eyn schön nützlich büchlein und underweisung der Kunst des Messens mit dem Zirckel, Richtscheidt oder Lineal* (1531).

elusive processes of human thought. The table of places at the beginning of a Ramist logic is designed to let the reader comprehend the subject at a glance, like the Ramist "synopses" of melancholy included in Burton's *Anatomy*. Burton's and the countless other Renaissance "anatomies" imply by their titles the opening up of a subject for the inspection of the reader. The science of anatomy itself, which lends its name to this visual concept of knowledge, could not have progressed without accurate perspective drawings.

Perspective puts space more firmly into the grasp of the imagination, makes it manipulable to the hand and eye and therefore more readily available as a category of thought. Renaissance historiography, for example, depends on a spatialization of past time foreign to the medieval chronicler (who reports what he hears): in the new scheme humanist scholarship had erected a special vantage point from which men could see back beyond the dark ages to a luminous ancient world. There is, as Panofsky has argued, an

> inward correspondence between perspective and what may be called the general mental attitude of the Renaissance: the process of projecting an object on a plane in such a way that the resulting image is determined by the distance and location of a "point of view" symbolized, as it were, the *Weltanschauung* of a period which had inserted a historical distance—quite comparable to the perspective one—between itself and the classical past.[18]

A perspective structure can be seen as well in Renaissance city planning, a field Alberti helped inaugurate. In the symmetrical star-shaped *città ideale* of Italian theory, space is organized by roads converging from the outer walls toward a central building. This building stands, like the viewer of a perspective painting, at the most advantageous vantage point, focusing and controlling the surrounding space.[19]

I have surveyed some major connections between perspective and other Renaissance concerns to suggest how much more than a graphic convenience Alberti's construction was. It is not surprising that perspective should have become a cognitive metaphor, its elements providing a set of terms for the act of thought itself—an observer, an object of perception, a point of view, a focal point, a horizon. Although the analogy between seeing and knowing is as old as Plato's *Republic,* and has been a vital mode of thought in both the Greek and the Christian traditions, linear perspective revitalized the analogy by making it more detailed and concrete. In the fifteenth and early sixteenth centuries, as I have tried to suggest, perspective arises out of and gives expression to a sense of certainty about man's place in the world and his ability to understand that world. This, indeed, has been the dominant meaning of the perspective metaphor—so that, in common usage, to see a thing "in perspective" is to see it from the proper vantage point, at a sufficient distance to make it fully manifest or properly set in its context, to see it clearly, unambiguously, in short, truly. However, the perspective conventions can themselves be regarded from another, less confident, point of view which came to fascinate the theorists of the later sixteenth and earlier seventeenth centuries who transmitted and perfected the teachings of the earlier masters.

Despite its geometrical elegance, the perspective scheme had serious limitations which qualified the claim, behind every line of Alberti's enthusiastic presentation, that here was a method capable of producing a perfect illusion of optical reality. For a perspective illusion to seem real, the viewer had to be deprived of any reference point outside the painting. The painting had to be seen not just from a predetermined point of view, but from one which was rigidly fixed—often, in the treatises, by placing an eye-hole at the proper location—and further, seen with one eye only. Though the theory allowed the spectator's point of view to be designated arbitrarily, in practice the artist could not make it too near or too far from the plane of the painting without producing an unnatural appearance. Alberti had to assume that the apparent height of an object in the painting is proportional to the distance from which it is viewed. This assumption was a revision of classical—that is, Euclidean—optics, which taught that height is proportional to the size of the angle through which an object is seen (the angle formed by the two visual rays, meeting in the eye, which touch the extremities of the object). Since visual images are actually projected on the curved surface of the retina rather than on a flat plane, the classical principle is more accurate. We know from Leonardo's notebooks that he was interested in this contradiction between perspective and visual appearance, and in the possibility of a truer perspective based on the ancient spherical optics.[20] Where the field of vision in a painting was relatively wide, a strict adherence to the Albertian scheme produced marginal distortions that painters quickly learned to camouflage or avoid by fudging the rules.

These technical misalignments between the perspective construction and the optical reality only point to other more subversive and paradoxical issues that Alberti does not pursue. If the spectator's position is the ideal vantage point for comprehending the world of the picture, it is at the same time only one of an infinite number of other points of view. The ideal spectator pays the price of absolute immobility; should he shift his place (or even look through *both* eyes) the world so carefully constructed for his benefit goes awry. A perspective painting conjures up a three-dimensional space in which every front has a back and a side, every figure and every scene generate an unlimited number of aspects—and yet it imprisons the spectator in a single point offering only a single view. The very fullness and definition of perspective space implies the radical incompleteness of our vision, and the point of view becomes a drastic limitation, a set of blinders, as well as an epistemological privilege.

The spectator's secure vantage point is undermined in another way, even as it seems to be firmly established. The more perfect the representation of reality achieved in a perspective picture, the more perfect is the deception practiced on the viewer. Alberti's window opens onto an *illusion* of *reality;* these two irreconcilable categories are joined in the perspective painting, which thus takes on an intriguing and complex dimension not found in conceptual art. Plato's critique of illusionism in Greek art (*Republic* 10) has a special force here: a work of art that claims to be in direct touch with the real world is nothing but an imitation at three removes, and for Plato a dangerously deceptive imitation if the viewer does not realize he is being taken in. And Socrates adds a comment, related to the question of point of view as much as to illusion, the effect of which is to challenge the ambitious claims of perspective:

> *Socrates:* If you look at a bed, or anything else, sideways or endways or from some other angle, does it make any difference to the bed? Isn't it merely that it looks different?
>
> *Glaucon:* Yes, it's the same bed, but it looks different.
>
> *Socrates:* Then consider—does the painter try to represent the bed or other object as it is, or as it appears? Does he represent it as it is, or as it looks?
>
> *Glaucon:* As it looks.
>
> *Socrates:* The artist's representation is therefore a long way removed from truth, and he is able to reproduce everything because he never penetrates beneath the superficial appearance of anything.[21]

Representing the bed "sideways" or "endways" is for Plato not merely an incomplete reproduction, a facet of the truth, but a falsification. In a perspective rendering, the "superficial appearance" is accomplished by foreshortenings and converging parallel lines that misrepresent the real form of the object.

Writers who recommend the perspective system, like Filarete, feel the need to protect it against the Platonic attack, but the awkwardness of their defense only call attention to the problem:

> You can say that it [perspective] is false, for it shows you a thing that is not. This is true; nevertheless it is true in drawing, for drawing itself is not true but a

demonstration of the thing you [are] drawing or wish
to show. Therefore it is true and perfect for this, and
without it the art of painting or sculpture cannot be
done well.[22]

In the seventeenth century, Descartes can dispose of the
question more simply because for him our ordinary accep-
tance of perspective drawing is proof of the deceitfulness
of the senses:

> According to the rules of perspective, [engravings]
> often represent circles by ovals rather than by other
> circles, and squares by diamonds rather than by other
> squares. Thus very often, in order to be more perfect
> *qua* images and to represent the object better, it is
> necessary for the engravings *not* to resemble it.[23]

Alberti's unexamined assumption that "the painter is
solely concerned with representing what can be seen"
bestows a double role on the painter as truth-teller and
liar, and on the viewer as either ideal perceiver or dupe; if
painting is an "embracing with art of what is presented on
the surface of the water," what perils for Narcissus lie in
that embrace?[24]

Treatises of the later sixteenth and early seventeenth
centuries show a growing fascination with these paradoxical implications of perspective theory even as they put the
Albertian method on a more sophisticated mathematical
basis. The earlier theory had submerged the illusory aspect
of the image beneath the claim of rationally accurate
representation. Later writers, while never abandoning the
goal of realism and geometric precision, begin to explore
how the rules of perspective can magnify or diminish, mul-

tiply or distort the image. They emphasize the illusion by playing with it and make our awareness of it part of our experience of the work of art. In the process, both the nature of the world depicted and of the viewer's relationship to it undergo a change. Alberti's world is fully manifest and comprehensible; the world implied in the writings of later perspectivists is shifting, multifaceted, and ambiguous. It has a mystery at its heart that is not open to rational comprehension, a complexity that can only be apprehended—touched and wondered at but not grasped.

After Alberti and Piero, perspective theory spread throughout Europe on the wings of dozens of treatises written mostly in Italy, France, and the low countries, but frequently translated and widely circulated. People studied it with enthusiasm, not only because it opened up an intriguing new branch of mathematics, but because it was immediately applicable to a range of practical needs outside the painter's studio. Here were, as the title of one seventeenth-century German handbook announced, "New geometrical and perspective inventions, various remarkable instruments useful for the perspective plans of drawings and fortresses as well as for the planimetric principles of cities, camps and landscapes."[25]

The architect Jacomo da Vignola, who taught mathematics and perspective in the middle years of the sixteenth century, is one of the important systematizers and purveyors of perspective theory. The substance of his teaching, published after his death and reprinted many times, appears in *Le due regole della prospettiva pratica* (Rome, 1583). The "two rules" of the title refer to the slightly different technical constructions of Alberti and

Piero della Francesca, which are explained and reconciled. Like most of the treatises that would follow it, Vignola's emphasizes the practical nature of the subject by including drawings of various perspective schemes for the draftsman to study. Among these, however, are illustrations for two kinds of perspective puzzle.[26] In the first a picture is cut into an array of strips, each of which is fastened to one face of a wooden triangular prism. When the prisms are lined up, the gaps between the faces make it impossible for the spectator to decipher the picture when he looks at it directly. Yet when he shifts his glance he sees the whole picture reflected, as if by magic, in a mirror attached to the display at the proper angle (diagram 2).

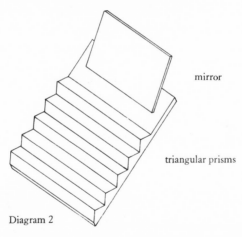

mirror

triangular prisms

Diagram 2

In a variation of this device, the artist could draw different pictures on each side of the corrugated surface, producing two images that changed one into the other as the viewer turned the instrument. Shakespeare's Cleopatra recalls such a device, or another with the same effect, a reversible portrait (figures 8, 9), as the appropriate emblem for her own emotional reversals at the news of Antony's marriage:

> Let him forever go!—let him not!—Charmian,
> Though he be painted one way like a Gorgon,
> The other way's a Mars.
>
> [*Antony and Cleopatra,* 2.5.115-17]

Similarly Chapman alludes to a "couzening picture, which one way/Shows like a crow, another like a swan" (*All Fools,* 1.1.47).[27]

The second puzzle is an anamorphosis, an image whose perspective is systematically distorted or skewed. This one is simple to construct: the grid which Alberti had recommended as an aid to drawing is placed over the image to be reproduced, but the squares, instead of serving as a guide for faithful reproduction, are now elongated. When the segments of the picture are drawn proportionally into the deformed squares, the whole image stretches itself out into an unrecognizable pattern of swirling lines. Only when the panel is seen from an unexpected point of view—from the side in a line of sight almost parallel to the picture plane—does the image appear undistorted (diagram 3).

Diagram 3

Vignola recommends that this construction be displayed in a deep box frame with a peephole at the correct point of view (diagram 4)—a "perspective box" like the one in Ben Jonson's *Every Man out of His Humour:* "I brought a dozen, or twentie gallants this morning to view 'hem (as you'ld do a piece of *Perspective*) in at a Key-hole" (4.3. 91-93).[28]

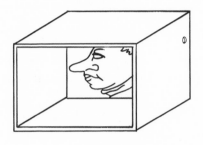

Diagram 4

Both of these figures present a warped, confused appearance precisely from the point of view at which the conventions of perspective lead the observer to expect clarity. He has to shift his point of view, to take up an unconventional stance, in order to make sense of the image before him. Here we have a kind of visual pun that demands to be seen in two ways; its effect lies in the viewer's dislocation and then his surprise as the confusion resolves itself. Such displays—trivial as they may seem next to the visual wizardry that we scarcely notice in our electronic environment— were much admired as feats of wit, no less marvelous than the sight of an insect magnified in a microscope, or of the moon brought up close in a "perspective glass." They are startling, too, because they use the rules of perspective, rigorously applied, to parody, almost to subvert, the purposes perspective is supposed to serve. An anamorphic picture questions the fit between appearance and reality that is quietly assumed in a proper perspective picture. Its appearance is carefully constructed to deceive, to conceal the optical truth and produce an experience of doubt and readjustment before it reveals itself.

Vignola's anamorphic figure, or other more technically sophisticated versions of it, appear in Daniello Barbaro's *Pratica della perspettiva* (Venice, 1559, 1568), in Samuel Marolois's *La perspective* (1614, published in Paris 1629), and in various Dutch and German handbooks.[29] The anamorphic figure also appears in Giovanni Paolo Lomazzo's *Trattato dell'arte de la pittura* (Milan, 1584), which was translated in part by Richard Haydocke as *A Tracte Containing the Artes of Curious Paintings, Caruing, and Building* (Oxford, 1598).[30] Lomazzo's account of the canon of proportion in his first book could well have been appended to Alberti's treatise of the previous century: God "taught Noah to builde the Arke" in

> the proportions of mans body: according to the similitude whereof, God . . . in his excellent wisdom framed the world, heaping all the perfections thereof in farre greater aboundance upon man, in such sorte, that one is called the greater world and the other the lesser.[31]

But in Lomazzo's fifth book, on perspective, the proportional similarity between the divine Artificer and man, man and his own artifacts, gives way to a new emphasis on the distortions of perspective, in which the skill "consisteth in shewing False and deceitfull sights insteede of the true."[33] He is interested in pictures drawn on irregular or curved surfaces such as barrel vaults, which appear optically correct from the special point of view from which they must be seen, but from elsewhere grotesquely distorted. In the context of such examples, the anamorphic picture—which switches the right and wrong points of view—becomes a witty extension, a teasing out, of the possibilities inherent in perspective.

This shift in emphasis can be seen in a treatise written forty years later by Pietro Accolti which takes *Lo inganno de gl'occhi* (Florence, 1625) as its title and major theme. Accolti prefaces his technical instructions for making an anamorphic image with a long passage on the "dilettosa operatione de Prospettiva" by which we are "maravigliosamente ingannati":

> From the above [anamorphic picture], it seems that we are constructing a strange and delightful perspective operation by which we are marvelously enchanted, because if this operation is presented to us in a drawing or painting, we are unable to guess what the painter meant to represent by his lines and colors, unless we solve the enigma with the help of a mirror placed so we can direct our gaze at it (because the mirror shows something other than what we see with our eye directly). We immediately recognize with astonishment that the picture is usually a portrait of people who are known and very dear to us—such is the strength, value, and power of perspective, in which everything entirely depends on appearances. Thus we must say, and believe, that drawing and painting have their codes and decoders ["cifra, & contracifra"] which can keep them hidden even from Argus. . . .[33]

Accolti has seen anamorphic drawings used as pictorial secret codes to transmit portraits or ground plans which would literally be indecipherable if they should fall into the wrong hands. The rules of perspective are applied to distort and conceal the image, to turn it into an "enigma" which must be "solved" (in this case by placing a mirror at the side to reflect the undistorted image the viewer would see if he stood at that point of view). If we think of this device as merely an amusing trick, we will be surprised by the fervor of Accolti's language. For him the anamorphosis partakes of the marvelous: such is its strength and power that the viewer, having been wondrously deceived by an appearance, is suddenly astonished to recognize a familiar face or scene in the mirror. This enigmatic appearance—a shapeless swirl which is nonetheless constructed with the nicest geometrical precision—is no longer Alberti's open window but a riddling, opaque surface, which in a flash reveals the truth hidden in it.

The most extravagant treatment of deceptive perspectives occurs in two French treatises of a slightly later date, the *Perspective curieuse* of Jean François Niceron (Paris, 1638) and the *Perspective pratique* of Jean Dubreuil (three volumes, Paris, 1640, 1647, 1649).[34] For Niceron perspective is a form of "magie artificielle" capable of producing "des effets merveilleux" no less amazing than the fabled sphere of Possidonius, which duplicated the movements of the planets, the flying wooden dove of Architas, or the speaking bronze head made for Albert the Great. Like these "automates" perspective is a "récréation de savants" but also a re*creation* of the natural world by "les plus admirables effets de l'industrie des hommes"—a case of art not simply imitating but rivaling nature.[35] But what the artificer creates is no longer an embodiment of the universal harmonies underlying all things; he is no longer a Noah building the ark according to the proportions of the human body. Instead, in these seventeenth-century treatises, he is a showman whose spectacular displays strike sparks of wonder and mystery, intriguing concealments and sudden revelations.

Both Niceron and Dubreuil divide their work into three general areas: anamorphoses, catoptrics, and dioptrics. In the first categroy Niceron suggests a complex variation on the anamorphic figure: several distorted drawings, organized from different points of view, are superimposed on a panel which already contains a straightforward image—resulting in a kaleidoscope of images which,

> according to the diversity of their appearance, represent two or three wholly different things, such that being seen from the front, they represent a human face; from the right side a death's head, and from the left something different.[36]

Niceron himself executed a large anamorphic painting of Saint John visible only from a special angle, hidden inside what was seen from the front as a landscape—an "excellent Perspective" which John Evelyn admired during his visit to Rome in 1645. Concealing a human figure in a landscape—a conceit also practiced in gardening (figure 3)—was considered no less witty than concealing a landscape or a still life in a human figure, as in Arcimboldesque painting: this is Crashaw's "wit of love! that thus could place / Fountain & Garden in one face."[37]

Figure 3. Athanasius Kircher, *Campus Anthropomorphus* (1646), anamorphic landscape in the Roman garden of Cardinal Montaldi (c. 1590). From *Avs Magna Lucis et Umbrae in Decem Libros Digesta* (Rome, 1646).

Both Niceron and Dubreuil illustrate ways an image "projected"* onto a pyramid, cone, or irregular solid can appear normal "provided that it be seen through a small aperture, or a fixed point."[38] Dubreuil's imagination extends to large-scale projects suitable for gardens, church oratories, and great houses—displays joining stationary painted panels with the *machina versatilis* of Renaissance stagecraft, a triangular form that can be rotated to display a different scene on each of its faces:

> For example, if for the first fixed frame, one makes the Perspective of a grand arcade which may appear in relief, and may extend four or five feet in appearance, and through this arcade, one sees a Perspective of beautiful buildings, painted on three or four triangles: These two Perspectives, detached one from the other, at whatever distance one wishes, will make a Palace, or several magnificent dwellings, appear. But if one takes the time necessary to pull a curtain behind this first frame, while one turns the triangles, one will no longer see these buildings through the arcade, but a landscape spring to view, or a beautiful pleasure garden with fountains or jets of water, walks, wooden fences, and so on.[39]

Dubreuil also provides instructions for painting a *trompe l'oeil* perspective view that will seem to extend the space around it, such as a panel cunningly placed at the end of one's garden to create the illusion of another garden stretching off into the distance.

*Projected: crudely, but accurately, using a candle to shine light through a pinholed pattern and onto the object; see Dubreuil, 3:123.

The sections in these treatises on catoptrics and dioptrics add further elements of ingenuity to the simpler anamorphic constructions through the use of mirrors and refracting lenses. Catoptrics, in Niceron's summary, teaches "the manner of constructing figures which cohere and represent by reflection something completely different from what they appear to be when viewed directly."[40] Here, as in Vignola and Accolti, a mirror is placed at the proper point of view for resolving the anamorphic image which it reflects. The effects of such devices—"admirables" and "prodigieux" as they are—can be further heightened by making the image decipherable only in a concave or convex, cylindrical or conic mirror (figure 4), a technique that enables the artist, as Robert Burton says, "To do strange miracles by glasses . . .[and] perspectives . . . to represent bodies, by cylinders and concaves." In this device the straightforward image is completely unrecognizable since it must be more strangely distorted than a planar anamorphic projection; as Dubreuil put it: "These pieces are extremely entertaining in that, from a mélange of colors which seem to be thrown onto the flat surface without any order, one sees a beautiful image in the Cylinder."[41]

In their arrangement in a room these images can be placed above or below the mirrors, on the walls or ceilings—or even hidden from sight so that a reflection seems to spring up onto the mirror from nowhere. Typically, Dubreuil's imagination spins out even more fanciful constructions on a larger scale: one can set mirrors all over a room, so the reflections from a single panel (or from several panels mounted on turning prisms) will bounce off

Figure 4. Jean Dubreuil, *Cabinet des anamorphoses catoptriques*, detail. From *La perspective pratique* (Paris, 1649).

each other, "such that, for five or six small figures, one sees an army; for two or three trees, a great forest; for two or three houses, entire towns."[42]

Dubreuil proposes another mirror construction similar in its effect to the regular image that conceals an anamorphosis within it: one can "paint on a flat surface, an image separated into diverse pieces, which being viewed in a prismatic mirror, or a mirror with several faces, will appear similar to its prototype."[43] If in the mirrored room of the previous example an image is multiplied, here an apparently fragmented image is unified in the prismatic mirror. And by skillfully painting another unrelated picture in and around the patches reflected in the prism, the artist can make them unrecognizable—and thereby heighten the viewer's surprise at the hidden image that the mirror is able to discover. The same idea can be given an even more marvelous form with the help of the refracting lens—the technological advance which made possible those "deux rares inventions," the telescope and the microscope, which in themselves provided a source of boundless fascination for the seventeenth century. Lenses revealed the irregularities on the surface of the moon to Galileo and to Robert Hooke the cellular structure of plant tissue. This made possible much of the philosophical and literary speculation to which the new science gave rise: neither the Pascalian vastnesses of space nor the interplanetary progress of Elizabeth Drury's soul would be imaginable without the refracting lens to open up new worlds to human perception.

Yet as the prospect of an infinite universe could be terrifying to one man but exhilarating to another, so the mechanical extension of sight could be regarded in two ways. It represents an "advancement," in Bacon's sense, of man's dominion over nature—as it is in Salomon's House, where Bacon has his investigators carry out experiments in telescopy and microscopy "to see small and minute bodies perfectly and distinctly, as the shapes and colours of small flies and worms, grains and flaws in gems, which cannot otherwise be seen." But the same lenses are studied for an understanding of the "delusions and deceits of the sight" which enables the investigators to reproduce "artificial rain-bows, halos, and circles about light. . . . all manner of reflexions, refractions, and multiplications of visual beams of objects."[44] It is important for Bacon to know how appearances can be manipulated and our perception tricked; lenses can exploit the weakness of our senses for which the Baconian method in general is designed to compensate. The view through the lens convinces us that what our unaided eye had taken for real was an imperfect appearance only, but that new reality is no more certain than the view it replaced: it is an evanescent appearance, a manipulation which can itself be changed by a shift in point of view, an adjustment in the angle of refraction.

Both Niceron and Dubreuil crown their treatises with a device that plays with these ambiguities of the lens. An eyepiece is fixed at a certain distance from a panel. At the end of the eyepiece is a lens, flat on the side near the eye and convex on the other, with the convex side cut into facets like a diamond. Light projected through the lens onto the panel will be broken up into separate areas corresponding to the facets, and these areas can be outlined with a pencil. Then the artist, looking through the lens himself, can draw a figure part by part in the fragmented areas of the panel. This figure will appear whole when viewed through the lens, but will be unrecognizable on the painted surface—the more so if the artist incorporates these fragmentary images into other pictures drawn around them. By shifting the eyepiece slightly, the artists can even hide another broken picture in the same panel. Thus, "on the flat surface of a painting where several figures or portraits are drawn in their just proportions, one can make visible another portrait, different from all those in the painting, similar to some given object or portrait"[45] (diagram 5).

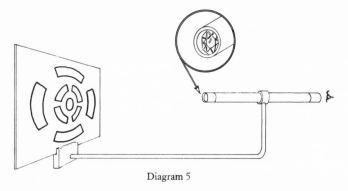

Diagram 5

This is the device Hobbes calls to mind when he pays D'Avenant a witty compliment:

> I believe (Sir) you have seen a curious kind of perspective, where, he that looks through a short hollow pipe, upon a picture containing diverse figures, sees none of those that are there painted, but some one person made of their parts, conveighed to the eye by the artificiall cutting of a glasse. I find in my imagi-

nation an effect not unlike it from your Poem. The virtues you distribute there amongst so many noble Persons represent (in the reading) the image but of one man's virtue to my fancy, which is your own.[46]

Hobbes's assumption that D'Avenant must surely have seen the "curious kind of perspective" is one piece of evidence—along with the allusions in the work of Shakespeare, Jonson, Chapman, Bacon, Crashaw, and other writers, and the translations of continental treatises into English—that the curious perspective was known and admired in England during the reign of wit.[47] The following chapter will offer further evidence as it sketches in the context of the visual arts in England.

2 The Curious Perspective in England

We have been following the development of the curious perspective, to adopt Niceron's and Hobbes's phrase to cover the variety of objects explained in the treatises: the anamorphic distortions, the double or reversible images, the unexpected concealments and clarifications made possible through the use of mirrors and lenses. These treatises present the technical elements of a witty style in the visual arts all the more clearly for their basis in the Albertian perspective, which they extend and manipulate. The curious perspective undermines the viewer's authority by dislocating him from the "centric point" and obliging him to see the work of art from multiple "perspectives" before he grasps it fully. The numerous "practical perspective" handbooks should not in themselves be overemphasized. They provide directions and diagrams for works of art rather than the thing itself, and often the drawings given are necessarily simplified, textbookish figures intended to have only an instructional value. Many people went to the treatises undoubtedly for straightforward demonstrations of the mechanics of perspective

drawing and considered the curious perspective a whimsical, though ingenious, adornment to a practical subject.
Yet these visual witticisms had a life of their own outside
the treatises, more vigorous and widespread than the few
remaining examples suggest.[1] Although most of them are
virtuoso pieces that we, at least, would be tempted to put
in a different category from serious art, the techniques of
the curious perspective find their way into paintings that
will deserve our attention, as well as into architecture and
theatrical design.

A brief and (given the evidence) necessarily sketchy
survey of the curious perspective in England will set the
context for witty poetry. If our focus were on the continent, we should probably find the need for a distinction
between a Mannerist and Baroque phase of the curious
perspective, for men could appreciate the same technique
for different reasons. Lomazzo's emphasis on the enigmas
of perspective manipulation reflects the problematic, un-
settling quality of Mannerist painting: Daniel DaVolterra's
Descent from the Cross (mid-sixteenth century), for example, incorporates two conflicting perspective schemes
that force the viewer to see the descent from a point both
above and below the body of Christ, while Parmigianino's
The Madonna with the Long Neck (c. 1535) makes the
viewer's relation to the space of the painting impossibly
ambiguous by placing a tiny figure next to a towering
Madonna. On the other hand, Niceron, Dubreuil, and their
fellow Jesuit "perspecteurs" of the 1630s and 1640s, fascinated as they were with the marvelous revelations of the
curious perspective, are unmistakably Baroque. Between
the two, the emphasis has shifted from the desire to pro-

voke a perceptual uncertainty to the pleasures of resolving it. These continental waves, however, broke late and practically together on the English coast. Indeed in the visual arts England had barely felt the impact of the Renaissance before the end of the sixteenth century, and when it did the succession of continental styles were more or less simultaneously available as options.[2]

Although the court of Henry VIII patronized a few northern artists besides Hans Holbein to do duty as portraitists, and although the miniatures of Nicholas Hilliard won him the place of Queen's Limner under Elizabeth, the great German painter was the sole major representative of the Renaissance, Northern or Southern, in sixteenth-century England. Otherwise, the whitewashing of Papist imagery, the endemic English xenophobia (especially where Italy was concerned), the lack of a studio tradition, and Elizabeth's own indifference to the visual arts all left little room for the new art to take root. Holbein had done commissioned portraits for merchants of the Hanseatic League quartered in the Steelyard (on the north bank, across from the site of the Globe), but in 1598 Elizabeth closed the Guildhall and expelled the German merchants—and, unfortunately, their pictures—from the kingdom.[3]

But with the new century, as if suddenly aware of the catching up they had to do, Englishmen began to study and acquire European art with great relish. Young gentlemen on the Grand Tour, newly tutored in at least the rudiments of drawing by such instructors as Henry Peacham, were preoccupied with looking at buildings and pictures, making sketches, and supplying themselves with a respectable cabinetful of art to take home along with

their French and Italian manners. The most talented of
these tourists was Inigo Jones, who would later turn to
his sketchbooks for inspiration in designing masque
costumes and sets. The great private collectors like the
Earl of Arundel—"the father of virtú" in England, according to Horace Walpole—and the Duke of Buckingham had
their agents combing the continent for buys to increase
their holdings. Arundel's Italian paintings and statues mark
the first large-scale importation of the Mediterranean
world into England. In 1623, while visiting Spain, Prince
Charles saw the work of Titian, Rubens, and the young
Velázquez. He began acquiring on his own, eventually
purchased the magnificent collection of the Duke of
Mantua, and succeeded in attracting Van Dyck, Rubens,
Orazio Gentileschi, and others to England for more or less
extended visits. Men of smaller means, like John Donne,
bought what they could afford.[4] During these years a
fascination with the curious perspective helped to shape
English taste both in what was admired abroad and cul-
tivated at home.

Men who had the leisure and the interest to pay attention to art found themselves in a visually witty world of
which popular emblem books and the vogue of *imprese*—
which have been so extensively documented by Mario
Praz and his followers—formed only a part. Praz contended
that these two latter forms provide sources, or at least
pictorial equivalents, for verbal wit. Yet, emblems and
devices, it is important to realize, have to be seen in the
larger context of visual wit that includes the curious perspective and suggests literary comparisons that have not
been considered in the debate over Praz's work. In archi-

tecture, for example, Praz suggests that, like the emblem, the deceptive perspective of the famous Borromini colonnade in the Palazzo Spada, in Rome, is a visual counterpart of the epigram: the condensation of the epigram is analogous to the exaggerated foreshortening of the colonnade.[5] Yet the "conciseness" of the colonnade—its being in fact much shorter than it appears to be until one actually walks through it—is only an element in the total effect it has on the viewer, which is precisely that of the curious perspective. Taken in by a deceptive impression of the length of the colonnade, the viewer first imagines that the statue visible at the other end is relatively large, only to discover, once he readjusts his angle of vision, that it is really much smaller than he thought. This is also the effect of the Bernini stairway into the Vatican from Saint Peter's, with its misleading impression of length, as well as of the baroque illusionistic ceiling: in a ceiling such as Guercino's *Aurora* (in the Villa Ludovisi, Rome) the viewer has to accommodate to the rapid shifts of scale in the simultaneous awareness of a flat ceiling surface, emphasized by the architectural supports, and an apparently limitless expanse of şky filled with birds, attendant figures, and the chariot of the goddess. In the apotheosis of King James, designed for the ceiling of the Banqueting House at Whitehall in the 1630s, Rubens demands the same visual gymnastics of the English viewer.

In painting, Hans Holbein's *Ambassadors* (1533) includes an anamorphic figure: in the lower foreground of this double portrait there is an elongated, indecipherable streak which, seen from the side, turns into a death's head (figure 7). An unknown imitator of Holbein painted an anamorphic portrait of the young Edward VI (1546, now in the National Gallery). It was seen in Whitehall in 1598 by a German traveler named Hentzner, who made an enthusiastic note of it in his *Itinerarium* (Nuremberg, 1612):

> A portrait of Edward VI King of England: at first sight a representation of some monstrosity; but if it be looked at straight through the hole in the lid or shutter, with which the picture is covered, it is seen in its proper proportions; an ingenious invention of the artist.[6]

Though the exact nature of the "lid or shutter" is not made clear in Hentzner's description, the painting was then evidently displayed in a deep boxlike frame like the ones frequently mentioned in seventeenth-century inventories of great collections.[7] Such a frame, with a cover presumably hinged at the side and furnished with a peephole that would offer the proper point of view once the cover was swung open, would add an extra element of surprise to this "ingenious invention." A similar portrait was done of Charles I,[8] and there were undoubtedly other English examples that did not survive the destruction of art (particularly of frivolous art) during the Protectorate.[9]

The Holbein and the portrait of Edward VI are related to the vogue for anamorphosis in Germany in the sixteenth and seventeenth centuries among such artists as Erhard Schön, J. H. Glaser, and Jacob van der Heyden.[10] Schön did several humorous woodcuts in the late 1530s. One, entitled *Aus, du alter Tor,* shows a girl being caressed by an old man, who does not see his faithless mistress giving his money to her young lover; this image is set next to an anamorphic blur that, viewed from the side, resolves into a scene of the young couple making love—revealing to us their secret that is literally hidden from the cuckold's point of view. Another blurry landscape done by Schön turns into a row of portraits of the four rulers, "Charles V, Ferdinand I, Paul III, Francis I"; meanwhile the frontal view reveals, when it is examined closely, tiny scenes that illustrate the exploits of each of the figures portrayed anamorphically. Glaser's engraving *The Fall* (1638) uses the anamorphic device more subtly: at the left of a long panel Adam and Eve are seen eating the fruit, while on the right is the explusion from Eden. In the middle, a strangely agitated lake turns into an image of Christ with the crown of thorns—he was there all along, the promise of redemption concealed from Adam and Eve as from us inside the natural landscape (figure 11).

A similar kind of visual punning, the concealment of two images in one, was practiced on the continent by Francesco Zucchi and by Guiseppe Arcimboldo in the 1570s. In his "allegorical portraits"—*Fire, The Librarian* and the four *Seasons*—Arcimboldo models human heads out of objects. In *Summer,* for example, the figure is formed out of a bunch of fruits and vegetables. Here, as in the anamorphosis, two points of view are required: from a distance, the portrait seems entirely natural as its elements blend into human features. Up close, the portrait turns into a still life. From a middle distance the *gestalt* of the pictures shifts back and forth between these two possibilities. Arcimboldo had his imitators all over Europe and was known in England and in the seventeenth century: an inventory of the Earl of Arundel's collection made in 1641 lists "Two Peeces belonging to the Four Seasons,"[11] which are thought to be either originals or copies of the Italian master.

In its delight with optical trickery the Stuart court enthusiastically patronized the physicist and inventor Cornelius Drebbel (1572–1634). In 1618 Drebbel put on a magic lantern performance at court in which he "projected pictures of himself in different costumes from beggar to king, one figure metamorphosing into the next through the social scale."[12] Drebbel also exhibited a camera obscura to enchanted audiences. This device— in its simplest form a box of whatever size with a convex lens on one side and a white screen, onto which the image is projected, on the opposite side—was known to Alberti, Barbaro, Kepler, and Niceron.[13] Though the principle behind it, incorporated in the photographic camera, is today taken quite for granted, the seventeenth century admired the camera as another instance of the marvelous and a testimony to the ingenuity of the artificer. Constantijn Huygens (1596–1687) saw Drebbel's camera in London in 1622 and wrote:

I have at home that other instrument of Drebbel's which certainly produces wonderful effects by the painting of reflection in a *camera obscura*; it is impossible for me to tell you the beauty of it in words; all painting is dead, for here is life itself or something so close to it if words don't fail me. For both the figure and the contour and the movements occur naturally and in a greatly pleasing fashion.[14]

English travelers also had an eye open for curiosities:
Thomas Coryate includes among his undigested crudities
an account of the bishop's palace in Padua where

> there are many curious pictures, in one whereof there
> is the exquisitest conveyance that I ever saw, which is
> a pretty little picture drawen in the form of an hand-
> kerchiefe with four corners, and inserted into another
> very large and faire picture. The lesser picture is so
> passing cunningly handled, that the lower corners of
> it seeme either to hang loose, and to be a pretty way
> distant from the ground of the maine picture, or to be
> pinned upon the other. And so will any stranger what-
> soever conceive at first sight thereof, as indeede I did,
> in so much that I durst have laid a great wager, even
> ten to one, that the lower corners of it had been loose
> or pinned on. But such is the admirable, and methinks
> inimitable curiosity of the worke, that it is all wrought
> upon the very ground of the other great picture, as the
> other several parts thereof are.[15]

In the same room there was also "a picture of Christ and
the Virgin Mary . . . excellently contrived in a faire looking
glass that hangeth at the side of the bedde." Elsewhere on
his itinerary Coryate observed an assortment of other
trompe l'oeil paintings and constructions like

> the picture of a Gentlewoman, whose eies were con-
> trived with that singularitie of cunning, that they
> moved up or down of themselves, not after a seeming
> manner, but truly and indeed. For I did very exactly
> view it. But I believe it was done by a device which the
> Grecians call αὐτόματον.[16]

Drummond of Hawthornden described for Sir George Keith the perspectives he had seen at the fair of Saint Germain:

> Here were many double Pictures, the first view shew old men and young Misers gathering carefully, the second view shew young men and prodigals spending riotously with *stultitiam patiuntur opes*. Churchmen and grave Senatours consulting and seriously deliberating, the one face of the Picture represented: the other Fools dancing, Souldiers dicing and fighting.[17]

These images were evidently superimposed (by what technical method Drummond does not say), and the viewer, looking first one way and then the other, could draw the appropriate moral from the contrast.

The *Diary* of John Evelyn, perhaps the most passionate and knowledgeable connoisseur among the English travelers, offers glimpses of the mirrored hall in the Villa Borghese at Rome, "which renders a strange multiplication of things, resembling divers most richly furnished rooms," of the garden in the Count de Liancourt's palace in Saint Germain, "which though very narrow, is yet by the addition of an excellently painted Perspective strangly enlarg'd to appearance," and of the magnificent variety of painted perspective scenery at the Venice opera. Back in London Evelyn was shown

> a prety Perspective & well represented in a triangular Box, the greate Church at Harlem in Holland, to be seene thro a small hole at one of the Corners, & contrived into an handsome Cabinet: It was so rarely don,

that all the Artists & Painters in Towne, came flocking
to see and admire it.[18]

This perspective box was apparently a peep show similar in
principle to one by Samuel von Hoogstraeten (1627–78)
now in the National Gallery: the viewer can look down
into the box through the top and assure himself that
it is empty, yet seen through a peephole in the side the
paintings on the inner walls create the powerful three-
dimensional illusion of a Dutch sitting room filled with
furniture.[19] The perspective box and the camera obscura
had their place in a gentleman's cabinet of rarities and
nourished in men like Evelyn a curiosity that we would
tend to see as an odd blend of the artistic and the scien-
tific. But the seventeenth century made no sharp distinction between these two impulses. Such productions
combined the laws of geometry, the draftsman's skill,
and the artist's genius into a witty display.

On a far more opulent scale, the spectacle of the English
court masque depends on a mastery of perspective techniques in scenic decoration. Unlike the platform stage of
the public playhouse, the deep rectangular masquing area
enclosed by painted panels becomes in effect a perspective
box writ large. The masque is influenced by classical
theories of dramatic representation which the Renaissance
pieced together or inferred from ancient texts. Studies of
Pollux, Cassiodorus, and especially Vitruvius's *De architectura* established on classical authority that the Greeks
and Romans had used two kinds of stage machine that
would reappear in the English masque: the *scena versatilis,*
a rotating triangular prism with a different scene painted

on each face, and the *scena ductilis,* the "tractable scene," that could be moved on and off stage in a groove or parted in the middle to reveal a new scene behind it.[20] Particularly influential in England as well as in Italy was Sebastiano Serlio's *De architettura,* which presents three perspective schemes for use on the stage.[21] Following the ancient genres Serlio reproduces his designs for the "tragicall," "comicall," and "satiricall" stages.[22] The third is of course a "rude & rustical" woodland scene, but the first two are carefully foreshortened architectural perspectives set on a checkerboard floor to create the illusion of a receding street or piazza. Two "houses," placed on either side of the stage, are made of canvas on a wooden frame and painted to resemble either the great houses of tragedy or the more modest ones of comedy. The lines in depth on these paintings are made to converge toward a central vanishing point on a painted backdrop which completes the illusion. Serlio's basic perspective scheme was incorporated in such Italian theaters as the one built for the Olympic Academy of Vicenza to house productions of classical plays,[23] and eventually in the English masque.

Serlio's praise for the power of illusionistic stagecraft could well be a description of the later English masque:

> Among all the things that may be made by mens hands, thereby to yield admiration, pleasure to sight, and to content the fantasies of men; I thinke it is placing of a Scene, as it is shewed to your sight, where a man in a small place may see built by Carpenters or Masons, skillful in Perspective worke, great Palaces, large Temples, and diverse Houses, both neere and

farre off; broad places filled with Houses, long streets
crost with other wayes: triumphant Arches, high Pillers
or Columnes, Pyramides Obeliscens, and a thousand
fayre things and buildings adorned with innumberable
lights. . . . There you may see the bright shining Moone
ascending only with her hornes, and already risen
up, before the spectators are ware of, or once saw it
ascend. . . . And when occasion serveth, you shall
see a God descending downe from Heaven; you also see
some Comets and Stars shoot in the Skyes. . . .[24]

The lights, the moon suddenly rising, the descending god,
the shooting stars and comets—these "motions" so popular
on the seventeenth-century Italian stage are central to the
masque. In the hands of Inigo Jones the masque came to
be so lavishly decorated and technically mysterious that
its scenic effects never ceased to astonish even its regular
royal audience. As well as using rotating and tractable
panels for the many scene changes required, Jones fitted
out his stage with drop curtains, light and sound effects,
and an assortment of carefully concealed winches, cables,
and levers that made it possible' for clouds to descend,
chariots to fly across the stage, and thrones to hover in
mid air. These effects and the perspective stage that contains them are not merely embellishments for a text, as
they might be in the drama. A masque is not a play—not
an imitation of an action—but a visual representation of
a poetic ideal. Stephen Orgel and Roy Strong make the
distinction clear in their recent study of Jones's work:
"The scenic machine is the setting for a play, and it may
provide its own momentary interludes of wonder as the
drama pauses. But the scenic machine is the *action* of a

masque, its metamorphoses, miracles, apotheoses."[25] The masque typically makes a "visual progress" from disorder to order, and this movement is embodied, not simply illustrated, in the changing scenes and machines of the masque spectacle.

The masque uses perspective to create, not a realistic scene (like the street setting of an Italianate comedy) but a "wonder"—to heighten the effect of myth and fantasy by making it optically plausible. The success of the production depends on its ability to carry off that illusion convincingly. As the court's symbolic vision of itself, the masque is an expression of what Orgel calls "Platonic politics." The masque usually ends with a scene of universal harmony restored after some challenge. This victory celebrates the proper subordination of passion to love, brutishness to reason, in man, the cosmos, and the state. In this the court saw an idealized reflection of its own virtue, the representation of a Platonic Idea realized in the person of the king, just as the realm of England existed as a reflection of the royal power. Those members of the court who took roles in the masque literally entered into the illusion, but its force also controlled the spectators (and organized the space of the masquing hall). The masque directed

the theatrical experience toward the single point in the hall from which the perspective achieved its fullest effect, the royal throne. . . . Through the use of perspective the monarch, always the ethical center of court productions, became in a physical and emblematic way the center as well. Jones' theater transformed its audience into a living and visible emblem

of the aristocratic hierarchy: the closer one sat to the
king, the "better" one's place was, and only the King's
seat was perfect.[26]

The real and the fictive world are interlocked by the perspective structure of the experience. At the end of the
performance, when the masquers take partners from
the audience for the final dance, these two worlds are
completely fused. The illusion incorporates the real into
itself.

For this reason, despite its marvelous devices and the
technical virtuosity of its perspective scheme, the masque
must itself be distinguished from the curious perspective
in one important respect. Politically and optically, the
masque allows the spectator only one point of view. The
masque reinforces the power of illusion and does its best
to conceal its own deceptions: it calls attention to its
illusionism only to confirm it and the ideology it represents. In his long and increasingly testy collaboration with
Inigo Jones, Ben Jonson succeeded in a few masques in
registering a dissent to the genre's unquestioning submission to an idealizing illusion. In *Love Restored* (1612)—
here Jonson had a free hand, since Jones was occupied
designing   another   project—the   antimasque   characters
satirically threaten the masque itself:

But masquing and revelling? Were not these ladies
and their gentlewomen more housewifely employed, a
dozen of 'em to a light, or twenty—the more the mer-
rier—to save charges, i' their chambers at home, and
their old nightgowns, at draw-gloves, riddles, dreams,
and other pretty purposes, rather than to wake here, in

their flaunting wires and tires, laced gowns, embroi-
dered petticoats and other taken-up braveries? Away, I
will no more of these superfluous excesses.[27]

That threat, posed by Plutus, is duly banished in the revels,
which celebrate not the niggardly god of money but the
generous Cupid whose love is embodied in the king and
gloriously reflected in such costly entertainments as the
masque: "This motion was of love begot." Still the telling
critique of the antimasque is by no means cancelled.
Jonson would insist that his language carries a greater
moral weight than lavish country houses "built to envious
show" or spectacles like Jones's; and after their final
break, he would malign Jones as the purveyor of "the mere
perspective of an Inch board."[28] But within the form of
the masque itself—as Jonson perhaps acknowledged by
abandoning the field—the mere perspective reigned un-
challenged. There is no way to lift the lid of Inigo Jones's
perspective box, or to gain another vantage point by looking at it from the side. The curious perspective questions
the illusions it creates by inviting that other view. It tests
out and plays with the fit between the fictive and the real
that is so powerfully affirmed in the masque.
  The masque helps to define by this difference the elements of a witty style in the visual arts that can be
summarized as follows: The curious perspective is self-
consciously riddling and gamelike, a "divertissement de
l'esprit,"[29] yet with a claim to be taken seriously as an
embodiment of the marvelous. It calls attention to itself
as a deception, and so raises questions about its own status
which, in Alberti's esthetic, were possible but unasked. We
no longer have an open window onto reality, but an object

that declares itself to be an illusion, and a precarious one
at that, which can be wiped away by a change in point of
view, or abruptly transformed into another, unexpected
image. Thus the style does an intriguing balancing act on
the borderline between the fictive and the real. *Trompe
l'oeil* images, or images projected in the camera obscura,
have a double nature; they are apparently real only because they are so consummately fictional, and that
duplicity is essential to their effect on the viewer as he
reaches out to touch the painted grapes. Using the same
rules which had earlier guaranteed clarity and perspicuity,
the curious perspective delights in creating visual complexity through its ability to distort, reflect, conceal, and
superimpose images.

Faced with a curious perspective, the viewer has a different, more strenuous role than he did with regard to Alberti. He finds that he is no longer able to see the world
unequivocally—with the eye of cool reason—from a secure
point of view. Instead he confronts an enigma that demands to be figured out, and his own relationship with
the work becomes problematical as it engages him in a
process of puzzlement and revelation. To the writers who
will be considered in the following chapters the curious
perspective offers a model for manipulating language—a
visual construct that reflects their confirmations and sus-
picions of their own medium, the two yoked by wit
together.

3 Tesauro on Visual and Verbal Wit

Thus far I have been describing the curious perspective as "witty" without trying to justify the term itself. The anamorphic paintings and mirror devices have been left to speak for themselves, to define their own category, however miscellaneous, as witty objects. The Renaissance commentators do little better when they speak of the prodigious, the marvelous, the rare, the enigmatic, the ingenious. These terms convey nothing more specific than the observer's enthusiasm for something new and striking—something the very novelty of which beggars description by the established critical vocabularies of, let us say, "imitation" or "storia." The same problem has made it difficult to find a language, old or new, for dealing with literary wit, especially in English writing. English criticism of the earlier seventeenth century produced a scattering of prefaces, commendatory poems, and elegies, but no body of theory or analysis to match the earlier rhetorical criticism of the sixteenth century or the neoclassicising criticism of the Restoration.

The Elizabethan rhetoricians had contributed the doc-

trine that a poem should be grounded, as Gascoigne said,
in a "fine invention." To Puttenham and Hoskins invention
meant the original and even surprising treatment of a subject, and their manuals instructed the poet in the use of
figures such as irony, catechresis, paradox, and litotes that
turn on dissimulation, discords, and contraries. For the
Elizabethans the term *wit* had the general sense of a lively
intelligence and, applied to writing, of the acuity or interest of a literary idea (the "invention" or "conceit" in-
forming a poem); but the rhetorical tradition prepared the
way for the more specialized sense "wit" began to acquire
for the Jacobeans, a quickness of mind in seeing resemblances between dissimilar things and capturing these
insights in unusual metaphors or engaging paradoxes. In
the seventeenth century "wit" continued to imply originality, as "invention" had earlier, though now originality
came to mean (rather unhelpfully) *not* writing Elizabethan verse. Like Carew in his "Elegy upon the death of . . .
Dr. John Donne," the champions of the new style praised
the "fresh invention" that liberates the witty poet from
"soft" imitations of Ovid or Pindar or Petrarch and enables
him to draw "a line/Of masculine expression" in his native
English.

The notion of wit in the new century is further complicated by a set of terms introduced into literary discussion
through the revival of interest in the curt, silver Latin style
of Tacitus and Seneca. Tacitus especially was "difficult"
and "dark"—but *difficilia quae pulchra.* In the Roman
historian's "obscurity" and "asperity" the Jacobeans saw
an energetic alternative not only to the orotund eloquence
of Ciceronian prose, but to the expansive and decorated

"sugared" style of Elizabethan poetry. As poets like Chapman began to pack their verse with "strong lines," any
poem that was elliptical, learned, terse, mysteriously
allegorical, enraptured, or otherwise "veiled" could be
considered "witty" on those grounds alone—as Jasper
Mayne said of Donne's poetry, "we are thought wits, when
'tis understood."[1] It is perhaps a sign of the seventeenth
century's failure to define its own achievement that later
opponents of the "metaphysical" style were left the task
of coining, and debasing, the critical epithets in circulation
since then. Earlier honorable usages gave way before those
critics who rejected the style and associated the term
conceit with outrageous metaphor and *wit* with a more or
less frivolous turn of mind, or a gift for social repartée,
that needed to be checked by the sober restraints of
judgment.

The shortage of sustained theoretical criticism in England before the Restoration has led those interested in
reconstructing a contemporary poetics of wit to Spanish
and Italian treatises by Gracián, Sforza-Pallavicino, Pelle-
grini, and Tesauro. The disadvantages of consulting these
continental writers are obvious. The poetics of an Italian
Jesuit like Tesauro, writing at mid-century, can be brought
to bear on an earlier English style only with the greatest
caution. Yet these writers are worth the risk, for reading
them leads us to see the rage for wit in its widest scope as
a European movement embracing the visual arts as well as
literature. Tesauro has the special advantage of making a
theoretical connection between poetic wit and the wit of
the curious perspective.

Il cannocchiale aristotelico (1654) is Emmanuele Tesauro's voluminous effort to find in Aristotle both a classical sanction and a theoretical basis for wit. His extension of Aristotle's scattered remarks on metaphor in the *Rhetoric* and the *Poetics* has led modern critics to argue for a "poetic of correspondence" behind the use of metaphor in witty poetry.[2] For Tesauro all witty expression, verbal and pictorial, is essentially metaphoric, replacing or conjoining one term with another according to an implied analogical connection. In Aristotle's famous example of the proportional metaphor: since the cup is to Dionysus as the shield is to Ares, one may speak metaphorically of the shield as the "cup of Ares" or the cup as the "shield of Dionysus." The philosopher also notes, later in the *Poetics,* that the ability to make good metaphor is the mark of genius because it implies an eye for resemblances, and, in the *Rhetoric,* that "smart sayings" (ἀστεῖα), jokes, and riddles are based on vivid metaphors.[3] Tesauro makes a larger claim for the faculty of *ingegno:* the two areas of experience joined by metaphor are not, as Dr. Johnson would later insist in the case of unusual comparisons, "heterogeneous ideas . . . yoked by violence together," that is, unnaturally or capriciously linked. Rather their connection embodies a correspondence that obtains in nature between apparently unrelated objects. Inventing a metaphor is therefore an act of discovery, an exploration of the subtle network of interrelationships knitting all things together; the more surprising and original the connection—the more conceited the metaphor—the greater is the poet's wit.

Tesauro supports the metaphysical framework for this notion of wit by arguing that God himself is the efficient

cause of wittiness, the creator of a witty universe. Not
only is the language of scripture ingeniously metaphoric—
at every opportunity connecting the literal event with a
corresponding tropological, allegorical, and anagogical
meaning—but the "metaphorical witticisms of God" are
evident everywhere in the book of creatures, from constellations to insects. Just as Christ's "physcial action" of
being born in a manger "contains in itself many symbols
and conceited witticisms," God's witty designs are such
that everything in nature can reveal hidden meanings to
the witty observer.[4] Wit is the method by which the
creator confers significance on the creation—and by which
the conceited poet explores and imitates the working of
the divine mind.

If, however, wit is an instrument for discovering truth, it
is paradoxically likewise a means of deception, for Tesauro
cannot ignore the dominant ornamental conception of
metaphor as a violation of the plain truth. Aristotle himself had defined metaphor as the "application of an alien
name" (*Poetics* 1475b), and the rhetorical tradition since
then had harbored a suspicion of metaphor as a linguistic impropriety. "Do you not know," Castiglione warns us,
"that figures of speech, which give so much grace and
luster to discourse, are all abuses of grammatical rules?"
Similarly, in his *Arte of English Poesie* (1589), Puttenham
approaches the "Figure of Transport," like the other
figures of speech, with typical caution:

As figures be the instruments of ornament in every
language, so be they also in a sorte abuses or rather
trespasses in speach, because they passe the ordinary

limits of common utterance, and be occupied of purpose to deceive the eare and also the minde, drawing
it from plainnesse and simplicitie to a certaine doublenesse, whereby our talke is the more guilefull &
abusing. . . .

When he speaks of metaphor as a "kinde of wresting of a
single word from his owne right signification, to another
not so naturall," Puttenham presupposes a norm of the
natural in language which metaphor transgresses however much it adds to the "pleasure and ornament of our
speach."[5]

Tesauro not only admits this deceptive aspect of metaphor, but seizes upon it with none of the scruples that gave
pause to the Elizabethan rhetorician. "The unique glory
of wit," Tesauro insists, "resides in knowing how to lie
well," while the most ingenious form of "the conceit is
nothing more than an urbanely fallacious enthymeme."[6]
The simplest metaphor, like "Achilles is a lion," reduces
logically to an invalid syllogism, "All lions are fierce,
Achilles is fierce, therefore Achilles is a lion." The wittiest
expressions expand these fallacies into arguments that
trick the intellect at first by appearing conclusive, only
to dissolve like the tempting apples of the Black Sea that
leave the mouth full of ashes and smoke. Donne proffers
such caviling fictions in poems like "The Flea" and "The
Good-morrow":

What ever dyes, was not mixt equally;
If our two loves be one, or, thou and I
Love so alike, that none doe slacken, none can die.[7]

This argument uses its logical form to create the expectation of a demonstrative syllogism, a true deduction, which is no sooner suggested than collapsed into a paralogical but highly witty denial of death. The two terms of the conceit—the stability of a well-mixed chemical compound and the permanence of love—are just enough alike to give the comparison an air of plausibility. God may create real connections; however men may imitate the divine process, they seem inextricably tied to the fictitious and the factitious.

A recent study of Tesauro subtitled "A Study of the Lie in the Arts" abandons the poetics of correspondence entirely in favor of what might be called a poetics of playful fallacy. In this view, *The Aristotelian Telescope* appears at a moment when belief in a universal system of analogies is at an end, and the metaphorical book of nature, once so luminous to the medieval mind, is no longer available for imitation in the books of men except by parody. Witty conceits are justified not by any claim to the truth but by their salutary effect on the reader, who (being a witty fellow himself) recognizes that wit is the imitation of a lie, a feigned falsehood. Its intent is not primarily to deceive but to please; by a kind of *trompe l'oeil* that Tesauro especially admired in the visual arts, wit creates the appearance of truth before revealing itself to the intellect as a fiction. It is in this rhythm of deception and discovery that the peculiar pleasure of wittiness is to be found.[8]

Tesauro cannot fully reconcile these two views of wit, and in a sense his sprawling book would be impoverished by a narrower consistency. Wit as an acute perception of the truth and as a potent force for artistic illusion lie side by side in the *Cannocchiale* in a fertile, if logically promis-

cuous, cohabitation—as in the following passage, where Tesauro draws a distinction between *ingegno* and *prudenza:*

> Wit is more acute; prudence is more judicious: the
> former is quicker; the latter more steadfast: the one
> deals in appearances, the other in truth: and where
> [prudence] has its own utility as an end, [wit] covets
> the admiration and applause of the people. Hence it is
> not without reason that ingenious men are called
> divine. For, just as God brings forth that which is out
> of that which is not, so wit makes something out of
> nothing: it makes the lion become a man and the eagle
> a city. It places a woman on top of a fish and invents
> a siren as the symbol of adultery. It joins the bust of a
> goat to the hindquarters of a serpent and forms the
> chimera as a hieroglyphic of madness. Whence some of
> the ancient philosophers called wit a particle of the
> divine mind, and others a gift given by God to those he
> holds most dear.[9]

Wit is a particle of the divine mind, a generative gift
analogous to God's power to creat *ex nihilo.* Yet the end
of wit is popular admiration, and its productions deal in
appearances rather than truth, in the pleasant fictions of
sirens and chimeras. Devising such whimsical, capricious
creations would seem very different from discovering cor-
respondences that obtain in nature—except insofar as
whimsy is in the nature of the divine mind. When Tesauro
claims that thunderbolts are "formidable witticisms and
symbolic works of nature, at once mute and vocal, having
the bolt for a body and the thunderclap as a motto," it is
difficult to tell from his tone how much metaphysical

weight the argument is meant to carry.[10] Does symbolic meaning inhere in the lightning bolt as a natural emblem crafted by the divine wit, or do we impose on it a witty, fallacious appearance for the sake of "l'applauso de' populari"? Here as elsewhere, Tesauro's treatment of wit flows from a joint religious and secular impulse that does not hesitate to wed theology with entertainment, profundity with play. His book is at once a Jesuit treatise in the tradition of Saint Ignatius of Loyola, a manual of preachable conceits, and a courtier's handbook in the manner of Castiglione.[11]

For all its categorizing, the *Cannocchiale* becomes finally an exuberant survey of wit everywhere and in everything. Like melancholy for Burton, wit for Tesauro is a portean spirit that overflows all the bonds set up to contain it. It appears not only in the direct manifestations of the "Argutezze di Dio" but indirectly in the oracles and dreams Tesauro groups under angelic wit as well as in the wit of nature—in stars, oak trees, apes, ants, snakes, and so on and on. Wittiness among the products of human art is equally universal. Epigrams and conceits, *imprese,* emblems and lapidary inscriptions are witty, no less than pictures and statues, polite retorts, costume balls, tournaments and pageants, games of chess, stage settings, clocks, mirrors and lenses, and architectural ornament—to name some examples from a seemingly inexhaustible list that demands, if the term is not too feeble, an interdisciplinary approach.

The common element in the various examples of human art, verbal and visual, is obviously not formal or thematic but rather that divine particle, a "maravigliosa forza

dell'Intelletto," that makes them all possible. This "ingegno naturale" consists of two talents, "perspicacia" and
"versabilità":

> Perspicaciousness penetrates the furthest and most
> minute particularities of any subject; such as sub-
> stance, material, form, accidents, properties, causes,
> effects, ends, sympathies, similitude, opposition,
> equality, greater, lesser, characteristics, proper names
> and equivocations: all of which are coiled up and hid-
> den in every subject. . . .
> Versatility rapidly compares all these particularities
> among themselves, or with the subject: it knots them
> together or divides them; increases or diminishes them;
> deduces one from the other; hints at one through an-
> other; and with a marvelous dexterity puts the one in
> the other's place, like the calculations of a juggler.
> And such is metaphor, the mother of poetry, of sym-
> bols, and of imprese.[12]

Perspicaciousness enables the mind to see clearly into any
matter, to unravel it and dispose it into its proper logical
categories. This analytic power might be sufficient for wit
in its general sense as intelligence, but the ingenious mind
must also have the versatility to dislocate ideas from their
ordinary logical connections, to knot them together or
take them apart, to increase or diminish them, deduce one
from the other, reveal one through the other, and put one
in the other's place. This marvelous dexterity, which suggests for Tesauro the agility of a juggler, is the essense of
metaphor—here considered not so much a figure of speech

as a habit of mind, a kind of mental acrobatics that gives grace and speed to the plodding logical categories of thought. "Perspicacia" moves deliberately and sequentially to isolate the component parts of a subject. In this respect its function is similar to Elizabethan "invention"—finding out what can be said on a given topic—and also to what Locke and the eighteenth century would call "judgment," the careful drawing of distinctions where a careless mind might see superficial resemblances. But what the sixteenth century had not fully defined, and what the eighteenth century would reject, is that juggling quality of the witty mind that Tesauro prizes so highly. "Versabilità" implies first that ideas do not release their full energy to a merely logical inspection, no matter how thorough, and second, that understanding itself—whether in the production or the appreciation of wit—is an activity rather than a passive state. The ingenious mind must train itself to experience ideas dynamically, their parts in constant motion like the juggler's balls, not filed neatly into categories.

Indeed, for the benefit of those not fortunate enough to be ingenious by nature or inspiration, Tesauro provides a regimen of mental calisthenics designed to strengthen that dexterity: the aspiring wit is taught how to construct an "indice categorico" in which he first tabulates any idea or subject into its substance, quantity, qualities, and the rest, and then practices juggling these categories metaphorically. Such exercises develop the perspicaciousness necessary to understand a logical concept and the versatility to turn it into a witty conceit.[13]

The notion of "versabilità" lies behind visual as well as

verbal wit. Tesauro's taste is eclectic but guided always by an appreciation for metaphoric agility. He praises the wittiness of composite pictures—a two-headed demon combining human and animal features, a figure with a column for one leg and a serpent for the other—which, like the siren and the chimera, join the parts of different subjects in unexpected ways. Such images, like metaphors of opposition, knot together two incompatible thoughts and are therefore exceedingly wondrous in their effect. For the same reason he thinks of bizarre architectural ornament and sculpture as "metaphors in stone" and automata as "metaphorical" (their interior mechanism is paradoxically joined to a lifelike exterior). Emblems are witty by their very nature of joining word and picture in a single meaning, each component serving so to speak as a metaphor of the other. The wittiest visual objects, however, are "le Optiche," which, "through certain proportions of perspective, with strange and ingenious appearances, make you see what you do not see."[14]

The juggling performed in language by metaphor proper—the deceptions, the diminutions and hyperbolic enlargements, the shifts and replacements—is accomplished visually by "metaphoric" manipulations of perspective. Here Tesauro admires the classical painting of Athena, whose eyes seemed to turn toward the observer wherever he stood (figure 5), and the statue of Diana, whose face would appear sad to worshippers entering her temple, but joyful to those leaving, as if to suggest wittily that the goddess had been placated by the offerings brought her. Still these legendary examples are far surpassed in wit for

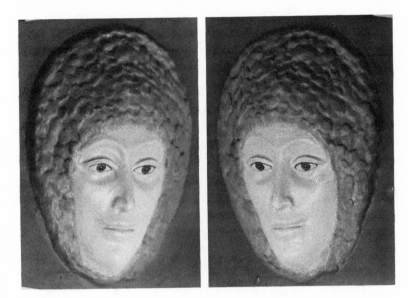

Figure 5. Two views of a detail from Achille Forgione's *Mythopoetic* (1974), a hypothetical reconstruction of a classical technique. A: seen from the right, B: seen from the left. Created for the 1975 exhibition at the Xerox Square Exhibit Center, Rochester, N.Y. Courtesy Lillian Silver.

Tesauro by the marvelous optical inventions of his own age—most notably the telescope, which

> with two glass windows, carries human sight through a hollow tube to where the birds cannot reach. With these you can cross the sea without a sail: you can see the pupil of the eye up close: even fly to the heavens in a flash; observe the spots in the sun; descry the horns of Vulcan in the forehead of Venus: measure the mountains and seas in the globe of the moon: number the children [i.e., the moons] of Jupiter: and whatever God conceals there, a little glass reveals to you.[15]

If metaphor is the "Aristotelian telescope," then the telescope is the Galilean metaphor. Both are instruments of discovery that equip the mind with the "versabilità" to regard its experience—visual and verbal—from new points of view; they make you see what you do not see, but they also reveal what divine wit conceals. Sight and logic are the ordinary tools of the rational intellect: the eye disposes the visual world into conventional relationships of size and distance just as the perspicuous mind disposes the topics before it into their proper categories. Shifts of perspective, like the "translations" of metaphor, reveal the limits of the ordinary means of methodizing nature by making unauthorized short-circuits across rational boundaries, and in that sense they lie: we no more see Athena move her eyes than we believe that Dionysus's cup is a shield. But they repay these trespasses by skillfully juggling the ordinary into the witty.

In a later passage that has attracted the attention of

Croce and Praz, Tesauro returns to the function of metaphor and again draws the analogy with visual perspectives:

> . . . metaphor packs everything tightly into a word:
> and in an almost miraculous way makes you see one
> thing inside another. Hence the greater is your delight:
> in the same way as it is a more curious and pleasing
> thing to see many objects through a perspective aper-
> ture [*per un' istraforo di perspettiva*] than the origi-
> nals themselves pass successively before the eye. A
> work (as our author says) not of the dull, but of the
> sharpest wit.[16]

With its characteristic "brevità" metaphor "packs" the
terms it compares (the image is one of forcefully wedging
things together), one within the other, into a single word.
Transcending common speech, in which subjects must be
marshalled one after the other, it compresses a sequence
of ideas into a single moment, and is thus primed to release
its "imparamente veloce," its flash of insight. So in such
metaphors as "Achilles the lion" or "Cleopatra the snake"
we are not merely to regard the animals as alien names for
the qualities of valor or treachery (or, for that matter, to
visualize a maned Achilles or a scaley Cleopatra): we are
rather to apprehend a new concept born of the union of
the two terms, a Cleopatrasnake or an Achilleslion, which
did not exist before in the everyday world of nonmeta-
phorical discourse. This notion of a new concept lies
behind Tesauro's claim that a witty metaphor does not
dress concepts in words—does not, that is, merely trim
what oft was thought in a new suit of verbal ornament—
but "the words themselves in concepts."[17]

Two examples from conceited English poems may suggest how the witty *concetto* performs like these textbook
metaphors, but with greater energy. Marvell's "A Dialogue
between the Soul and Body" plays on the metaphor, common to both devotional lyric and emblem, of the body
as the soul's "dungeon"; but here the soul gives his traditional complaint a witty turn:

> O who shall, from this Dungeon, raise
> A Soul inslav'd so many ways?
> With bolts of Bones, that fetter'd stands
> In Feet; and manacled in Hands.[18]

The words *fetter'd* and *manacled* each fuse the ideas of
bondage and body to point the extremities of the soul's
anguish. In these etymological conceits, to be fettered is,
in the root sense of the word, to have feet, while the body
is inevitably manacled (*manicula* = "little hand") by its
hands. As the "wit of love" in Crashaw's "The Weeper"
could place "Fountaine and Garden in one face," the witty
soul sees corporeality and bondage in one word. The third
stanza of Henry King's "The Exequy" is governed by an
equally commonplace metaphor comparing the poet's
dead wife to the setting sun:

> Nor wonder if my time go thus
> Backward and most preposterous;
> Thou has benighted me, thy set
> This Eve of blackness did beget,
> Who was't my day, (though overcast
> Before thou had'st thy Noon-tide past)
> And I remember must in tears,
> Thou scarce had'st seen so many years

> As Day tells houres. By thy cleer Sun
> My life and Fortune first did run;
>
> [21–30]

The stanza ends with a fine display of versatility:

> But thou wilt never more appear
> Folded within my Hemisphear,
> Since both thy light and motion
> Like a fled Star is fall'n and gon,
> And twixt me and my soules dear wish
> The earth now interposed is,
> Which such a strange eclipse doth make
> As ne're was read in Almanake.[19]
>
> [31–38]

The school explications of tenor and vehicle will not fit these lines. The poet runs two parallel tracks of meaning, the astronomical and the personal, that intersect in extraordinarily intense points of thought and feeling. While it continues the cosmic figure of earth and sun, line 32 suddenly and simultaneously shifts the focus back to an intimate image of the wife "Folded" within the "Hemisphear" of her husband's arms; the couple are turned into a microcosm, but their tender, private gesture retains the amplitude of the heavenly comparison. The tracks cross, and spark, again in line 36: "The earth now interposed is" between the benighted poet and his "fled Star," who has dropped beneath the horizon and been eclipsed by the earth. Here the bluntly literal fact of death asserts itself in the very language of the cosmic metaphor as we realize, with a mild shock, that we are now speaking of graves. We experience the "imparamente veloce" generated in these two conflated senses of earth—that a few feet of "earth" are as great an interposition as the "earth" itself in the "strange eclipse" of an untimely death. King's ability to pack everything tightly into one word animates the beginning of the stanza, if we attend to it: the one who should have died last having gone first, the widower's hours go "Backward and most preposterous," absurd and meaningless to him because, in the cosmic realm, time's due order is perverted (*prae* = "before," *posterus* = "coming after").

This capacity of witty metaphor for superimposing two ideas, embedding one within the other, suggests to Tesauro the analogy with perspective: " . . . it is a more curious and pleasing thing to see many objects [i.e., at once] *per un' istrafóro di perspettiva* than the originals themselves pass successively before the eye." Mario Praz translates the Italian phrase as "from a perspective angle," giving it the general sense of an advantageous point of view, a prospect from which the observer can take in many objects with a single glance.[20] I believe it is more likely that Tesauro is thinking of the more literal "perspective aperture": the eyepiece of a telescope, or of a perspective device such as Niceron and Dubreuil describe, through which a new image is discovered in the first, or the aperture designating the special point of view from which an anamorphic picture must be seen. By combining and contrasting multiple images, compressing them in space as verbal wit compresses ideas in time, these perspective devices perform the same feats visually as witty metaphor performs in language.

This analogy between the picture and the word is itself neatly depicted in Tesauro's frontispiece (figure 6). At

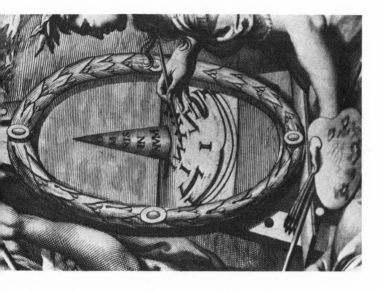

Figure 6. Frontispiece to Emmanuele Tesauro's *Il Cannocchiale Aristotelico* (Torino, 1670).

the left a figure representing Poesis peers through a telescope steadied for her by Aristotle. As the Latin tag at
the bottom explains, she is studying the spots in the sun
("she reproves the blemishes on a perfect body") revealed
to her through the perspective aperture.[21] Meanwhile, at
the right, Pictura paints a catoptric device which at once
(rather wittily) proclaims and enacts the motto: *omnis
in unum.*

These theoretical connections between verbal and visual
wit complete the analogy to be tested out in the following
chapters: the language of wit is to the rules of logical discourse, and to the poetic styles that obey them, as the
curious perspective is to the Albertian rules of perspective
drawing. Alberti's mathematically exact perspective constructions are paralleled by the logical and rhetorical
principles of orderly exposition and appropriate figurative
language. The reader or viewer familiar with the rules will
find the meaning of a regular work of art clear; his experience of it will be immediate and unquestioned because
its conventions will be transparent. So long as he can see
through them without having to think about either his
own authority as an understander or the adequacy of the
rules themselves as vehicles of understanding, he can safely
master the work of art. The poem or picture may be difficult to interpret for other reasons, but in this fundamental
respect it yields itself up fully and unambiguously to his
rational grasp.

Wit delights in breaking the rules of the rational game,
or at least in putting them under strain: to the awe of
Donne's "imperious wit," says Carew, "Our stubborne
language bends." By a kind of parodic internal subversion,

wit deforms the conventions of expository logic in the one case, and of linear perspective in the other. To the steady light of perspicuity, wit prefers the darkness of a coiled enigma with a flash of insight at its core.

Tesauro's emphasis on the link between literary and pictorial wit reminds us that seventeenth-century poets had available to them, "through the perspective aperture," a visual equivalent for their own witty practices, one which they might make explicit if they chose with some confidence that the force of the allusion would not be lost on the witty reader. For us as for them, the double vision demanded by the curious perspective offers a model for the experience of a witty poem—or even a witty play about a witty king, as we discover when we look through Shakespeare's "perspectives."

4 Richard II and the Perspectives of History

The cautionary preface to Arthur Fairchild's survey *Shakespeare and the Arts of Design* holds now as it did in 1937: "While there has been some casual discussion of Shakespeare and the fine arts, no systematic treatment of them has yet appeared, nor is it my purpose to attempt one"; to which Fairchild adds what must have been a somber reflection for one about to launch a lengthy monograph, "Shakespeare was not actively interested in the fine arts." The scholarship since then has been so various in subject matter and approach as to suggest that, in the absence of any unified interest on Shakespeare's part, the topic naturally splinters into smaller, unrelated studies focused less on the plays than on whatever aspect of the visual arts appeals to the writer. There have been emblem studies arguing that a verbal motif (for example, "She sat like Patience on a monument," *Twelfth Night*), a bit of stage business (Falstaff's pillow), or the staging of entire scenes would remind Shakespeare's audience of well-known emblems and the symbolic meanings they carried.[1] Other studies have traced explicit references to the visual arts (such as the *imprese* designed for the five knights in *Pericles* or the mention of Julio Romano in the *Winter's Tale*), and implicit or suspected allusions (such as Shakespeare's debt—so Panofsky believed—to Titian in his descriptions of Venus and Adonis). There have also been analyses of ekphrastic passages like the long account of an imaginary painting of the fall of Troy in *The Rape of Lucrece* or Enobarbus's description of Cleopatra's barge; works on stage design and properties; and more general speculation linking Shakespeare on stylistic or thematic grounds to the Mannerist or Baroque spirit.[2]

The very range of these studies suggests at least the breadth of reference to the visual arts that Shakespeare could command. To the growing list we should add his appreciation for the possibilities of perspective itself. In Sonnet 24 the poet (playing on the root sense of *perspectiva*) instructs his love that

> . . . perspective it is best painter's art.
> For through the painter you must see his skill
> To find where your true image picture lies. . . .
>   [4–6]

Perspective is best dramatist's art as well: the analogy points to Shakespeare's fundamental concern, beneath whatever emblems and other visual motifs he may call to our attention, with the complex activity of witnessing a play. Shakespeare's viewer is typically asked to see not just the drama, but "through" the dramatist to his "skill"—to the technical bones and sinews of playwriting that both support the dramatic illusion and reveal the fragility of its surface. Furthermore, like his fellow poets of the seventeenth century, Shakespeare associated the word *perspective* not only with the painter's *perspectiva artificialis* but also with the curious perspective. Thus Cleopatra has a reversible portrait in mind when she says of her two-faced Antony, "Though he be painted one way like a Gorgon,/The other way's a Mars" (2.5.116–17); Orsino (as we shall see in chapter 5) thinks of optical trickery when, seeing Viola and Sebastian together at last, he marvels, "One face, one voice, one habit, and two persons!/A natural perspective, that is and is not" (5.1. 208–09); and France's bantering with Henry V turns on a joke about hidden landscapes:

> *King.* . . . and you may, some of you, thank love for my blindness, who cannot see a fair French city for one fair French maid that stands in my way.
> *Fr. King.* Yes, my lord, you see them perspectively, the cities turned into a maid; for they are all girdled with maiden walls that war hath never entered.
>
> > [5.2.311–16]

Our own ability to "see" *Richard II* "perspectively" may be somewhat clouded unless we look more closely than students have so far[3] at Shakespeare's most elaborate use of the perspective image, for it proposes in effect that the play itself is to be regarded as a kind of perspective device.

At the end of 2.1 we have just seen Richard leave for the Irish wars and Northumberland tell the other disaffected nobles that the exiled Bolingbroke is about to land at Ravenspurgh. In a moment Green will report the chilling news to the queen, but before he rushes in the queen confides in Bushy that she feels the weight of some unknown

grief, nameless and yet heavier to bear than the mere sad-
ness of Richard's absence:

> Yet again, methinks,
> Some unborn sorrow, ripe in fortunes womb,
> Is coming towards me, and my inward soul
> With nothing trembles. At something it grieves
> More than with parting from my lord the King.
> [2.2.9–13]

Bushy's reply ingeniously plays on the scholastic distinction between substance and shadow, something and
nothing, to invent a consolation for grief that he—if not
the queen with her premonition, or the viewer with his
experience of the previous scene—will find convincing:

> Each substance of a grief hath twenty shadows,
> Which shows like grief itself, but is not so;
> For sorrow's eye, glazed with blinding tears,
> Divides one thing entire to many objects,
> Like perspectives, which rightly gazed upon,
> Show nothing but confusion—eyed awry,
> Distinguish form. So your sweet majesty,
> Looking awry upon your lord's departure,
> Find shapes of grief more than himself to wail,
> Which, looked on as it is, is naught but shadows
> Of what it is not. Then, thrice-gracious queen,
> More than your lord's departure weep not.
>   More's not seen;
> Or if it be, 'tis with false sorrow's eye,
> Which for things true weeps things imaginary.
> [2.2.14–27]

Bushy would have the queen believe she has "nothing" to fear. In this he is precisely, if ironically, correct. The play will demonstrate that having "nothing" to fear is hardly a consolation. This "heavy nothing," this "nameless woe," will soon become substantial enough when Green arrives:

> *Queen.* So, Green, thou art the midwife to my woe,
> And Bolingbroke my sorrow's dismal heir.
> Now hath my soul brought forth her prodigy;
> And I, a gasping new-delivered mother,
> Have woe to woe, sorrow to sorrow joined.
> [2.2.62–66]

For Richard the "shadows" of what is not—the fore-shadows of the nothing ahead—are even more ominous. Like Lear (reduced, says the Fool, to "Lear's shadow," "an O without a figure") Richard will have to endure the loss of his power, his crown, the very name of king, finally his life. "Are you contented to resign the crown?" asks Bolingbroke in the deposition scene (4.1.200). Richard's "Ay, no; no, ay; for I must nothing be" (201) is the properly ambiguous response of a "great minor poet" always sensitive to a quibble.[4] For if he is "contented"—willing—to resign, he is then certainly not contented in the other sense, substantially the king, full with the royal authority. Bolingbroke is now full, Richard empty, and in an equally empty ceremony the crown changes hands in token of the shifted weight of political power. And in the moments before his murder in the keep of Pomfret Castle, Richard struggles with his contradictory thoughts, none of them "contented":

> Sometimes am I king;
> Then treasons make me wish myself a beggar,
> And so I am. Then crushing penury
> Persuades me I was better when a king;
> Then I am kinged again; and by and by
> Think that I am unkinged by Bolingbroke,
> And straight am nothing. But whate'er I be,
> Nor I, nor any man that but man is,
> With nothing shall be pleased till he be eased
> With being nothing.
>
> [5.5.32–41]

These thoughts are "still-breeding" (8), endlessly gener-
ating yet stillborn, barren, and thus the last paradoxical
echo of the queen as a "gasping new-delivered mother"
of the "nothing" in fortune's womb.

All this is beyond Bushy's ken, for in 2.2 the irony of
Bolingbroke's return, of the empty shadow becoming the
terrifying substance, is directed against his attempt to
explain (away) the queen's sorrow. By the time he loses
his head and is "graved in the hollow ground" (3.2.140),
he will have learned the meaning of a "nothing" grief, but
now he is made to speak more than he knows: while he
argues that Richard's leaving can be understood unambiguously if one only regards it from the right point of view,
his analogy with the curious perspective suggests that there
are several points of view, and further that it is not as
simple as it seems to choose the "right" way of looking.

Bushy maintains that there is only a single "true" grief
falsely multiplied into twenty "imaginary" shadows by the
tears in sorrow's eye, as if by a multifaceted refracting
lens. These deceitful perceptions are "like perspectives,"

anamorphic pictures, which *"rightly* gazed upon,/ Show
nothing but confusion—eyed *awry,* Distinguish form."[5]
But how are they "like"? Which is the deceitful point of
view? The conceit in these lines turns on a punning reversal of the usual meanings of the words I have emphasized. "Rightly" here means, "at right angles," "directly,"
and hence the *wrong* way to look at an anamorphic
image; the right way is to look "awry," that is, obliquely.
The queen finds too many "shapes of grief . . . to wail"
because (in line 21) she looks "awry" upon her lord's
departure—but which way is that? If the second "awry" in
line 21 carries on the metaphor of lines 18–20 and means
"obliquely but technically correct for an anamorphic
picture," then Bushy is saying: It is a mistake to look
obliquely and thereby to distinguish multiple shapes of
grief. Look at it "as it is" (that is, "rightly"—straight
on, and in this case correctly) and you will see that what
you fear is just (needless) confusion and (empty) shadows.
But if "awry" in line 21 means "wrongly" in the usual
sense, then Bushy's advice becomes: You look wrongly
to look rightly (straight on) at your lord's departure and
find there delusive shapes of grief. See it instead "as it
is" (obliquely) and realize that the terrifying confusion in
the direct point of view is in fact naught but the harmless
shadows of one limited grief.

In the best tradition of the *Variorum* editor and his
predecessors, I have just cut a logical path through the
forest of puns in Bushy's speech.[6] However, with this
prose version to guide us, we run the risk of not seeing
the forest for the footnotes: to untangle the knotted
complexities of the text is to overlook its effect on the

reader or the playgoer. In our actual experience of Bushy's speech the criss-crossing double meanings of "rightly" and "awry" make the passage itself like an anamorphic perspective which conflates two images into one and requires of the witness the kind of mental juggling act Tesauro would have approved as the touchstone of a witty conceit. This is the same experience Stanley Fish describes in his reading of the "shifting relationships" in the final couplet of Herbert's "The Crosse":

> Reading these lines is like looking at a gestalt figure in which first one and then another pattern emerge from the same physical (here verbal) components. . . . until finally there is only one pattern made up of two declarations which, if they were laid side by side, would be perceived as mutually contradictory, but here, occupying the same linguistic space, they constitute a triumph of discursive language.[7]

I have singled out Bushy's speech because both the notion of a double perspective and the experience of seeing double that Fish describes are central to the play. Shakespeare's use of the painter's "perspective" as a metaphor for the understanding is one of the earliest in English. The word was common in English before the seventeenth century, as Claudio Guillén points out, in a more literal sense which referred first to the rules and devices of optics and later to the artificial perspective of the artist. Through the Christian association of optics with magic, pagan soothsaying, and the vanity of appearances on the one hand, and the pictorial illusionism of the artist's perspective on the other, the perspective

metaphor was often used to figure a deception of the eye
and mind, as in Drummond of Hawthornden's "All we
can set our eyes upon in these intricate mazes of Life is
but Alchimie, vain Perspective, and deceiving Shadows."[8]
In the seventeenth century, perspective provides a metaphor for cognition as well as illusion. It contributes a
vocabulary for speaking of the mind's point of view as
an observer of its own contents or the facts of experience;
like the figures in a painting, the objects of knowledge are
"seen" at various distances or in different aspects in a
conceptual space, as in Bacon's metaphor: "We have en-
deavored in these our partitions [of the *Advancement*]
to observe a kind of perspective, that one part may cast
light upon another."[9] Similarly the perspective conceit in
Ben Jonson's "Epigram.—In Authorem," originally printed
before Nicholas Breton's *Melancholike Humours* (1600),
demonstrates that those who fail to appreciate Breton's
verse must be looking at it from the wrong point of
view:

> Look here on BRETON'S work, the master print,
>   Where such perfections to the life do rise;
> If they seem wry to such as look asquint,
>   The fault's not in the object, but their eyes.
> For, as one coming with a lateral view,
>   Unto a cunning piece wrought perspective,
> Wants faculty to make a censure true;
>   So with this author's readers will it thrive;
> Which being eyed directly, I divine,
> His proof their praise'll incite, as in this line.

In the later seventeenth century the perspective metaphor becomes important for Leibniz as a way of imagining

the unity of the universe from a divine point of view beyond the multiplicity of our individual perceptions. In the *Monadologie* he compares the universe with a city whose aspect changes with the observer's point of view; "comme multipliée perspectivement," but which is nonetheless the same city.[10] The varieties of individual experience are thus seen as valid, though partial "perspectives" on a perfect whole, and a metaphor based on the anamorphic perspective serves him, in another place, as an assurance of universal harmony:

> It is as in the inventions of perspective, where certain lovely drawings appear only as confusion, until one finds their true point of view or sees them by means of a certain glass or mirror. . . . Thus the apparent deformities of our little world come together as beauties in the greater world, and there is nothing opposed to the unity of a universally perfect principle.[11]

Shakespeare's metaphor has the same form as Liebniz's but none of the philosopher's rational delight in the certainty of our knowledge or his assurance that the world we seek to understand is perfect and harmonious. In *Richard II* the painter's anamorphic "perspectives" lend the playwright not just a local metaphor but, as I hope to show, a conceptual model for seeing the chronicle of English history. We must see the play, like the queen her "nothing" grief, both "rightly" (awry) and "awry" (rightly)—as a wedged contrariety that contains two opposed points of view, neither offering the consolation of complete certainty, but both necessary for a fuller, if paradoxical, apprehension of a truth beyond our logical reach. This perspective is akin to the Shakespearean "mode of vision" which Norman Rabkin, borrowing a term from Einsteinian physics, calls "complementarity." The term, coined by Niels Bohr and popularized by Robert Oppenheimer, describes the theoretical necessity to regard light as both wavelike *and* corpuscular according to the experiment one is performing. For Rabkin this is analogous to the literary technique which is certainly not Shakespeare's alone, but his preeminently, of "presenting a pair of opposed ideals or groups of ideals and putting a double valuation on each."[12] But we need not ally Shakespeare with such distinguished if historically remote colleagues from the pure science faculties when the playwright offers us a comparison closer at hand in the curious perspective.

Before putting the play in that perspective, we might pause over Holbein's *The Ambassadors* (figure 7), the finest example of anamorphic painting done in England, and indeed one Shakespeare could well have had in mind when he wrote *Richard II*.[13]

The figures in Holbein's double portrait are French envoys to the court of Henry VIII, Jean de Dinteville and Georges de Selve. Between them they represent the temporal and spiritual arms of the French legation—Dinteville, on the left, is Seigneur de Polisy and Selve the Bishop of Lavour—with the poise, solidity, and magnificence that characterize Henry in Holbein's famous portrait of 1540. Dinteville is the more imposing figure in his black velvet surcoat lined with ermine and set off with rose-red satin sleeves. The gold neck chain carrying the badge of the order of Saint Michael and the ornate golden sheath of the dagger in his right hand emphasize the gorgeous variety of

Figure 7. Hans Holbein, *The Ambassadors* (1533). Courtesy National Gallery, London.

color and texture in Dinteville's costume. Although Selve's purple brocaded robe is more subdued and his pose less commanding, he makes almost as forceful an impression: the two share an authoritative but wary look that joins the studied poise of men who know their own importance in the public eye with the shrewd, critical detachment of practiced courtiers in a foreign land.

In Holbein's composition their authority rests symbolically, as their elbows do in fact, on a table displaying the tools of mastery over the liberal arts. The lower shelf contains, on the side near Selve, a lute and open hymnal; on the other side are the more practical instruments of worldly management suited to Dinteville: a terrestrial globe showing the papal line of demarcation between Spanish and Portuguese possessions in the new world, a T-square and compasses, and a partially opened book that can be identified as Peter Apian's *Well-grounded Instruction in all Merchant's Arithmetic.* The objects on the "higher" shelf, including an astrolabe, a solar clock, and a celestial globe, complete the symbolization of the four arts of the quadrivium by adding astronomy to arithmetic, geometry, and music. Pictorially the collection stresses the interrelationship of the arts by balancing the lute against the celestial globe, upon which all earthly harmony depends, and the celestial globe against the earthly to point the analogy between the "upper" and "lower" spheres of knowledge represented on the two shelves. There may also be an allusion to the *perspectiva artificialis,* that other liberal art which the Renaissance had added to the inherited list: Holbein's lute is shown in almost the exact position as the lute Dürer had chosen a few years earlier as the subject of his woodcut demonstrating a precise mechanical method of perspective drawing.[14]

Such still-life objects are of course common in late Renaissance painting either as the subjects of smaller works such as inlaid panels or as significant background for other figures.[15] Here these objects, meticulously detailed, lighted, and foreshortened, are at once emblems of the worldly knowledge associated with the ambassadors and a center of attention in themselves nearly as prominent as the main figures. The heavy table and the men flanking it form a single rectangular grouping welded by the horizontals of the shelves and the verticals of the figures, fully defined in surface and volume, convincingly represented to the eye. These men and the world at their command are, we tell ourselves, palpable, undeniably, "there."

So far, if we are looking "rightly," we experience the painting as an affirmation of the solidity and power of human achievement—of the instruments of policy, measurement, and exploration displayed before us, of the men who use them, and of the artist's power to image both in his own medium. Still we must reconcile this view with several small but disturbing details. The lute has one broken string, which in the inconographical tradition changes it from an emblem of harmony to an emblem of discord.[16] Richard has the emblematic significance of a broken string in mind during his prison solioquy:

> Music do I hear?
> Ha—ha—keep time! How sour sweet music is
> When time is broke and no proportion kept!
> So it is in the music of men's lives.

And here have I the daintiness of ear
To check time broke in a disordered string;
But, for the concord of my state and time,
Had not an ear to hear my true time broke.
I wasted time, and now doth time waste me.

[5.5.41–49]

The open book next to Selve is a Lutheran hymnal, the pages of which hint at another harmony beyond the discord of the earthly lute: Luther's German translation of the "Veni Creator Spiritus," "Kom Heiligen Geyst," is legible on the left, and on the right the introduction to his shortened version of the Decalogue, in which he enjoins obedience to the divine law. We might also notice a tiny silver crucifix in the upper left corner (almost obscured by the folds of the curtain), an even smaller death's head device in Dinteville's cap, and this: the decorative pattern of the floor places the scene unmistakably in the sanctuary of Westminster Abbey, though the interior of the church is hidden from view behind the green drapery in the background.

It has been suggested that the discordant string alludes to the failure of the League of Cognac in 1533, which ended seven years of fragile alliance between England and France, or that Selve is shown with a copy of Luther's hymns because the French cleric was dedicated to healing the religious schism, itself the most strident discord of the age. Still there is the suggestion in these nearly submerged details of sacred imagery that the scene before us is somehow discordant and deceptive in its very solidity (the empty lute case can just be seen under the table).

These men posed like acolytes on either side of the altar of human competence—in a kind of compositional parody of a religious scene—only conceal a truth which may be found on the altar behind the curtain.

That suggestion becomes part of the viewer's experience of the painting when he regards it "awry," in the perspective required by the anamorphic streak in the foreground. Seen from the right edge of the painting, the streak resolves itself into a skull. This bit of visual trickery, in part a clever signature (*holbein* means "hollow bone"), takes on a special significance in relation to the main theme of the work: it is a *memento mori* and an emblem of *vanitas* posed against a vital image of worldly prowess. Holbein had earlier used the death's head device in the woodcut *Death's Coat of Arms* (1526), where, placed between two robust figures, it gapes out its somber reminder.[17] *The Ambassadors* achieves the same effect more forcefully by creating the second point of view, for as the skull takes shape the rest of the painting becomes as blurry and indistinct as the streak was before. The "right" view goes "awry" as the wry view turns into a visual demonstration *de incertitudine et vanitate scientiarum et artium atque excellentia verba Dei.*[18] These wittily superimposed images join the two sides of Holbein's career. The secular portraitist and official recorder of the glories of the Tudor court controls one perspective, but the other is in the charge of the painter of the Basel altarpieces, the designer of the *Dance of Death* woodcuts, and the illustrator of Luther's Bible and Erasmus's *Praise of Folly*.

As Holbein celebrates and negates the two ambassadors, so the same ambiguity extends to the painting itself, which asserts both the power of perspective to create an illusion of reality and the emptiness, the *vanitas,* of that illusion.[19] That duplicity carries with it a similar process of loss and gain in the role of the viewer. The shifting perspectives undercut *his* authority as the ideal observer, but substitute a different kind of knowledge—an awareness of the reach and limitations of his own perceptions, and a disillusioned understanding that things are and are not what they seem.

That *Richard II* is capable of yielding the same understanding is a mark of its greater maturity over the first tetralogy and its kinship with the later tragedies. Given the limitations of the *Henry VI* plays—their episodic structure, their one-dimensional characters like Talbot, their vigorous heroics and unclouded patriotism—*Richard II* represents not only a considerable technical advance but a deepened insight into the problems of history and human motivation. Even *Richard III* seems crudely conceived beside it, despite the brilliance of the hunchback king's Machiavellianism which sustains the play. As Richard III bustles from one hateful villainy to the next, and finally to a bloody dog's death in Bosworth Field, the play moves toward its swift and untroubled resolution, reenacting a key chapter in the official Tudor explanation of English history. The Wars of the Roses, according to the chronicler Hall, showed "what mischiefe hath insurged in realmes by intestine devision . . . by domestical discord & unnatural controversy"; but this controversy

by the union of Matrimony celebrate and consummate betwene the high and mighty Prince King Henry the seventh and the lady Elizabeth his moste worthy Quene, the one beeying indubitate heire of the house of Lancastre, and the other of Yorke was suspended and appalled in the person of their most noble, puissant and mighty heire King Henry the eight; and by hym clerely buried and perpetually extinct.

The lesson of Henry's victory was plain: "that all men (more clerer than the sonne) may apparently perceive, that as by discord greate thyngs decaie and fall to ruine, so the same by concord be revived and erected." As the wars had issued from a breach of harmony, the union of Henry and Elizabeth "erected" fallen England to a state of sacramental integrity exemplified not only by "man & woman in marriage" but by the union of the "Godhed to the manhod," for in Christ "manne was joyned to God whiche before by the temptacion of the subtle serpent was from hym segregate and divided."[20] The defeat of Richard III, the last and most vicious fomenter of discord, was nothing short of an act of redemption, a national resurrection.

So in Shakespeare's *Richard III,* England awakes from the old king's "dead midnight" to a new morning under Richmond, whose prayer at the end has the full moral weight of the play behind it:

> . . . as we have ta'en the sacrament,
> we will unite the White Rose and the Red.
> Smile heaven upon this fair conjunction,
> That long have frowned upon their enmity!
> What traitor hears me, and says not amen?
> England hath long been mad and scarred herself;
> . . . .
> All this divided York and Lancaster,
> Divided in their dire division,

O, now let Richmond and Elizabeth,
The true succeeders of each royal house,
By God's fair ordinance conjoin together!
And their their heirs (God, if they will be so)
Enrich the time to come with smooth-faced peace
With smiling plenty, and fair prosperous days!

                                        [5.5.18-23, 27-34]

Richard II returns to the origins of the division and also
records the overthrow of a king and the installation of a
new regime. But where *Richard III* has its moral poles
clearly marked—on one side Richard, "determined to be
a villain," and on the other the pious Richmond, a captain
of the Lord and a minister of chastisement—*Richard II*,
without abandoning the framework of Tudor political
theology, confronts the ambiguities inherent in the ortho-
dox interpretation of English history.*

---

*Using terms similar to mine ("doubleness," "ambivalence"), A. P.
Rossiter, in his essay "Angel with Horns," finds *Richard III* the
better play on the grounds that the crook-backed king is a subversive figure (like Falstaff) who directs a fierce, comic energy against
the "repulsiveness, humanly speaking" (p. 20) of an unremitting
and naive conception of English history as "retributive reaction"
(p. 42). The "doubleness" of history therefore pits individual
dynamism against the grim working out of God's vengeance; and
where that dynamism is lacking, as in the case of the mere "precios-
ity and self-regarding sentiment" of Richard II (p. 57), the history
play collapses into an "obscure tragedy"—not fully tragic or fully
comic—displaying the "Frustration, the inadequacy of the Individual" helpless against the "national Destiny" (p. 42). See *Angel With
Horns,* ed. Graham Storey (New York: Theatre Arts Books and
Longmans, Green and Co., Ltd., 1961). My argument works toward
rehabilitating *Richard II* from such a charge by noting its focus on
the crucial "doubleness" of providential history itself, more soberly

These ambiguities arise first of all from the chroniclers' attempt to impose a providential design on the historical record. Richard II, though not malicious of heart, suffered from the "frailties of wanton youth," ruled wilfully rather than justly, and gave himself overmuch to his pleasures. To this extent, and because he had been unlawfully used at Richard's hand, Bolingbroke's revolt could be justified, and Holinshed could discern the "providence of God" at work in the deposition. Nevertheless Bolingbroke was the "first author" of discord; as Henry IV he and his line were "scourged afterwards as a due punishment unto rebellious subjects."[21] This paradox was sharped by the elaboration, under Elizabeth I, of the doctrine of the king's divinity. In the late fourteenth century the historical Richard had ruled as *primus inter pares.* At the deposition, as reported in Holinshed, the Bishop of Carlisle is concerned with the injustice of passing judgment on a king in his absence. But Shakespeare's Carlisle, influenced by late Tudor political theology of the king's divine right, argues Richard's immunity from human judgment: "What subject can give sentence on his king?/And who sits here that is not Richard's subject?" (4.1.121–22).[22]

The claims of divine right were elaborated in a series of homilies issued by the crown from 1547 on. Distributed to every parish in the kingdom, the homilies taught the duty of passive "obedience to Rulers and Magistrates" as the Lord's deputies on earth, and the sinfulness of rebellion even against an evil king: "Shall the subjects both by

---

contemplated by the dramatist than Rossiter's prejudice would allow, and brilliantly reflected in Richard's language and character, precious though they may be, as well as in the structure of the play.

their wickedness provoke God for their deserved punishment, to give them an undiscreet or evil prince, and also
rebel against him, and withal against God, who for the
punishment of their sins did give them such a prince?"[23]
This theological doctrine of the king's divinely ordained
rule was reflected in English law, as Ernst Kantorowicz
has shown, in the concept of the "king's two bodies."[24]
Possessed of an immortal "body politic" (in effect the
"body" of the state, with its citizenry the "members"
and the king its "head") as well as a perishable "body
natural," the king combined within himself the divine
and the human—in a union analogous to the Church's
status in canon law as a *corpus mysticum,* and ultimately
based on the dual nature of Christ.

The potential paradox of a king who both enjoys the
special sanction of divinity and suffers the infirmities of
the flesh did not trouble the Tudor jurists. In fact the ambiguity of this legal fiction was an asset in that it permitted
the courts to argue with equal validity the divine or the
human aspect of kingship according to the case before
them. But applied retrospectively to an event like the deposition of Richard II, the doctrine of the king's divinity
could only complicate historical interpretation. If, despite
his unfitness for rule, Richard stood above human judgment, then his deposition and murder by a subject could
be nothing but the most impious treachery. Indeed, a
"deposition" engineered by the sword could only be futile
since the crown is an alienable possession that only sepa-
rates itself from the king's person upon the death of his
natural body, whereupon it invests itself in the proper successor. Nor can Richard the man effectively consent in his

own deposition, even to preserve the nothing that is left him without the name of king, for the king cannot act against his own interest—"what the king does in his Body politic cannot be invalidated or frustrated by an Disability in his Natural Body." Yet that deposition must have fallen into God's larger plan, and the mantle of divinity must have passed to the usurper—especially if the usurper was to be the paternal ancestor of the Tudor line. From a providential point of view the glorious union of the white and red roses required the deposition of Richard II as prologue, just as Christ's salvation required the fall of Adam. The Tudor lawyers had emphasized the seamless unity of the king's dual nature, "a Body natural and a Body politic together indivisible . . . incorporated in one Person."[25] But the dramatist's concern lies with testing the fit between the physical and the metaphysical, between human action and providential design, in a case where the king's two bodies are violently separated.

When Richard is dethroned his royal identity is shattered like the mirror in the deposition scene, the glass which reflects, as Kantorowicz says, only the "banal face and insignificant *physis* of a miserable man, a *physis* now devoid of any *metaphysis* whatever."[26] He is left with a self defined only by deprivation and the fear of death; for Richard as for Holbein, the splendor of power dissolves into the imagery of the grave, of the "hollow crown" where death keeps his court. Deprived of the power of action and reduced to "Bolingbroke's 'Jack of the clock'" (5.5.60)—an automaton ticking off another man's hours— Richard falls back on a desperate theatricality, on acting. Kingship becomes a role for Richard to play as he becomes the mere "shadow" of a substantial king. (In the Renaissance the word *shadow* included "actor" among its many meanings.)

It is the hopeless attempt to reconstruct the shattered fragments of his identity that turns Richard into a witty poet as well. Critics have regarded Richard's strained, punning language as a sign of the play's immaturity. The later Shakespeare, like Berowne in *Love's Labor's Lost,* would forswear "Three-piled hyperboles, spruce affectation,/Figures pedantical," the "summer flies" of a style full of "maggot ostentation" (5.2.408–09). *Richard II* has been soberly pronounced "a qualified achievement in the consciously artificial manner."[27] But this judgment fails to realize that artifice is Richard's only resource, that his langauge is excessive and conceited because it must stretch itself around the paradox of a king unkinged. Richard seizes obsessively on the words spoken to him and splits them in two. His language sets "the word itself/Against the word" (5.5.13–14), for only a double language, painfully aware of the opposite meanings lurking in words, is adequate to Richard's own double condition:

> *Boling.* Go some of you, convey him to the Tower.
> *K. Rich.* O, good! Convey? Conveyers are you all,
>   That rise thus nimbly by a true king's fall.
>   [4.1.316–18]

Richard's "conveyers" become both "royal escorts" and "thieves," as his "still-breeding thoughts" are both fertile and stillborn, and his anguished "Ay, no; no, ay" a knotted pun of conflicting impulses. Bolingbroke can afford to be, as Richard calls him, a "silent king" (4.1.

290), or, when he speaks, a skilled but conventional rhetorician concealing as much as he reveals: "Henry Bolingbroke/On both his knees doth kiss King Richard's hand . . ." (3.3.35-36). His real meanings have no need for public utterance because they are attached to actions and backed with the weight of political power. Compared with Richard's frantic ostentation, Bolingbroke's reticence is powerful enough to topple a king without his once declaring his intentions. Bolingbroke not surprisingly has little patience with Richard's wordplay, but Richard persists in ruling the only realm where he still holds sway, persists in hammering his verbal subjects into linguistic models of his own paradoxical state.

But the effort is unavailing: Richard can never fashion his splintering words into a language that will reestablish connections. His final attempt to "compare/This prison where I live unto the world" (5.5.1-2)—to rejoin the shrunken kingdom of his own natural body to the greater world from which he has been severed—must fail. The only solution to his grief is the dissolution of the metaphysical and the physical in death: "Mount, mount, my soul! thy seat is up on high;/Whilst my gross flesh sinks downward, here to die" (5.5.111-12).

By setting Shakespeare's king next to Holbein's ambassadors I have hoped to suggest that Richard's character and language must be seen from the two points of view of the curious perspective, generated, in Richard's case, by his double nature as king and man. In him the perspectives of imperishable authority and fragile mortality are joined in an unstable union, a discord, that requires us to see both the crown and the hollowness at its center. One analogue for Richard's character may be found in mortuary sculpture which presents two reposing figures of the deceased, one fully fleshed and lifelike on the lid of a carved tomb and the second, a skeletal corpse, inside the tomb.[28] Another visual model which conflates the two aspects into a single figure is the reversible perspective portrait like the seventeenth-century French woodcut entitled *Il faut Mourir* (figure 8). I would like to propose further that our need to see Richard rightly and awry extends to our experience of the play as a whole.

The "seeing" with which I have been concerned so far is a kind of intellectual balancing act in the presence of a double character speaking a double language. But of course we see a play in the literal sense as well: whether in performance or in the mind's eye, the drama depends upon our visual experience more directly than the lyric or the novel, which may or may not call up relevant imagery for the individual reader. The composition of figures onstage and the rhythm of their movement and gesture are crucial to what Michael Goldman terms the "energies of drama."[29] For the playgoer the carefully posed, often ritualized, scenes of *Richard II* serve more than the narrative purpose of advancing the plot through time: they form an overall visual composition, a pattern as well as a sequence.

The first four scenes of the play alternate between public ceremony and private conversation. The public scenes, Bolingbroke's challenge (1.1) and the aborted combat (1.3), are visually identical: two opponents take their places on either side of King Richard, who (with the viewer) must make a choice between them. The characters'

Figure 8. Reversible Portraits: Esme de Boulonnois, *Il Faut Mourir* (seventeenth century). Courtesy Metropolitan Museum of Art.

movement onstage, like their language, is restricted to the few ritual acts prescribed by the solemn occasion. Standing "face to face,/And frowning brow to brow" (1.1.15–16) Mowbray and Bolingbroke throw down the gage in turn and accept the other's challenge. In 1.3 the locale has shifted to the lists at Coventry, where there are perhaps more "Nobles" in attendance, the combatants are now armed, and a marshall replaces Gaunt as an interlocutor between them and the king; otherwise this scene echoes the first in both its balanced composition and rigid formality. With Richard in the center (whether on a balcony above the "field" or on the platform stage), Bolingbroke and Mowbray enter from either side and "orderly proceed" to announce their name and cause, profess their loyalty to the king and receive the lance. They are posed in a formal tableau which is all the more static because the action we suppose will issue from all this ceremony is frustrated. Having refused to be reconciled, they will now not be permitted to fight:

> *Mar.* Sound trumpets, and set forward combatants.
>   [*a charge sounded*]
>   Stay! The king hath thrown his warder down.
> *King.* Let them lay by their helmets and their spears
>   And both return back to their chairs again.
>   [1.3.117–20]

The judicial forms of challenge and combat are intended to make conflicting claims manifest, a part of the public record, and to resolve them by the certain test of battle. Yet here nothing happens and no judgment is rendered except for Richard's apparently capricious decision to sus-

pend the contest and banish both parties. It is left for the
smaller scenes to reveal what lies hidden in the public
spectacle. Richard explains his verdict publicly as a pre-
caution against shedding kindred blood in civil strife, but
in 1.4 he tells Aumerle that his private motive for the
banishment lay in his fear of Bolingbroke's ambition and
popularity. We know further from Gaunt in 1.2 that
Richard is already spotted with kindred blood for his com-
plicity in the murder of the Duke of Gloucester—that
when Bolingbroke accuses Richard's agent Mowbray of
spilling Gloucester's blood, "Which blood like sacrificing
Abel's, cries/. . . To me for justice and rough chastisement" (1.1.104, 106), it is the king himself who stands
guilty by proxy of committing the sin of Cain. The public
scenes appear to be richly significant with all the trappings
of history; but counterpointed against what is said out of
public hearing, they become opaque. Their color and detail, their rhetoric, their very factuality, form an ornate
surface concealing the truth beneath it. The high ceremony
is there not merely to recreate a nostalgic picture of a lost
medieval order, as Tillyard believed,[30] but to suggest that
history itself—for all its high-stomached language—is an
articulate dumbshow.

I have emphasized the visual composition of scenes 1.1
and 1.3 because the same pattern recurs at three other
points in the play, twice in the deposition scene, 4.1, and
again in 5.3. Schematically, the three principal figures onstage—in 1.1 and 1.3 Bolingbroke, Richard, and Mowbray—form a kind of triptych with the central character in
the judgment seat: ⁀⁀⁀ . This is a scenic equivalent for
the Gardener's judicial image of Bolingbroke and Richard

"weighed" in the balance (which in production the Gardener will certainly make a living emblem by extending his arms like a pair of scales):

> Their fortunes both are weighed.
> In your lord's scale is nothing but himself,
> And some few vanities that make him light;
> But in the balance of great Bolingbroke,
> Besides himself, are all the English peers,
> And with that odds he weighs King Richard down.
> [3.4.84–89]

In each recurrence a dual judgment is to be made, that of the character at the fulcrum about the two contenders in the balances, and that of the viewer about the scene itself. These scenes together form a larger set of balances that weigh the crucial dilemma of the play.

At the beginning of 4.1, when Bolingbroke has the power if not the crown, the "woeful pageant" of deposition opens with a formal challenge between Bagot and Aumerle over which the new king must preside. The captured Bagot is called to testify what he knows of "noble Gloucester's death;/Who wrought it with the king, and who performed/The bloody office of his timeless end" (3–5). He accuses Aumerle, who is brought forward and told to "look upon that man" (7) as Bagot levels his charge:

> In that dead time when Gloucester's death was plotted,
> I heard you say, "Is not my arm of length,
> That reacheth from the restful English court
> As far as Calais to mine uncle's head?"
> Amongst much other talk that very time

I heard you say that you had rather refuse
The offer of an hundred thousand crowns
Than Bolingbroke's return to England;
Adding withal, how blest this land would be
In this your cousin's death.

[10-19]

Visually and thematically the scene reenacts the challenge in 1.1 and 1.3, which also concerned responsibility for Gloucester's death, with different actors in the key positions (diagram 6).

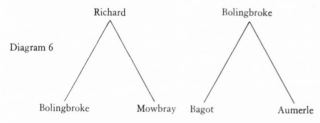

Diagram 6

Richard · Bolingbroke · Mowbray · Bagot · Aumerle · Bolingbroke

Although Aumerle denies the charge, it seems at first that the balance has tipped decisively against him as three other witnesses line up on Bagot's side: Fitzwater supports Bagot's testimony from personal knowledge ("I heard thee say, and vauntingly thou spak'st it,/That thou wert cause of noble Gloucester's death"), Percy throws down the gage to defend Fitzwater's honor, and "Another Lord" add his own gage to the pile as he declares Aumerle forsworn and treacherous (36-37, 44-48, 52-56). At this moment, however, Surrey steps in as an eye-witness to the conversation between Aumerle and Fitzwater: "My Lord Fitzwater, I do remember well/The very time Aumerle and you did talk" (60-61). Fitzwater acknowledges that Surrey was there and looks to him for support, whereupon

Surrey flatly contradicts Fitzwater's accusation and the two fall into a quarrel of their own:

> *Fitz.* 'Tis very true. You were in presence then,
>   And you can witness with me this is true.
> *Surrey.* As false, by heaven, as heaven itself is true!
> *Fitz.* Surrey, thou liest.
> *Surrey.* Dishonorable boy!
>
> [62–65]

Since this is Surrey's first appearance in the play we have no voucher for his honesty or, indeed, for Fitzwater's, Bagot's, or Aumerle's. With one eyewitness for each side, the case reaches an impasse that can only be broken by calling yet another witness—for now Fitzwater remembers having "heard the banished [Mowbray, Duke of] Norfolk say/That thou, Aumerle, didst send two of thy men/To execute the noble Duke at Calais" (80–82). Bolingbroke is willing to have the conclusive witness repealed; but Norfolk, he is told, has died in exile, and he has no choice but to leave all these differences unresolved—"under gage" until some future "days of trial" which are never appointed in the course of the play (105–06).

This episode, inconclusive and apparently unrelated to the deposition which follows, is nevertheless reconstructed with some care out of a few details in Holinshed's chronicle. There Sir John Bagot is reported to have given a deposition containing "certeine evill practises of king Richard" and affirming Richard's "great affection" for the Duke of Aumerle. Bagot also testified to a private conversation with Mowbray in which the latter, having denied any part in Gloucester's death, named Aumerle as the one who carried out the king's murderous wishes. The next day, according to Holinshed, Fitzwater appealed Aumerle for treason and "twentie other lords also . . . threw downe their hoods, in pledge to prove the like matter against the duke of Aumerle." Bolingbroke then licensed the return of Mowbray to answer the charges against him and learned of Mowbray's death.[31] While Holinshed makes no mention of anyone speaking *for* Aumerle, who in his account stands condemned on all sides, Shakespeare deliberately adds the character of Surrey to balance the scales, and further makes Aumerle's case depend on the unobtainable testimony Mowbray carried with him to the grave. With these changes Shakespeare creates a scene where a matter of historical judgment becomes ambiguous: Surrey and Fitzwater see the past from conflicting points of view, and neither we nor Bolingbroke can decide which is "right" and which is "awry." That "dead time when Gloucester's death was plotted" is not just past but dead as Mowbray is dead—silent and beyond recall. Like one of Richard's double words, the past has split into opposites that cannot be reconciled.

By its parallelism to the earlier judgment triptychs this scene makes the question of Gloucester's murder all the more uncertain (given that Richard wanted it done, who carried it out? Mowbray? Aumerle?) and reminds us of the stasis and concealment, the inconclusiveness, of the history open to public view. The scene's importance as a prelude to the deposition becomes clear if we realize one obvious but vital aspect of our own relationship to this history play. Bolingbroke's vantage point on the history of Bagot and Aumerle is analogous to our vantage point on the history of Richard II and Henry IV: we are spectators at a reenactment, an attempted resuscitation, of a dead past, but the replica is necessarily a death mask and not the living flesh. Because we cannot see more than the preserved public face we can never attain the certainty of knowing the private heart.

That limitation first of all gives special point to Carlisle's speech, which follows next. "What subject can give sentence on his king?" warns not merely against the offense of judging God's deputy but against the presumption of judging at all. If Bolingbroke cannot in conscience give sentence on two of Richard's underlings, how can he give sentence on Richard? The same caution must apply to the audience's judgment of the deposition. For Richard, acting as the stage manager of his own deposition, will maneuver Bolingbroke into the same position Bagot and Aumerle were in a moment before. Taking the crown (from York or one of the officers who has carried it into the room), Richard invites Bolingbroke to "seize" it, and the figures hold the pose, each with a hand on the crown between them, while Richard speaks:

> Give me the crown. Here, cousin, seize the crown.
> Here, cousin,
> On this side my hand, and on that side yours.
> Now is this golden crown like a deep well
> That owes two buckets, filling one another,
> The emptier ever dancing in the air,
> The other down, unseen, and full of water,
> That bucket down and full of tears am I
> Drinking my griefs whilst you mount up on high.
>   [4.1.181–89]

Richard's conceit of the crown as a "deep well/That owes two buckets" echoes the Gardener's scales as a figure of the shifting fortunes of the two men and the difficulty of the judgment we have to make between them. The banishment of Bolingbroke and Gaunt's prophetic denunciation of Richard in act 1 had been followed by an announcement of Bolingbroke's return. Now the deposition of Richard and Carlisle's prophetic denunciation of Bolingbroke are followed (at 4.1.326–34) by the laying of a plot against the new king. As the beginning of the new regime reenacts the end of the old, our judgment is suspended in an equilibrium which carefully balances their competing claims.

The final triptych occurs in 5.3, where Henry must decide between two supplicants. On one side Aumerle (seconded by his mother) begs the king's forgiveness for his part in the conspiracy which has just come to light; on the other Aumerle's father, the Duke of York, urges the king to condemn Aumerle for treason (diagram 7).

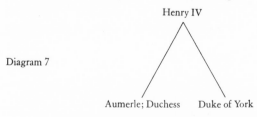

Henry IV

Diagram 7

Aumerle; Duchess   Duke of York

An uncle to both Richard and Bolingbroke, York had been torn between them but finally bound his allegiance to the new king so securely that—even though Henry is inclined to be lenient—he now demands his own son's death. Henry, angry as he is with Aumerle, is also half amused at these proceedings, for the old duke and his persistent wife make a faintly ridiculous pair (79–82); and what is held up for ridicule in the warm light of Henry's generosity is York's vindictive code of "honor" and "dishonor" which places political loyalty over the natural affection of fathers for their children:

> *York.* Mine honor lives when his dishonor dies,
>   Or my shaded life in his dishonor lies.
>   Thou kill'st me in his life; giving him breath
>   The traitor lives, the true man's put to death.
>   [70–73]

Henry chooses mercy over this harsh brand of justice, a new way of life over the death demanded of him by the last survivor of the old generation, and his forgiveness is as complete as Aumerle's guilt. York urges him to say his pardon in French—to "say 'pardonne moy'" (119)—but the king refuses to quibble. He will not "set the word itself against the word" (122) but rather speak it plainly, "I pardon him, as God shall pardon me" (131); and to leave no doubt he grants the duchess's plea that he speak it twice:

> *Duch.* Speak it again.
>   Twice saying "pardon" doth not pardon twain,
>   But makes one pardon strong.
> *Boling.* With all my heart
>   I pardon him.
>   [133–36]

Balanced against the play's opening triptych, this scene completes one view of the historical process—let us call it the "right" view—that justifies the deposition morally and metaphysically, suggesting (as York had earlier put it) that "heaven hath a hand in these events" (5.2.37). In the first act Richard had ruled in a case of treason and, to keep his own guilt hidden, had dispensed not justice but vengeance on both parties. By exiling and then dispossessing Bolingbroke of his inheritance, he had taken "from Time / His charters and his customary rights" and so broken the chain of "fair sequence and succession" by which he could claim his own authority. In this view Bolingbroke, as Henry IV, has rejuvenated the political order by putting time back into joint: he has created a "new world" (Fitzwater, 4.1.78) and a "new spring of time" (York, 5.2.50). Richard has the blood of Abel on his hands. Like the Gardener he is "old Adam's likeness," and his fall signifies a "second fall of cursed man" (3.4.73, 76). Although at the deposition Richard had played the role of a betrayed Christ—"Did they not sometime cry 'All hail!' to me / So Judas did to Christ" (4.1.169–70)—this was nothing but a shadowy performance, for the substance of divine kingship had passed to another man. Now when Henry pardons Aumerle the duchess corretly proclaims him a "god on earth," and leads her son off stage with the words, "Come, my old son; I pray God make thee new" (5.3.136, 146). The old Aumerle is forgiven under a new dispensation of mercy, and his pardon is the emblem of a regenerate kingdom. In short the "right" view is that English history recapitualtes spiritual history as a redemptive movement from sinfulness to grace.

If the play ended here it would be another version of *Richard III*, moving from "Richard's night to Bolingbroke's [= Richmond's] fair day" (3.2.218), but the con-

cluding three scenes establish the second, "wry" point of
view. First Exton and a servant remain onstage:

> *Exton.* Didst thou not mark the king, what words he
>   spake?
>   "Have I no friend will rid me of this living fear?"
>   Was it not so?
> *Man.*   These were his very words.
> *Exton.* "Have I no friend?" quoth he. He spake it twice
>   And urged it twice together, did he not?
> *Man.* He did.
>
> [5.4.1–6]

Having just twice spoken the words of pardon, Henry
(evidently before the scene with Aumerle) had already
twice spoken the words of treachery and murder. Having
just refused to set the word itself against the word in a
French pun, Henry now presents us with a far more disturbing contradiction—which is echoed a moment later
in the language of Richard's prison soliloquy. For among
Richard's discontented thoughts, the

> thoughts of things divine, are intermixed
> With scruples, and do set the word itself
> Against the word:
> As thus, "Come, little ones," and then again,
> "It is as hard to come as for a camel
> To thread the postern of a small needle's eye."
>
> [5.5.12–17]

Weighing his own fate, Richard is caught on the dilemma
of reconciling the scripture's promise of mercy with its

threat of retribution. The same dilemma confronts the spectator in the juxtaposition of 5.3 and 5.4, which presents the equivalent (and equivocal) problem of interpreting King Henry (diagram 8).

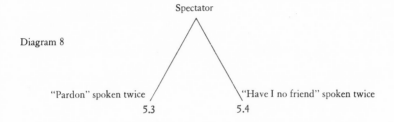

Diagram 8

Spectator

"Pardon" spoken twice   "Have I no friend" spoken twice

5.3   5.4

Henry's final action in the play, the banishing of Exton, completes the "wry" perspective by recalling the allusion to Abel in 1.1: "They love not poison that do poison need,/Nor do I these. . . . With Cain go wander thorough shades of night" (5.6.38–39, 43). Exton is Henry's man as Mowbray was Richard's and through these exiled surrogates both the deposed king and his successor bear the guilt of a kindred murder. In the "wry" view English history recapitulates the sin of Cain, recording a cycle of homicide rather than a spiritual progress. The "right" view permits us to discern the hand of a merciful God in the local design of English history, a God who leads his chosen people ("Come, little ones") along the path of salvation charted, through scripture, in the larger design of sacred history. In this view the scales tip decisively toward Henry IV in his divine aspect, and the end of the play (insofar as it seems about to end with the pardon at 5.3) completes the form of a divine comedy mirrored in the human comedy of the king's charity. The "wry" view, on the other

hand, sets this sense of an ending against what is in effect
an alternative and tragic conclusion: it sets the word of the
play against the word. We are now reminded that in
the balance of the judgment we are called upon to make of
Henry, the career of this guilt-stricken and prematurely
weary man is intermixed with "scruples" (literally, and
appropriately, the minute weights used to counterpoise
what is weighed in a scale). We are reminded that cal-
culation and naked power have advanced him to the
throne; that those same arts will be employed to secure the
throne through the murder of Richard; that despite, or
perhaps within, God's more comforting designs, fallen men
enact the woeful pageant of history by reenacting the role
of Cain on the stage of public events. The difficulty of
balancing God's two awesome attributes, his mercy and his
justice, not only preoccupies Richard's anguished thoughts
in prison, it also supplies the terms of the play's double
ending. For if a merciful God justifies Bolingbroke's rise,
a just God will exact a century of national suffering as the
penance for his fall. We look both ways and ask: "Is this
the promised end?" The question does not appear in this
play but in *King Lear,* when Kent has just seen the end of
Goneril and Regan but must now witness a howling Lear
with Cordelia in his arms.

These two perspectives together comprise the play's two
bodies, a spiritual and a physical nature paradoxically incorporate in one dramatic form. The play is bracketed by
two opposing structural symmetries, corresponding to two
opposed patterns of meaning, which may be represented
schematically (diagram 9).

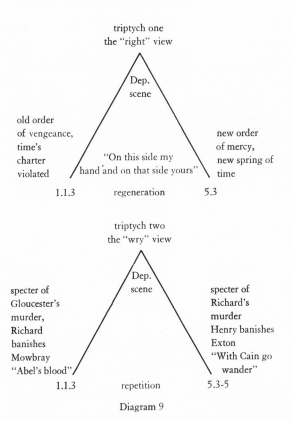

triptych one
the "right" view

Dep.
scene

old order
of vengeance,
time's
charter
violated

"On this side my
hand and on that side yours"

new order
of mercy,
new spring of
time

1.1.3   regeneration   5.3

triptych two
the "wry" view

Dep.
scene

specter of
Gloucester's
murder,
Richard
banishes
Mowbray
"Abel's blood",

specter of
Richard's
murder
Henry banishes
Exton
"With Cain go
wander"

1.1.3   repetition   5.3-5

Diagram 9

In our experience of the play the "right" and "wry" points of view are superimposed in a way that forces us to hold both configurations in mind. As the model of a double character generates a witty double language, it also imbeds two modes of explanation in the same historical event, or rather discovers in one event two necessary, if logically incompatible, meanings. The play neither endorses nor denies the Tudor myth but builds on its premises to show that the providential theory of the king's double nature necessarily requires a complex kind of doublethink for which the curious perspective is the visual model. Confronted with these shifting patterns of meaning, the witness can have no unequivocal point of view. Instead he is put in the difficult role of balancing conflicting but equally valid perceptions. He must see both the "controlling majesty" of kingship and the vanity of the "hollow crown."

5 The "Natural Perspective" of Shakespearean Comedy: *Twelfth Night* and *A Midsummer Night's Dream*

> . . . painting [uses] perspectiue and forshortning of lines, with due shadoing according to the rule of the eye, by falshood to express truth. . . . For perspectiue, to define it brefly, is an art taken from or by the efect or jugment of the eye, for a man to express anything in short'ned lines and shadowes, to deseaue bothe the vnderstanding and the eye.[1]

"Two persons" together onstage for the first time, each a mirror image of the other, both sharing "One face, one voice, one habit," Viola and Sebastian become a perfect visual ambiguity. Their joint presence at the climactic moment of *Twelfth Night* finally unties the tangle of mistaken identities that had been growing hopelessly, if predictably, snarled; it is a moment designed "to expresse truth" by reasserting, and then revealing, the "falshood" of Viola's disguise. It initiates an unmasking that fulfills Viola's trust, when she first takes on the "form" of Cesario, in the clarifying power of time. Yet, as we have come to expect by the fifth act of a play obsessed in its language, plot, and spectacle with double forms, the final revelation strikes Orsino as just possibly the final deception. Caught between astonishment and suspicion, belief and incredulity, he registers the wonder of "one" split into "two persons" by seeing it as a piece of perspective trickery, "A natural perspective that is and is not" (5.1.209).

On the page, and even more in production (the brother and sister must stand transfixed in their surprise, a vivid speaking picture), the scene enforces itself as imaginatively essential. It would seem to embody the play's central concern with identity and disguise and to present itself to Orsino as a valuable instant of instruction in seeing and role playing. As always in Shakespeare, such moments implicate the audience as well as the character onstage and explore the dramatist's concern with the complex activity of witnessing a play. Orsino's calling the moment a "perspective" can hardly be a casual choice on the playwright's part.

I have argued that in the case of *Richard II* the characters' and the audience's "perspectives" on English history may become a mode of dramatic understanding more precise than our usually vague metaphor, if we attend to the full meaning of the queen's griefs as "perspectives, which rightly gazed upon,/Show nothing but confusion—eyed awry,/Distinguish form" (2.2.18–20). There Shakespeare invites the audience to see in a local passage—and more importantly, to envision as a concept governing the whole play—a kind of witty picture built on an oblique (anamorphic) perspective schema and comprehensible only from a sidelong point of view. The "perspectives" in the second act of *Richard II* generate an elaborate metaphysical conceit whose verbal complexities image the difficulty of regarding the past unequivocally from a certain vantage point—to see "rightly" (that is, straight on) is to see wrongly; the right view is paradoxically "awry." By offering itself as a kind of picture—an opaque surface for all its rich detail and apparent depth—the history play both asserts and questions its own ability to re-present a dead past. We respond to the playwright's imitations of history as Bassanio does to "Fair Portia's counterfeit," the miniature portrait in *The Merchant of Venice:* "What demigod/Hath come so near creation," and yet, "this shadow doth limp behind the substance" (3.2.115–16, 128–29). Orsino's view of Viola and Sebastian—a perception that "is" and "is not," a simultaneous truth and falsehood—functions similarly as a visual epitome of *Twelfth Night* and permits us to focus on a crucial "perspective" of Shakespearean comedy in such other plays as *A Midsummer Night's Dream.*

The word itself as we have seen has its root meaning for the Renaissance in the context of technical optics, where "perspectiva naturalis" designates the study of eyesight on a geometrical model. By applying the rules of "natural" vision to the problems of pictorial composition, Alberti and his followers formulated the painter's "perspectiva artificialis." The intrigue of the "artificial" perspective lay in its ability to fashion an exact visual match of the "natural world—to transform a flat surface into an "open window" through which, as it were, the observer could see an optically correct representation of objects in a three-dimensional space. This "perspective," says Shakespeare in Sonnet 24, "is best painter's art." In a broader sense any picture, such as a panoramic landscape or an architectual vista, that conspicuously used this art to create the illusion of spatial depth or *trompe l'oeil* verisimilitude could be called a "perspective." Those who appreciated "perspectives" in art might transfer the term back to the non-pictorial world and pronounce certain real views pleasing natural "perspectives"—pleasing because composed like perspective pictures.

The witty interplay possible between the "natural" and "artificial" perspective is reflected in the Renaissance fascination with juxtaposing the two realms in theatrical spectacle and in illusionistic mural painting. In the masque (Twelfth Night was the chief occasion for presenting spectacular entertainments) artfully concealed stage machinery could make clouds and chariots bearing the royal masquers seem to fly naturally through a space created by foreshortened backdrops.[2] By way of Serlio and Lomazzo, Elizabethans knew not only of the Italian perspective stage, but also of such feats as Peruzzi's *Sala delle Prospective* in the Villa Farnesina, where a frescoed wall continues the architectural logic of the whole room as it appears to open onto an outer balustrade and, beyond, to an expansive view of Rome.[3] In 1612 Salomon de Caus published his treatise *La perspective* at London. There the French engineer, who as "Prince Henry's drawing master" had redesigned the gardens at Greenwich and Richmond Palace, gave directions for painting a *trompe l'oeil* garden on the wall of an actual garden, or for "painting on the end of a gallery, another gallery, so that to a person entering there will seem to be still another gallery, or two, or three, just as long as the natural one."[4] It is this power of perspective to duplicate the natural that points one emphasis in Orsino's exclamation: "A *natural* perspective that is and is not." In Viola and Sebastian nature alone has apparently created an effect that would be less surprising if art had had a hand in it. Of course, Viola's artful disguise is responsible for her likeness to her brother, and the entire "natural" perspective Orsino sees exists within an encompassing artifice called *Twelfth Night,* itself juxtaposed to the actuality of a theater—these are nuances that should not be lost on a Shakespearean audience.

The convincing verisimilitude which linear perspective makes possible sharpens the sense of paradox (Orsino's "perspective that *is* and *is not*") in Renaissance discussions of pictorial imitation: the most faithful representation was understood to be not merely a shadow of the real thing (as the Platonists would maintain about any image) but a willfull, methodical deception—to seem round in perspective, a circle must be misrepresented as an oblong. Nicholas Hilliard, quoted in the epigraph to this chapter, is typical of the English writers who provide a context for Shakespeare's "perspective" allusion. Translating Lomazzo, Richard Haydocke finds that "the skill of the workeman" occupied with foreshortenings and converging parallel lines "consisteth in shewing False and deceitfull sights insteede of the true," while Henry Peacham devotes a chapter of his *Gentleman's Exercise* to the "manifold deceptions of the sight by perspective." The best miniaturist in the generation after Hilliard, Edward Norgate, writes that impressions of depth in landscape painting are "nothing but Deceptive visions, a kind of cousning or cheating your owne Eyes, by (y)our owne consent and assistance."[5] None of these writers, content as they often are with the commonplace, considers why we should particularly enjoy being cozened or what we gain by our "consent." The later Baroque—in the theorizing of Tesauro, the art of Bernini, the poetry of Crashaw—would see the flicker of illusion and disillusion as a spark of the divine *ingegno,* at once a game and a flash of transcendent insight.[6] Francis Junius is closer to the comic temper of *Twelfth Night* when he defines the "delight of admiration" common to poetry and painting and so makes a connection between the two suggested in Orsino's allusion to the sister art:

> . . . [painting and poetry] make us in such an astonishment of wonder to stare upon the Imitation of things naturall, as if we saw the true things themselves; in so much that we do not love, though we finde ourselves mis-led, to have this our joy interrupted, but we do rather entertaine it with all possible care and studie . . . we suffer our hearts wittingly and willingly to be seduced and beguiled.
>
> This deceit, sayth Philostratus, as it is pleasant, so doth it not deserve reproach: for to be so possessed with things that are not, as if they were; and to be so led with them, as that we (without suffering any hurt by them) should think them to be; cannot but be proper for the reviving of our mind. . . .[7]

The coupling of "wittingly and willingly" describes a finely balanced perception of art more emotionally charged and more paradoxical than a "willing suspension of disbelief." Coleridge's formula implies chiefly the act of a controlling intellect "willing" hypothetically to entertain something incredible: it is pointedly not a willing belief. Junius, and Shakespeare, yoke presence of mind with wonder. Their asethetic supposes the same rational detachment but also speaks the rapture of a heart "possessed," joyfully "seduced and beguiled" as if in love.

The language of enchantment here, at once erotic and magical, suggests another context for Orsino's "perspective," which he imagines, a few lines later in the scene, as a "glass": "If this be so, as yet the glass seems true, / I shall have share in this most happy wreck" (5.1.257–58). He is likely to have in mind one of those "woondrous devises" described in a contemporary account of the "miraculous sights and conceipts made and contained in glasse . . . whereto the art perspective is verie necessary."[8] One branch of perspective art (Lomazzo's *Specularia*) teaches how "you may have glasses so made, as what image or favour soever you print in your imagination, you shall thinke you see the same therein"—glasses to multiply images, to break white light into a spectrum of color, to create distorted or deceptive reflections, to magnify distant objects, to set fires by concentrating the rays of the sun.[9] An understanding of perspective can explain away much of the wonder of such devices as the gaping of the innocent in an age when refracting lenses (and indeed, in England, perspective pictures) were just ceasing to be a novelty.[10] "Tut, that's no news," scoffs a character in one of Jonson's masques after hearing a tale of the moon "made . . . great as a drumhead . . . and brought . . . within the length of this room": "your perspexive perplexive glasses are common."[11] But even for one who had learned, say, from Lomazzo, "all the properties and deceits" of glasses, something of the mystery might remain. The long catalog of perspectives from which the examples above are taken appears in a sixteenth-century *Discoverie of Witchcraft;* the writer's list of "illusions" includes a number of magical ones soberly reported ("you may perceive man flieng in the air") and ends by endorsing Augustine's opinion that "some hidden mysterie" lies therein.[12]

Indeed, despite Jonson's testier gibes at the superficiality of Inigo Jones's art ("ye mere perspectiue of an Inch board"), perspective was associated with the conjuring of the magus and the necromancer, in whose hands a "glass" could allow the eye to pierce through to the truth of things. Perspectives were instruments of "that famous art/Wherein all nature's treasure is contain'd," that "magic, magic" which so "ravish'd" Marlowe's Faustus (1.1.75–76, 111). Faustus would be as "cunning as Agrippa" (1.1.118), that "abundant scholar" who is credited by Thomas Nashe (among many such reports of his skill) with having produced a vision of King Henry VII "in a perspective glass" hundreds of miles from Windsor forest, where the sovereign was on a hunt.[13] The Faustian Friar Bacon, in Robert Greene's play, likewise emulates Cornelius Agrippa with his own "glass prospective," wherein distance presents no barrier to men seeing "What their thoughts or hearts' desire could wish."[14] But Greene also sets a moral limit to the unhindered gratification of the eye and the will represented by such a glass. Two friends who, with the aid of Bacon's device, have just witnessed their fathers kill one another in a duel reenact the same tragedy by falling upon each other. Bacon reproaches himself and breaks his glass:

> This glass prospective worketh many woes;
> And therefore, seeing these brave lusty brutes,

> These friendly youths, did perish by thine art,
> End all thy magic and thine art at once.
> The poniard that did end the fatal lives
> Shall break the cause efficiat of their woes.
> So fade the glass, and end with it the shows
> That nigromancy did infuse the crystal with.
>
> [Scene 13, ll. 75–83]

The images in the glass are true—"the fathers both lie dead" (74)—but they are "shows" nonetheless, airy nothings lacking the moral weight that Jonson also found wanting in country houses "built to envious show" and in Jones's spectacle:

> O Showes! Showes! Mighty Showes!
> The Eloquence of Masques! What need of prose
> Or Verse, or Sense t'express Immortall you?[15]

These shows are sufficiently compelling to vanquish reason and friendship. The unfortunate sons in Greene's play are the victims of an artifice, a mere appearance dangerous enough in itself to be "the cause efficiat of their woes." Nature imitates art: they become what they see.

The "glass prospective" in *Friar Bacon and Friar Bungay* would have been familiar enough to many members of Shakespeare's audience, and certainly to Shakespeare himself, for Orsino's "natural perspective" to point the allusion to the black arts, and to suggest the connections as Greene had done more explicitly, between the pretenses and delusions of love and the seductively dangerous illusions of the magician.[16] When Greene's Prince Edward announces his infatuation for Margaret, the fool proposes that he and Edward exchange clothing to "beguile Love" (scene 1, l. 33), a theme that continues in the main plot

with the courtier Lacy wooing Margaret for his master in
the guise of a country swain, and in the subplot with
Edward determined to get Bacon's help, for "it must be
nigromantic spells/And charms of art that must enchain
her love" (scene 1, ll. 122–23). And when Lacy's own love
for Margaret breaks through the rude disguise and the role
of surrogate wooer, Edward uses the powers of the glass
to spy on the couple and then to disrupt their betrothal:

> *Edward.* Gog's wounds, Bacon, they kiss! I'll stab
> them!
> *Bacon.* Oh, hold your hands, my lord, it is the glass!
> *Edward.* Choler to see the traitors gree so well
> Made me think the shadows substances.
>
> [Scene 6, ll. 127–30]

Edward's angry confusion, his mistaking "shadows" in
the glass for "substances," is important. The Renaissance
puns on "shadow" ("illusion," "actor") remind us that
the deceiver is here appropriately deceived: he had sent a
shadow to pretend love, he now overplays the role of the
betrayed lover, and he forgets that he has a more important role to fulfill, as the prince, in accepting the hand
of Eleanor of Castile in a marriage of state. The later scene
in which Bacon cracks the dangerous glass is followed
immediately by a parallel renunciation in the love plot as
Margaret—whose artful coyness caused the duel between
the two fathers—prepares to give up her own fatal magic
for a nun's habit. Lacy has just written her that he must
have been deceived to love her ("Eyes are dissemblers,"
he says) and that he has now chosen a Spanish lady. The
letter itself is a deception, a test of Margaret's loyalty. Her

sudden contempt for the "vain illusions of this flattering world" (scene 14, l. 10) has the ring of a role being tried on, a pious "show" that passes the moment Lacy returns: "Off goes the habit of a maiden's heart,/ . . . And all the show of holy nuns, farewell" (scene 14, ll. 89–91).

Compared with the "choler" provoked in Edward by Bacon's glass, Orsino's "natural perspective" is a therapeutic vision. Orsino has been suffering the enchantments of love—a general contagion in *Twelfth Night,* present in its acute form in Malvolio. The symptoms are a difficulty in distinguishing between shadows and substance, roles and realities, and an unfortunage singleminded tendency to trap oneself inside more or less foolish roles—the cross-gartered lover, the grieving sister, the languishing wooer. Orsino's recognition of the doubleness of his "perspective" signals a final rebalancing of the mind on a vantage point between the two halves of a full, if paradoxical, awareness. What Orsino gains is the kind of poise that Malvolio and Sir Andrew will never have, that Viola and preeminently Feste never lack, and that the audience of *Twelfth Night* must learn to exercise. With the "natural perspective" as its emblem, the play offers its characters and its audience a lesson in the complexities of sight.

"Oh, when mine eyes did see Olivia first," sighs Orsino at the beginning of the play,

> Methought she purged the air of pestilence.
> That instant was I turned into a hart,
> And my desires, like fell and cruel hounds,
> E'er since pursue me.
>
> [1.1.20–24]

Olivia's "purge" seems particularly ineffective. The air still hangs heavy with the excess of Orsino's first speech (1.1.1–15), his language surfeited with music, food, and the sweetness of violets all synaesthetically melted into something formless and engulfing that "Receiveth as the sea" (1.1.11). Now the sense of threat to the self continues just beneath the surface of the Ovidian repartee and the quibbling on "hart"; the allusion transforms Orsino into an Actaeon hunted by his own desires. His love, as he will say later, "is all as hungry as the sea / And can digest as much" (2.4.99–100). He has mistaken the disease for the cure, a delusion Olivia avoids though she is no less susceptible to love at first sight:

> Even so quickly may one catch the plague?
> Methinks I feel this youth's perfections
> With an invisible and subtle stealth
> To creep in at mine eyes.
>
> [1.5.281–84]

Both Olivia and Orsino have been "charmed" (as Viola fears) by the "outside" of those they imagine they love (2.2.17) and are now pursued by their own desire reflected off the surface of another. Olivia is the more completely deceived in her Cesario, but she herself presents only an outside to Orsino, and in fact does not intend to show her face for the next seven years:

> But like a cloistress she will veiled walk,
> And water once a day her chamber round
> With eye-offending brine: all this to season
> A dead brother's love. . . .
>
> [1.1.29–32]

Actaeon at least saw the goddess naked for his pains. These severe vows are the appropriate counterpart to Orsino's passion, itself a cloistered and solitary thing, a syrup of langorous frustration to be sipped at leisure, and unseen. Like Olivia in her "dead brother's love," Orsino indulges in a kind of funerary ritual centered on himself: "Away before me to sweet beds of flow'rs; Love-thoughts lie rich when canopied with bow'rs" (1.1.41–42). He is "sick of self love"—so Olivia will diagnose the malady in Malvolio—and tastes "with a distempered appetite" (1.5.85).

The second scene is set antiphonally against the first to introduce a healthier strain than Orsino's "dying fall" and a more hopeful picture than the death of Actaeon. Viola has also lost a brother, but she is admirably practical and brusque in questioning the sea captain; her activity contrasts with Olivia's mournful posing in the same way that Sebastian's heroics in trying to save himself from the sea contrast with Orsino's willingness to be engulfed. "I saw your brother," reports the captain,

> Most provident in peril, bind himself
> (Courage and hope both teaching him the practice)
> To a strong mast that lived upon the sea;
> Where, like Arion on the dolphin's back,
> I saw him hold acquaintance with the waves
> So long as I could see.
>
> [1.2.11–17]

If Orsino is an Actaeon, changed into a beast and cloyed with a distempered music, Sebastian is an Arion who rescues himself by a music that tames the beasts. The stress in the captain's account on Sebastian's survival as a *seen* event emphasizes its pictorial quality: a shipwrecked man clinging (if not lashed, here an added detail of Odyssean self-restraint against the sirens' song) to the mast is a common Renaissance allegory for hope.

Sebastian's mast prepares emblematically for his sister's disguise, which on the level of plot and motivation is never quite satisfactorily explained. The mast and the disguise are both instruments of self-preservation, means of riding the dolphin's back over a consuming sea. In Illyria there is no escaping disguises. What meets the eye in the play's conception of character is necessarily a constructed exterior self. The sea captain, Viola is certain, has "a mind that suits" with his visible appearance, but in others "a beauteous wall/Doth oft close in pollution" (1.2.48–51). Viola is not to be "devoured" (as Sebastian will fear) by the "blind waves and surges" (5.1.221). She will preserve her sight in Orsino's court through a role knowingly played—an ironic double awareness, which she shares with the fool, of the art she practices and the nature beneath. The sea captain is sworn to keep the secret of Viola's deceptive appearance; his vow points the paradoxical coupling in the play between concealment and vision: "When my tongue blabs, then let mine eyes not see" (1.2.63).

The themes of blindness and sight, disguises and truths, twine through the play, joining the main plot with the comic subplot. Sir Toby Belch's genial conning of Sir Andrew; Viola's disguised love for Orsino; Feste as Sir Topas deceiving the benighted Malvolio; Viola and Sir Andrew squared off for their duel, each misled into thinking the other a fearsome opponent; Antonio arriving just in time to confuse matters further by mistaking Viola for her brother—people come into view as a series of shifting appearances that flicker one into the next like perspective images. This sense of illusions concealed and revealed is reinforced by the play's references to painting. Toby rallies Andrew Aguecheek, who has been boasting of his talent for dancing "in Masques and revels," "Wherefore are these things hid? Wherefore have these gifts a curtain before 'em? Are they like to take dust, like Mistress Mall's picture?" (1.3.112-14). If the curtain is apt to conceal a sorry portrait of Andrew as a dancer, a fairer image is revealed to Viola when Olivia unveils herself: "We will draw the curtain and show you the picture" (1.5.220). Olivia is at that moment falling in love with a deceitful picture—Viola's outward curtain as Cesario—which will eventually turn into the true portrait of Sebastian. No wonder that Sebastian should finally be ready to distrust his eyes, and to half believe (as "Master Parson" had just been trying to persuade Malvolio) that madness is the only reasonable explanation for such strange appearances.

It is Feste who knows what kind of pictures are the most instructive:

> *Toby.* Here comes the fool, i'faith.
> *Clown.* How now, my hearts? Did you never see the picture of We Three?
>
> [2.3.14-16]

"We Three" is the motto on a common piece of visual wit in the Renaissance, a picture showing only *two* fools or asses; the viewer gets the point when he realizes that he makes the third. Crude as the conceit may be, its lesson in self-knowledge involves the onlooker in a neat paradox that is central to the perspective of *Twelfth Night.* The painted fiction reaches into an adjacent reality to complete itself. To see the whole, you must keep an eye on both and understand that two is not three. If you have the wisdom to include yourself in the picture as the third fool, then you no longer belong there; if you don't, the picture makes a fool out of you. You have to be willing to play the fool—and know what you are about—if you wish to escape being played for the fool in earnest. For that role Feste is the most clearly qualified. He is dressed in the fool's costume, but as he assures us at the outset, "cucullus non facit monachum. That's as much as to say as, I wear not motley in my brain" (1.5.50–53). He is not a natural (that is, feeble-minded) fool but a natural perspective fool who is and is not what he seems. To Viola—whose own role as Cesario is similarly a double one, and who recognizes that "This fellow is wise enough to play the fool" (3.1.58)—Feste defines his function at Olivia's court more precisely: "I am indeed not her fool, but her corrupter of words" (3.1.34–35). The fool's job, put suggestively in terms of a detail of costume, is to exploit the duplicities of language as he does his own appearance: "A sentence is but a chev'ril glove to a good wit. How quickly the wrong side may be turned outward!" (3.1.11–13).

Indeed, language itself is a kind of perspective device for the fool to manipulate. Those who, like Sir Andrew and Malvolio, lack the wit to see through the surface of words and the versatility to turn them inside out will naturally mistake the cowl for the monk. Andrew, like Toby, is a holiday figure who believes that life consists in eating and drinking and ignoring the clock, and he will not confine himself within the modest limits of order. Malvolio is (in Toby's opinion) a "niggardly rascally sheep-biter" (2.5. 4–5) opposed to bear-baiting and enjoyment in general, one who even in his fantasy life imagines himself winding up his watch. The other lovers (and the clown) occupy a seriously playful middle region from which both these are excluded. Opposed in temperament but equally single-minded, Andrew and Malvolio share a common blindness to the perspectives of love. This perceptual handicap makes them the butt of the comedy and disqualifies them from playing the game.

While Feste can skillfully juggle the word *dry* ("give the dry fool drink, then is the fool not dry"), Sir Andrew cannot follow Maria's playing on the same word, and so cannot understand that he is being played on as well:

Andrew.   . . . and here's my hand.
Maria. Now, sir, thought is free, I pray you, bring your
    hand to th' butt'ry bar and let it drink.
Andrew. Wherefore, sweetheart? What's your meta-
    phor?
Maria. It's dry sir.
Andrew. Why, I think so. I am not such an ass but I
    can keep my hand dry. But what's your jest?
Maria. A dry jest, sir.

[1.3.62–69]

Her metaphor and the witty riposte behind it remain opaque to Sir Andrew, as does the figurative sense of *dry* as a "stale" expression. He would make the word as literal and plain as his own hand. The effect of such a metaphor (here Puttenham speaks of the "figure of Transport" as others speak of the painter's perspective) is "to deceive the eare and also the minde, drawing it from plainnesse and simplicitie to a certaine doublenesse, whereby our talke is the more guilefull and abusing."[17] Sir Andrew's predicament is to be deceived for not realizing that he is in the presence of a deceit: he is pecking at the painted grapes.

Malvolio is just as blind to the perspectives of language—how could he not be, his own speech is so pedantic and cramped—and he is especially intolerant of the fool's witty corruptions of words. He is, in fact, a thorough-going literalist, and thus all the more ripe to be abused by a forged love letter from Olivia:

> By my life, this is my lady's hand. These be her very
> C's, her U's, and her T's; and thus makes she her great
> P's. It is, in contempt of question, her hand.
>
> [2.5.80–82]

Malvolio reads the letter by fastening on its grossest outward form, the lady's penmanship, without realizing that this "hand," too, is a chev'ril glove that should be turned inside out. His attempt to find his own name reflected in the letter's riddling "M.O.A.I. doth sway my life" (2.5. 100) suggests a characteristic belligerence:

> M,O,A,I. This simulation is not as the former; and yet,
> to crush this a little, it would bow to be, for every one
> of these letters are in my name.   [2.5.127–29]

He had a moment before imagined himself holding court as Olivia's husband and compelling a general reformation on Toby and Sir Andrew; now he would "crush" the very letters into a "simulation" of himself. As if in revenge, the letter re-forms Malvolio into its own simulation—a yellow-stockinged, cross-gartered fool. Viola had knowingly adopted her disguise as the "form" of her "intent" (1.2. 55). Malvolio has (if not greatness) a foolish disguise thrust upon him: "Thou cam'st in smiling," says Olivia, "And in such forms which were here presupposed/Upon thee in the letter" (5.1.339–41). It is Malvolio's astigmatic impulse to conform the world to the narrow images of his own self-love that draws upon him the ironically apt punishment of being confined in a dark room and tormented by Feste, who dexterously plays a double role as the fool and as Sir Topas the curate.

The fool's "vain bibble babble" (to turn his own phrase against him) at the beginning of that scene echoes significantly the one bit of language play that has by now become obsessive in *Twelfth Night:*

> . . . as the old hermit of Prague, that never saw pen and ink, very wittily said to a niece of King Gorboduc, "That that is is"; so, I, being Master Parson, am Master Parson; for what is "that" but that, and "is" but is?
> [4.2.12–16]

Such foolishly tautological questions have been posed verbally and visually all along. "What is . . . is but is" receives its definitive answer with the relevation of the natural perspective in act 5: what *is,* in this dramatic fiction, "is and is not." Not to see that is to end up in Malvolio's darkness, "more puzzled than the Egyptians in their fog." Andrew had thought logically enough that "to be up late is to be up late" (2.3.4–5). "A false conclusion," insists Toby. His explanation tutors the audience, if not the puzzled Sir Andrew, in the subtler logic of *Twelfth Night*: "To be up after midnight, and to go to bed then, is early; so that to go to bed after midnight is to go to bed betimes" (2.3.6–8)–that is, to be up late is and is not to be up late. Viola, who at the moment "is" Cesario, tells Olivia, "I am not what I am," and warns her that in her beguiled love, "you do think you are not what you are" (3.1.137–39). Feste himself registers the comic exasperation generated in the play by the dilemma of what "is" when he cannot understand how Sebastian cannot be the person he knows as Cesario:

> No, I do not know you; nor I am not sent to you by my lady, to bid you come speak with her; nor your name is not Master Cesario; nor this is not my nose neither. Nothing that is so is so.   [4.1.5–8]

The copulative verb mutually defines the terms it joins by proposing an identity more or less absolute between them. Tautologies leave nothing out of the equation, and in that sense may be considered the most complete form of definition, the absolute truth. They are also absolutely meaningless, and ponderously funny–like a missile nosing over a moment after launch to blow itself up on its own pad. A tautological sentence merely turns itself inside out. Sick of self-love, it reflects back on itself, a linguistic vanity. "A nose is a nose" says everything and nothing about a nose. The "is" carries an invisible but potent negative charge, just as Feste's "nor this is not my nose neither" ends up perversely positive. "Is" becomes especially unstable in a play that exploits the ambiguities of identity–of our self-definitions and our mutual definitions–in situations where the faces people present are artful constructions, conventional outward poses. "Being" in the role of "Master Parson," Feste is (and is not) "Master Parson" as truly as at other times he is a clown, or as Viola is Cesario, or as the boy-actor who plays her playing him is Viola. The complexities of "is" are evident when Malvolio has just performed his cross-gartered act and been facetiously pronounced mad. "Is't possible?" Toby asks. The reply wittily places Malvolio's performance within the larger perspective of the play itself as a dramatic artifice: "If this were played upon a stage now, I could condemn it as an improbable fiction" (3.4.118–20). Yet Malvolio has meanwhile identified himself so completely with the role—"his very genius hath taken the infection of the device"—that Fabian for one begins to fear, "Why, we shall make him mad indeed" (3.4.121–22, 124).

Coming after such self-conscious play with shifting levels of reality, Orsino's "perspective" may strike an audience as a visual tautology that focuses the comic energies of *Twelfth Night* into a final, luminous scenic image. As an optical redundancy, Viola and Sebastian seem to be one split into "two persons"—"How have you made division of yourself?" Antonio wonders (5.1.214). Yet their reunion seems, as though in the magic of a glass, a reunion of two halves into a single androgynous whole with "one face, one voice, one habit"; Olivia is "betrothed," Sebastian tells her rather too placidly, "both to a maid and man" (5.1. 255). This image of one twinning into two, two merging into one, offers a salutary exercise in perception for both the characters and the audience, "proper for the reviving of our mind." The air of madness and infection is purged at last in a moment of clearsightedness that recognizes, and accepts, a complementary juncture of artifice and truth—in love, and in the drama. In both realms, art and nature are opposed yet essentially identical.

The picture of Viola and Sebastian is framed off as an art object with its own status separate from, yet analogous to, the larger dramatic fabric that encloses it. Designated explicitly as an artifice like the illusory surface of a painter's or magician's "perspective," the scene offers the playwright a chance to comment obliquely on the value of his own creation: conventions that depend upon falsehood and deception yield truth and pleasure to those who are foolish enough to be beguiled and wise enough to know they are beguiled. That statement roughly describes not only the Renaissance aesthetic of perspective painting, but the action of *Twelfth Night,* and *Twelfth Night* itself as a theatrical illusion "played upon a stage." "But that's all one," as the fool will say (twice) at the end (5.1.362–63, 396). Orsino's "perspective" connects the inside and the outside of the dramatic chev'ril glove by making the play a tautological reflection of its own thematic concern with the illusions of love. His wonder at the twins directs our response to the play; we are finally invited to witness *Twelfth Night* as a "natural perspective that is and is not." Like a perspective picture, the play holds a mirror up to nature to produce a deceptive appearance whose power over us comes only with our acquiescence in its falsehoods. Its resemblance to life is no more an identity than Feste "is" Master Parson—and no less. If we yield ourselves knowingly to it wittingly and willingly—as if in love, as if entering into the marriages that perfect the comedy—it joins us to itself in a complete and satisfying copulation.

Twelfth Night's lessons in perception are fundamental as well for the experience of Shakespeare's other comedies—particularly so for *A Midsummer Night's Dream*, a dramatic artifice that reflects directly upon its own relationship with the spectator. Bottom's double nature is the focal point for two conflicting perspectives that the play asks us to unite. If Shakespeare's King Richard II paradoxically combines in himself the body politic and the body natural, Bottom is his comic counterpart: an unlikely amalgam of the body human and the body bestial. He is—like the play, whose emblem he becomes in this respect—a kind of reversible portrait whose shape and significance change with our vantage point (figure 9).

From the point of view of "cool reason," to use Theseus's criterion, Bottom is an ass indeed, the animal that symbolizes brute sexual drive with no rational control. In him the proper subordination of sense to intellect is overthrown in a topsy-turvy metamorphosis that puts his "bottom" faculties on top. Titania's infatuation with this odd creature is a parody of the equally blind love that afflicts the other characters. Titania, Bottom, and the four interchangeable Athenian lovers suffer from an unnatural "dotage," a midsummer madness from which, once freed of the fairy enchantment, they will awake as from a "dream and fruitless vision" (3.2.371) into the clear Athenian daylight. As a sudden enchantment, love is a "hateful imperfection" of the eyes. Helena, pursuing Demetrius beyond all reason, wonders what "wicked and dissembling glass" made her compare herself with Hermia's "sphery eyne" (2.2.98–99); but Lysander instantly forgets those eyes when his own are blinded by the "hateful fantasies" of Puck's flower and he finds himself in the pres-

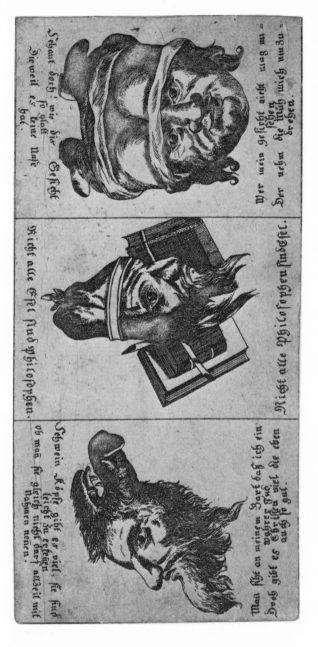

Figure 9. Reversible Portraits: *Heads and Beasts* (eighteenth-century German). Courtesy Metropolitan Museum of Art.

ence of what he takes to be a clearer vision: "Transparent Helena, Nature shows art,/That through thy bosom makes me see thy heart" (2.2.104–05). His contempt for Hermia only reflects the distortions of his own sight—as Bertram says of himself in *All's Well that Ends Well:*

> Contempt his scornful perspective did lend me,
> Which warped the line of every other favor,
> Scorned a fair color or expressed it stol'n,
> Extended or contracted all proportions
> To a most hideous object.
>
> [5.3.48–52]

Blind love viewed rightly from the reasonable point of view is dangerous awry. Cured of this affliction, Titania will acknowledge her proper submission to Oberon by relinquishing the Indian boy, Bottom will return to his proper station as a rude mechanical, and Hermia, it seems, will have to look with her father's judgment rather than with the eyes of love.

But Bottom's dream "hath no bottom"; it is both groundless and profound. The synaesthetic confusion of Bottom's speech at 4.1.199–216 is the daytime remnant of a nonrational experience past the wit of man to expound, an experience which is the proof of Helena's earlier contention that "Things base and vile . . ./Love can transpose to form and dignity" (1.1.232–33). Bottom's garbling of 1 Corinthians 2:9 suggests a sacred dimension to the experience, for in the same epistle Paul argues that God "hath chosen the foolish things of the world to confound the wise" (1:27) and that the "hidden wisdom" of God appears only in mystery (2:7). In *The Golden Ass,* whose

echoes lie just behind the biblical ones, once Apuleius is
released from the ass's shape he is granted an ineffable
vision of the goddess Isis and an initiation into her mysteries. Frank Kermode has summarized the resonant tradition behind this alternate interpretation of blind love:

> To Pico, to Cornelius Agrippa, to Bruno, who distin-
> guished nine kinds of fruitful love-blindness, this
> exaltation of the blindness of love was both Christian
> and Orphic; Orpheus said that love was eyeless; St.
> Paul and David that God dwells in darkness and be-
> yond knowledge. Bottom is there to tell us that the
> blindness of love . . . can be interpreted as a means to
> grace as well as to irrational animalism.[18]

Bottom has not been merely "translated"—as Helena
wishes she might be to Hermia's shape—but, as Hippolyta
will say of the lovers, "transfigured" by an experience
"strange and admirable."

These two aspects of Bottom's dream belong to two
larger clusters of opposed values that critics have isolated
in the play: everyday and holiday (C. L. Barber), reason
and love (Norman Rabkin), reason and intuition (Terence
Hawkes), as well as reality and imagination, actuality and
acting, day and night, waking and dreaming, Athens and
the wood.[19] Theseus's and Hippolyta's different responses
to the lovers' story at the beginning of act 5 reflect this
opposition and also connect the value of the lover's story
with the value of poetry:

> *Hippolyta.* 'Tis strange, my Theseus, that these lovers
> speak of.
> *Theseus.* More strange than true. I never may believe
> These antic fables nor these fairy toys.

Lovers and madmen have such seething brains,
Such shaping fantasies, that apprehend
More than cool reason every comprehends.
The lunatic, the lover, and the poet
Are of imagination all compact.
One sees more devils than vast hell can hold:
That is the madman. The lover, all as frantic,
Sees Helen's beauty in a brow of Egypt.
The poet's eye, in a fine frenzy rolling,
Doth glance from heaven to earth, from earth to
      heaven;
And as imagination bodies forth
The forms of things unknown, the poet's pen
Turns them to shapes, and gives to airy nothing
A local habitation and a name.
Such tricks hath strong imagination
That, if it would but apprehend some joy,
It comprehends some bringer of that joy;
Or in the night, imagining some fear,
How easy is a bush supposed a bear!
  Hippolyta. But all the story of the night told over,
And all their minds transfigured so together,
More witnesseth than fancy's images
And grows to something of great constancy;
But howsoever, strange and admirable.

[5.1.1–27]

Using these passages as a key, critics have generally en-
rolled themselves as Theseans or Hippolytans in their reading of the play.

The former, like Ernest Schanzer, find Theseus a "cho-
rus" voicing the poet's opinion of lovers whose unre-
strained imagination leads them to see "Helen's beauty in a

brow of Egypt."[20] Paul A. Olson reminds us that Theseus was traditionally considered the mirror of the reasonable man and the model ruler who rightly subdues Hippolyta; while the Amazon queen in her wild, premarital state symbolized the domination of reason by sense and (like Eve's influence over Adam) a violation of the due sexual order.[21] Theseus, for whom the *furor poeticus* is equivalent to the frenzy of love, supplies the healthy note of rational skepticism that should guide our response to the story we have just witnessed. Hippolytans, on the other hand, find in the queen's retort a brief for the imagination: the test of the lovers' story (and of the play itself) is not its believability but its "constancy"—its coherence, stability, and permanence. It fills a measure of certainty gauged not by a factual test of every bush to make sure it is not a bear but by the story's power to "transfigure" the minds of those who share it. Fantasy may indeed "apprehend" a larger world than discursive reason can "comprehend"; rationality is circumscribed, imagination boundless.[22]

The Thesean position supports a reading of the play as a satire on love which the audience should enjoy wittingly in a Puckish mood of superior, amused detachment: "Lord, what fools these mortals be!" In this reading the antics of the mechanicals are naturally the best thing in the play. But from a Hippolytan persuasion the play's center lies in its romantic, magical element to which we willingly succumb; Athens merely provides a frame, and the mechanicals a low comic interlude, in a work of fancy nearly more suited to the pure lyricism of music and dance than to language. In this work, the audience must be transfigured rather than amused. These differences in interpretation are usually sharper in performance than on the page, and the play's production history has reflected the two tendencies clearly. One is the practice of staging the mechanicals' scenes independently as a droll, as in *The Merry Conceits of Bottom the Weaver* (1646) or John Rich's production of *A Comique Masque of Pyramus and Thisbe* (1716), intended as a burlesque of Italian opera. The broad comedy of these earlier versions was revived most recently in the slapstick style of Peter Brooke's 1970 production for the Royal Shakespeare Company. The other is the operatic, spectacular tradition that includes the Tieck revival in Berlin (1827) for which Mendelssohn's overture was written; the eight-year-old Ellen Terry rising on a mushroom through a trap door in an 1856 production; Beerbohm Tree's lavish production of 1900, featuring live rabbits in prominent roles; and Max Reinhardt's infamous film version of 1935.[23]

The best criticism recognizes that the play balances the arguements of Theseus and Hippolyta in a "comic equilibrium" or a "complementary" union, which I would prefer to call the double perspectives of comedy to point the comparison with the historical perspectives of *Richard II*.[24] The history dramatizes the tensions between the king's two bodies and between the deposition as the flourishing of a new spring and the repetition of an old fall—the disjunctions of experience that would fly apart if they were not forcibly constrained by the bands of paradox. But comedy emphasizes the final harmony of conflicting perspectives despite oppositions that would be fatal in the non-comic world. As Howard Nemerov remarks sensibly enough, Theseus and Hippolyta "do get married."[25] Outside the play such a marriage between apprehension and comprehension, enchantment and detachment, would be unlikely; in the theater it is the essence of the comic experience, as the spectator—like the figure of Reason pondering the wondrous union of "The Phoenix and Turtle"—sees "division grow together" (42). Comedy fosters the ideal of reconciliation within a shared community to which the spectator is invited to belong; it joins "rival enemies" in a "gentle concord" that Theseus himself must admire (4.1.142–43).

The threat to this harmony comes in *Twelfth Night* from Malvolio, here from Egeus, who invokes the "ancient privilege of Athens" and the authority of a father to offer Hermia a potentially tragic either/or choice:

> As she is mine, I may dispose of her,
> Which shall be either to this gentleman
> Or to her death. . . .
>
> [1.1.42–44]

Theseus softens the penalty—Hermia must be ready "either to die the death, or to abjure/For ever the society of men" (1.1.65–66)—but at best she can expect a barren life of "single blessedness." But through the magic of the wood the play overcomes these harsh oppositions, and, at the dawn, grants the lovers a moment of special awareness—which, like Bottom's recollection of his own rare vision and Orsino's "natural perspective," is also a moment of special confusion:

> *Hermia.* Methinks I see these things with parted eye,
>   When everything seems double.
> *Helena.* So methinks;
>   And I have found Demetrius like a jewel,

> Mine own and not mine own.
> *Demetrius.* Are you sure
>   That we are awake? It seems to me
>   That yet we sleep, we dream.
>
>   [4.1.188-93]

"Half sleep, half waking" (4.1.146), the lovers occupy a mid-point between two modes of experience and are capable for that moment of an apprehension that touches both worlds. Against the disjunctive "either/or" logic of Athenian law, the law of comedy proposes its own logic in which "both/and" is the governing conjunction. The lovers' double vision also corresponds to the audience's experience of the play, for we watch with parted eye, simultaneously aware that the dramatic illusion before us is both an airy nothing and something of great constancy.

Just how the audience is expected to respond becomes an issue in the play itself as Peter Quince and company discuss the problems of staging their production of "Pyramus and Thisby" (3.1.1-67). Fearful that the ladies will be shocked by Pyramus's suicide, they decide to include a prologue explaining that

> we will do no harm with our swords, and that Pyramus is not killed indeed; and for the more better assurance, tell them that I Pyramus am not Pyramus, but Bottom the weaver. This will put them out of fear.

Similar precautions must be taken to prevent the terror that is sure to sweep the audience at the appearance of the lion:

> Nay, you must name his name [in another prologue], and half his face must be seen through the lion's neck,

and he himself must speak through, saying thus, or to the same defect: "Ladies," or "Fair ladies,—I would wish you" or "I would request you" or "I would entreat you—not to fear, not to tremble. My life for yours! If you think I come hither as a lion, it were pity of my life. No! I am no such thing. I am a man as other men are." And there, indeed, let him name his name and tell them plainly he is Snug the joiner.

Even with these cautionary prologues, two problems of a different nature remain. First, how "to bring moonlight into a chamber; for you know Pyramus and Thisby meet by moonlight." To accomplish this feat they decide they must either open the window of the chamber where the play will be staged (the almanac having predicted a moonlit night), "Or else one must come in with a bush of thorns and a lantern, and say he comes to disfigure, or to present, the person of Moonshine." And second, the need for a wall to separate Pyramus and Thisby admits of an equally concrete solution in which even the chink is given a real, physical presence:

> You can never bring in a wall. What say you, Bottom? Some man or other must present Wall; and let him have some plaster, or some loam, or some roughcast about him to signify wall; and let him hold his fingers thus; and through that cranny shall Pyramus and Thisby whisper.

In their naiveté about the theater the mechanicals first suppose that their audience will react like the deluded spectator in Dr. Johnson's "Preface to Shakespeare" who, "when the play opens . . . really imagines himself at Alexandria, and believes that his walk to the theatre has been a voyage to Egypt, and that he lives in the days of Antony and Cleopatra. Surely he that imagines this, may imagine more." They believe that Pyramus's suicide and the lion will create a dramatic illusion so convincing and so terrifying that its power must be denied. The audience must be told that Pyramus is not Pyramus, shown the actor's face beneath the lion's mask, and reminded that they are actually seeing Bottom the weaver and Snug the joiner. On the other hand their decision to "present" wall and moonshine (which is so beautifully evoked in the imagery of *A Midsummer Night's Dream*) arises from the opposite misconception: the audience's imagination is so deficient and the dramatic illusion so weak that they must be reinforced with plaster and roughcast. The mechanicals assume that the audience first suffers from advanced Hippolytanism—what Dr. Johnson would diagnose as a "state of elevation above the reach of reason, or of truth," a mind "wandering in extasy"—and then from terminal Thesean rationality. In fact the audience of *A Midsummer Night's Dream* will find the whole debate amusing because they can see that the man with the sword is both "Pyramus" and "not Pyramus" and that moonshine suggested by less solid means is both more insubstantial and more potent.

The exercise and refinement of that double vision is one of the main tasks Shakespearean comedy imposes on its audience.[26] *A Midsummer Night's Dream* in particular extends its interest in transformations to our experience of the play and, with an adroit self-consciousness, nudges us back and forth across the border of the illusory and the real. Like Puck eluding Demetrius in the forest, the play runs before us, "shifting every place," undermining the stable frames of reference that usually separate the audience from the work of art. In this play, which was probably written as an entertainment for a royal wedding, we watch Theseus and Hippolyta watching a play, "Pyramus and Thisby," written as an entertainment for a royal wedding. Peter Quince's troupe rehearse their play in the forest, where they create the unadorned necessities of a theater out of the stuff of fancy—the imagined greenwood—into which Shakespeare has already transformed his own bare stage: "This green plot shall be our stage, this hawthorn break our tiring house" (3.1.3-4). In the forest the theatrical metaphor reigns. Coming upon the mechanicals' rehearsal, Puck will "be an auditor;/An actor, too, perhaps," if he sees cause (3.1.70-71). Puck and Oberon delight in watching the "fond pageant" of Lysander wooing the wrong girl, and Oberon arranges the proper outcome by taking the production into his own hands as director (3.2.354-77). The fairy Oberon works his magic on the lovers, and the effects of fairyland persist into daytime Athens, where Theseus—himself a character out of old legends, and at the moment the creation of a poet's shaping fantasy—professes never to "believe/These antic fables nor these fairy toys."

As in *Richard II,* the ambiguities of the word *shadow* point to the larger ambiguities at work in the play. Oberon is the "king of shadows" (3.2.347), of darkness and dreams and deceiving simulacra, but also, in the Renais-

sance meaning, of *actors*. These meanings are both present
in Puck's epilogue:

> If we shadows have offended,
> Think but this, and all is mended—
> That you have but slumb'red here
> While these visions did appear.
> And this weak and idle theme,
> No more yielding but a dream,
> Gentles, do not reprehend.
> If you pardon, we will mend.
> . . . .
> So, good night unto you all.
> Give me your hands, if we be friends,
> And Robin shall restore amends.
> > [5.1.412–19; 425–27]

If we feel offended, if we find this the silliest stuff that
ever we heard, we should think of the play as yielding no
more (and no less) than a dream. We are invited to imagine
ourselves in the same relation to the "shadows" onstage
as the lovers were to the "shadows" in the forest. We recall
that Bottom was determined to write a ballad called "Bottom's Dream" which would be sung "in the latter end of
our play" (4.1.213–14); it is this transformation of dream
to art that we are asked to witness in *A Midsummer
Night's Dream,* except, as Puck suggests, it is our dream
that we observe. The play, like a dream, is an interlude
more strange than true in our waking life, and our relationship to it is one of mutual responsibility. Puck asks not
only for our applause but for our "hands" in friendship,

assuring us that he will "restore amends." He tactfully concedes that the play is a "weak and idle" dream, but if it is our dream we are also obliged to "amend" it:

> *Theseus.* The best in this kind are but shadows; and
>   the worst are no worse if imagination amend them.
> *Hippolyta.* It must be your imagination then, and not
>   theirs.
>
>   [5.1.209–12]

We are the coauthors of a work that is our own and not our own—a fiction imposed on our cool reason, but one which takes on life as we transfigure it into a shadow of our own mind.

For the contrast it offers to this comic partnership we might recall the relation between spectator and spectacle established in the masque. When the masquers choose partners from the audience for the final dance they symbolically incorporate the spectator into a single political and visual point of view—the idealization of the Stuart court—which the masque is designed to celebrate. This fusion obliterates any distinction between the real and the illusory by absorbing the viewer totally into its own fictional realm. The Shakespearean perspective preserves that distinction and refines it into a complex statement about our interaction with the work of art. We have as the motto for that relationship Orsino's "A natural perspective that is and is not." John Donne balances his reader on the same point at the center of "The Canonization," where the wit of love wedges bawdry and mystery into a single conceit:

> The Phoenix ridle hath more wit
> By us, we two being one, are it.

> So to one neutrall thing both sexes fit,
> Wee dye and rise the same, and prove
> Mysterious by this love.[27]

"Wee dye and rise the same": the line, like the love, must be seen both rightly and awry, as biological self-consumption and spiritual rebirth. This kind of poise, and the sanity it requires and fosters, also describes the witness's experience of the multiple perspectives of Shakespearean comedy.

In *A Midsummer Night's Dream* the viewer is a dreamer conscious of his dream, looking with parted eye at the representation of a bottomless experience that he must both share and suspect. He must be aware above all that he is a spectator at a play; though he has one foot in Thebes he has the other in a theater. The point seems obvious enough as a truism that applies to almost any kind of theatrical experience, but Shakespeare turns the basic fact of a theater to brilliant advantage by making his audience simultaneously conscious of the power and precariousness of the dramatic illusion. Whether the viewer is watching Richard play the role of king or the mechanicals debate the problems of stagecraft, he is always reminded that the lion's mask has an actor's face behind it.

This sophisticated manipulation of the conventions of his art which allies Shakespeare with perspective trickery is the hallmark of his later work: of the subsequent plays within plays, of characters ranging from Iago to Prospero who in their different ways direct the dramatic action in which they appear, and of the procession of actors on Shakespeare's stage from Hamlet to Cleopatra.[28] Hamlet will be disgusted with role playing—indeed with words themselves—but will depend on a play to catch the conscience of a king. Cleopatra will contemptuously imagine the actor who boys her greatness on the Roman stage, yet that greatness is the creation of her own skill as a consummate actress (and of the skill of the squeaking boy who plays her role on Shakespeare's stage). These double perspectives question the efficacy of the drama and expose its limitations even as they assert its power to prove mysterious after all.

The poetry of religious wit in the seventeenth century harbors a similar suspicion of the value of its medium and shares a similar desire to emulate the Phoenix. In the distorted perspective of the language available to men, what hope can there be for a right view of the divine? The following chapter will consider that question in the work of Donne, Herbert, and Greville.

6 The Pauline Perspectives in Donne, Herbert, and Greville

As an image of human understanding the reflecting glass has held a special and ambiguous fascination. It is the traditional emblem of sight, the noblest of the senses, and hence the *cognitionis via*—the way to enlightenment through the eye.[1] The inquiring mind holds the mirror up to nature, and, most importantly (following the Socratic injunction to know thyself), to its own nature. Fifteenth-century artists painted mirrors into their scenes, perhaps as a reminder of Alberti's counsel that the mirror is the painter's master and may, in fact, serve as an aid to exact composition. In representations of Saint Luke painting the Virgin and child, the saintly painter's studio is usually equipped with a looking-glass—appropriately so, since the Virgin is, in the medieval epithet, the *speculum immaculatum*. At German church festivals mirrors were sold as mementos in which pilgrims could collect and take home the holy rays emanating from the relics on display.[2] On a higher plane of speculation the sixteenth-century neoplatonists would teach that the divine beauty

shines from the one, self-same face of God into three

mirrors placed in this order: the angel, the soul, and the body. In the first mirror, because of its nearness to God, it shines brightest; in the second, farther away, it is less bright; in the third, the farthest, it is very obscured.[3]

Yet the obscurity of the reflection in the body suggests that the mirror may be seen as an instrument of deception as well as clarification—like the shadows on Plato's cave, a delusion which can easily be mistaken for the truth it dimly reflects. As a mirror for magistrates or a mirror for Narcissus, the glass symbolizes both Prudence and Vanity.[4]

The Pauline mirror figures in the same ambiguity in Christian thought and implicitly poses the central question for a Christian writer: how can he fashion an earthly language adequate to a divine object? In 2 Corinthians (3:12–18) Saint Paul contrasts his own "plainness of speech" (*Vulgate: Multa fiducia utimur,* faithful speech) with that of Moses, who when he brought the law down from Sinai and still bore the glow of the divine presence, "Put a veil over his face, that the children of Israel could not steadfastly look to the end of that which is abolished." This veil blinded the minds of the Israelites, and "even until this day, when Moses is read, the veil is upon their heart." But the veil "is done away in Christ": the veil of the temple was rent as the Crucifixion, through which Christ consecrated for us a "new and living way . . . through the veil, that is to say, his flesh" (Hebrews 10:20). By turning our heart to Christ, "we all, with open face beholding as in a glass [*speculantes*] the glory of the Lord, are changed into the same image from glory to glory [*a claritate in clarita-*

tem], even as by the Spirit of the Lord." In Christ we know openly what was veiled in Genesis 1:27, that "God created man in his own image." The passage guarantees every Christian a face-to-face experience of the divine so intimate that it overcomes the gap between flesh and spirit and merges the knower and the object of his knowledge in a single image. The mirror becomes transparent and offers a revelation of the eternal, like Saint John's of the New Jerusalem, of "pure gold, like unto clear glass."

Here Paul speaks in the present tense of the knowledge open to the Christian heart now, but in 1 Corinthians 12:18 he insists on the crucial distinction between what we can know "now" and "then." When "that which is perfect is come," tongues shall cease and knowledge shall vanish away, "For now we see through a glass, darkly [*per speculum in aenigmate*], but then face to face: now I know in part; but then shall I know even as also I am known." Donne glosses "These two termes in our Text, *Nunc* and *Tunc,* Now and Then," in his 1628 Easter sermon: " . . . one designes the whole Age of this world from the Creation, to the dissolution thereof (for, all that is comprehended in this word, Now) And the other designes the everlastingness of the next world, (for that incomprehensibleness is comprehended in the other word, Then)."[5] In these verses the apostle looks forward to the perfection of our knowledge of God that will come only at the general resurrection; until then we must be satisfied with an obscure reflection. Donne explains the difference between the two:

For our sight of God here, our Theatre, the place where we sit and see him, is the whole world, the whole house and frame of nature, and our medium, our glasse, is the Booke of Creatures, and our light by which we see him, is the light of Naturall Reason. And then, for our knowledge of God here, our Place, our Academy, our University is the Church, our medium, is the Ordinance of God in his Church, Preaching and Sacraments; and our light is the light of faith. . . . But for our sight of God in heaven, our place, our Spheare is heaven it selfe, our medium is the Patefaction, the Manifestation, the Revelation of God himselfe, and our light is the light of Glory. And then, for our knowledge of God there, God himself is All; God himself is the place, we see Him, in Him; God is our medium, we see Him, by him; God is our light; not a light which is His, but a light which is He; not a light which flowes from him, no, nor a light which is in him, but that light which is He himself.[6]

The brightest earthly beacon is the light of faith, but "Faith is itself but darknesse in respect of the vision of God in heaven. . . . all the world is but *Speculum,* a glasse, in which we see God; the Church itself, and that which the Ordinance of the Curch begets in us, faith itself, is but aenigma, a dark representation of God to us, till we come to that state, to see God face to face, and to know as also we are knowen."[7]

The *nunc* and the *tunc* converge on earth only in the miraculous intersections of the human and the divine. "Moses saw God," says Donne, "in that conversation which he had with him in the Mount, . . . Removed from all benefit and assistance of bodily senses, (He needed not that Glasse, the helpe of the Creature)."[8] The Incarnation

joined the two realms in one body, as Donne reminds his
Easter congregants: "These two words, that design two
such Ages, are now met in one Day; in this Day, in which
we celebrate all Resurrections in the roote, in the Resurrection of our Lord." The preacher's words commemo-
rating the Easter miracle offer "some sight," but "perfect
sight" must await the fulfillment of time.[9]

But what of the poet's words? If tongues must cease in
the face of perfection, how can the poet speak faithfully
on a topic language cannot comprehend? Even if the heart
is turned to Christ and the mind is granted a private
moment of vision through the glass, the tongue can only
record *in aenigmate* its own failure to capture more than
a dim reflection of the experience. "O how scant is speech
and how feeble to my conception!" cries the pilgrim Dante
as his sight becomes pure and enters into the beam of
eternal light:

> From that moment my vision was greater than our
> speech, which fails at such a sight, and memory too
> fails at such excess. Like him that sees in a dream and
> after the dream the passion wrought by it remains and
> the rest returns not to his mind, such am I; for my
> vision almost wholly fades, and still there drops within
> my heart the sweetness that was born of it. Thus the
> snow loses its imprint in the sun; thus in the wind on
> the light leaves the Sibyl's oracle was lost.[10]

"*Our* speech," the common medium, cannot accommodate
"*my* vision" except in images of loss, in faded dreams,
melted snow, and scattered leaves. Though he gropes to
describe how his sight gained strength until he was himself

transformed and absorbed into the circling light, his own
reflection and the divine merged into one, he must finally
confess that "Like the geometer who sets all his mind to
the squaring of the circle, and for all his thinking does not
discover the principle he needs, such was I at that strange
sight."[11]

The Pauline mirror recurs in devotional literature as an
image of our imperfect understanding, and wherever it
appears it carries a concern with the limits of language
and a dynamics of the mind striving for illumination
against its own darkness. Saint Augustine begins the tenth
book of the *Confessions* with a prayer paraphrased from
1 Corinthians: "Let me know you, for you are the God
who knows me; let me recognize you as you have recognized me."[12] Augustine's creator knows "all there is to
know of him," but how is Augustine to know in return?
Now "I am looking at a confused reflection in a mirror,
not yet face to face, and therefore, as long as I am away
from you, during my pilgrimage, I am more aware of myself than of you." Autobiography takes on a sacred dimension in Augustine as his discovery of the self becomes a
discovery, by reflection, of the divine: "I shall therefore
confess both what I know of myself and what I do not
know. For even what I know about myself I only know
because your light shines upon me; and what I do not
know about myself I shall continue not to know until
I see you face to face and my dusk is noonday."[13] Feeling
out the path of spiritual exploration that Bonaventura
would later methodize in *The Journey of the Mind to God*
and Ignatius adapt in the *Spiritual Exercises,* Augustine
"rises by stages" to God, turning first outward to the book

of creatures and then inward to the evidence of his own mind. As it moves from outward sense to the higher faculty of memory, however, Augustine's journey becomes tangled in paradox. The "vast cloister" of the memory—its power and reach, its capacity for remembering even forgetfulness—testifies to the divine presence, but the more Augustine probes it the less can he explain it to himself: "Although it is part of my nature, I cannot understand all that I am. . . . the mind is too narrow to contain itself entirely. . . . I am lost in wonder when I consider this problem. It bewilders me."[14] For Augustine the journey, so far as it can go on earth, must end beyond language in the contemplation of Christ.

Language directly reflects the limitations of the writer's mind but yields only a faint glimpse of the divine image. The laws of discourse, like the laws of Moses for Calvin, are a "looking glasse wherein we behold, first our weaknesse, and by that our wickednesse, and last of all by them both our accursednesse, even as a glasse representeth unto us the spots of our face."[15] The writer must work with the paradox, built into his medium, of trying to achieve a true reflection in a distorting mirror (figure 10). As geometry lacks the principles for squaring the circle, words are ill-equipped to describe the ineffable and the invisible; they attempt to mediate between the speaker and his experience, but when they enter the realm of the spirit—which is governed by a greater Mediator—they cannot communicate the immediate unity of the soul with God. The one sure way of saying nothing inadequate about God is to say nothing at all, to practice the perfect eloquence of silence on a subject that utterance can only falsify. In a strict ap-

Figure 10. Parmigianino, *Self-portrait in a Convex Mirror* (1524). Courtesy Kunsthistorisches Museum, Vienna.

plication of the negative theology, a true language would have to deny its every statement about a God beyond human predication; yet if the Christian poet like Henry Vaughan would continue to speak, he must find a way to pierce the veil of language:

> Weake beames, and fires flash'd to my sight,
> Like a young East, or Moone-shine night,
> Which shew'd me in a nook cast by
> A peece of much antiquity,
> With Hyerogliphicks quite dismembred,
> And broken letters scarce remembred.
> I tooke them up, and (much Joy'd) went about
> T' unite those peeces, hoping to find out
> The mystery; but this neer done,
> That little light I had was gone:
> It griev'd me much. At last, said I,
> Since in these veyls my Ecclips'd Eye
> May not approach thee, for at night
> Who can have commerce with the light?
> I'le disapparell, and to buy
> But one half glaunce, most gladly dye.[16]

Since the eclipsed eye is too dark to remember—either to call to memory or reassemble—the letters, broken in the fall, the poet must take the negative way to "disapparell" or dismember his words of their earthly dress, to be content with dealing in the debased fragments of meaning, in the hope of buying "But one half glaunce" of eternity.

In the Renaissance the Pauline mirror assumes richer metaphoric possibilities by association with the curious perspective: conical or cylindrical "glasses" could deform images or clarify others distorted anamorphically, while the range of the word *glass* now extended to the marvels of the new optics, refracting lenses, prisms, and telescopes ("perspective glasses"). Those in heaven, according to Sir Thomas Browne, "easily outsee the Sunne, and behold without a Perspective the extremest distances," while we on earth behold God "but asquint upon reflex or shadow."[17] Until the resurrection, writes Vaughan, the soul sees "darkly in a glasse/But mists, and shadows passe," illuminated only by its "owne weake Shine"; finding himself lingering in the dark after others "are all gone into the world of light," the poet prays:

> Either disperse these mists which blot and fill
>   My perspective (still) as they pass,
> Or else remove me hence unto that hill,
>   Where I shall need no glass.[18]

Still Sir John Davies assures us in *Nosce Teipsum* that

> . . . whoso makes a mirror of his mind
> And doth with patience view himself therein
> His soul's eternity shall clearly find,
> Though th'other beauties be defaced with sin.[19]

And if the other John Davies, of Hereford, could write a sonnet comparing the triangular prism ("dark earth, though made diaphanall") with the "cleare mirror" of the Trinity ("a glorious yet dark mystery!"), Dr. Johnson need not have been surprised at Donne for comparing a good man with a telescope in "Obsequies to the Lord Harrington."[20]

Donne's "Obsequies" (1614) is a kind of inferior third

"Anniversary"; crabbed and merely clever through most of its 258 lines of mechanical elegizing, it might be taken for self-parody. Yet, echoing "A Nocturnall upon S. Lucies day" and "The Canonization" as well as the two "Anniversaries," it formulates the modes of Pauline vision at work in his better verse by playing on the ambiguity of the "glasse"—as both the clear magnifying lens of the "perspective" and the opaque reflecting surface of the mirror. The speaker asks the "Fair-soule" of the deceased Harrington—"If looking up to God; or downe to us" he finds "that any way is pervious/Twixt heav'n and earth"—to "See, and with joy, mee to that good degree/Of goodnesse growne, that I can studie thee" (6-7, 9-10).[21] As in the "Nocturnall," the hour is "midnight," "Times dead-low water" (15, 16), but when Harrington's "Sunne rises to me, midnight's noone,"

> All the world growes transparent, and I see
> Through all, both Church and State, in seeing thee;
> And I discerne by favour of this light,
> My selfe, the hardest object of the sight.
> God is the glasse; as thou when thou dost see
> Him who sees all, seest all concerning thee,
> So, yet unglorified, I comprehend
> All, in these mirrors of thy wayes, and end.
> Though God be our true glasse, through which we see
> All, since the beeing of all things is hee,
> Yet are the trunkes which doe to us derive
> Things, in proportion fit, by perspective,
> Deeds of good men; for by their living here,
> Vertues, indeed remote, seeme to be neare.
>
> [27-40]

When Harrington's glorified soul sees the divine "glasse" in heaven there is no longer a distinction between direct and reflected sight: there is just "all." But on earth the glass must be accommodated to human perception by the "Deeds of good men," whose "trunkes" are both reflections in the flesh of a pure soul and the tubes aligning the eye with the telescopic image of the divine visible, "by perspective," to the living. In this kind of spiritual vision, "goodnesse," like the resolving power of a lens, enables the man who has the more acute instrument to focus more sharply on the divine image. Preachers may have a special calling to speak "As Angels out of clouds" (so Donne writes "To Mr. Tilman after he had taken orders"):

> If then th'Astronomers, whereas they spie
> A new-found Starre, their Opticks magnifie,
> How brave are those, who with their Engine, can
> Bring man to heaven, and heaven againe to man.[22]

Yet if the speaker's goodness is grown strong enough, he can "see/Through all" to his own image, which is also the divine image, reflected in the light of the glorified soul; and as the world becomes "transparent" to him, the heavenly glass puts life and death in a new perspective:

> Now I grow sure, that if a man would have
> Good companie, his entry is a grave.
> Mee thinkes all Cities, now, but Anthills bee,
> Where, when the severall labourers I see,
> For Children, house, Provision, taking paine,
> They are all but Ants, carrying eggs, straw, and grain;
> And Church-yards are but cities, until which
> The most repaire, that are in goodnesse rich.

[165–72]

The importance of the soul as a heavenly telescope helps to explain the poet's otherwise excessive praise for Elizabeth Drury in the two "Anniversary" poems. In "The Canonization" the language of sainthood is wittily applied to secular love as the speaker predicts that he and his lady will be posthumously invoked to "Beg from above/A patterne of your love": the love which he had first defended as harmlessly insignificant proves mysterious in the end as the lovers encompass the "whole worlds soule" in their mutual gaze. The two become "such mirrors" (each reflecting the other's face) and "such spies" (each seeing "Countries, Townes, Courts" in the spy glasses of the other's eyes) that they epitomize the greater world in their own microcosm. Having included us in their vision, they qualify, as the saints of love, to intercede for all earthly lovers.[23] And as they reflect an ideal "patterne" of love, so Elizabeth Drury, though dead at fifteen and hardly a piece of chronicle, is nevertheless fit for meditative verse as a "patterne" for life and death (2.524)—she represents (as Donne is supposed to have told Ben Jonson) "the Idea of a Woman, and not as she was."[24] Jonson's remark was that "if it had been written of the Virgin Marie it had been something," but to the Protestant mind no Christian soul need await official sanctification to mediate between man and God. Meditating on the "Idea" of Elizabeth Drury, on the perfection of her glorified soul in the sight of God, on the divine Idea in her, in whose image God has created all souls, becomes an exercise in Pauline vision for the reader of the "Anniversaries."

The reader must "see and judge, and follow worthinesse" (1.4) by celebrating Elizabeth Drury, but he cannot depend on ordinary sight. Indeed in "The first Anniversary"

Donne anatomizes the weakness of earthly vision that prevents us from seeing her "Whose composition was miraculous/Being all colour, all Diaphanous" (365–66): In a moribund world, sight may be "the noblest sense of any one,/Yet sight hath only colur to feed on,/And colour is decai'd" (353–55). Since she is gone, "no other way there is/But goodnesse, to see her, whom all would see," and so "All must endeavour to be good as shee" (16–18). Still,

> a glimmering light,
> A faint weake love of vertue, and of good,
> Reflects from her, on them which understood
> Her worth. . . .
>
> [70–73]

Those who can perceive this reflection by the "twilight of her memory" share the illumination of a new world free "from the carcasse of the old" (74–75), and "all assum'd unto this dignitie" are transformed into "so many weedlesse Paradises" (81–82). This act of commemoration, the first step in meditative practice, not only re-presents Elizabeth Drury to the mind's eye, but through her refracts as well the Edenic purity of the soul before its glass was stained by sin.

Yet the glimmering light of "The first Anniversary" only makes visible the darkest corners of the poet's skepticism. The two other meditative faculties,[25] the understanding ("judge") and the moral will ("follow"), here focus on the single theme, relentlessly amplified, of the "frailty and decay of this whole World." "Shee, shee is dead; shee's dead," is the refrain: "when thou knowest this," thou knowest that our life in the body is an ambulatory death. Man is a poor and trifling thing, and his world a dry cinder. "What Artist," therefore,

> now dares boast that he can bring
> Heaven hither, or constellate any thing,
> So as the influence of those starres may bee
> Imprison'd in an Hearbe, or Charme, or Tree,
> And doe by touch, all which those stars could doe?
> The art is lost, and correspondence too.
>
> [391–96]

Though her "name refines course lines, and makes prose song" (446), with proportion dead and all coherence gone from the world, language cannot comprehend one who is "now a part both of the Quire, and Song" (10), a "partaker, and a part" (434) of heaven's rich joys. With "correspondence" lost, the poet's words cannot bring heaven hither except by analogies that ironically point the disproportion between her state and ours, for since comparisons between heaven and earth must have one foot in the ground, language sucks up the general infection:

> But as some Serpents poyson hurtheth not,
> Except it be from the live Serpent shot,
> So doth her vertue need her here, to fit
> That unto us; shee working more then it.
>
> [409–12]

Reflected all too dimly in that "Serpents poyson" is the *figura* of Christ as the "serpent of brass" (Numbers 21:9) whose sight cures the mortal sting:

And Moses made a serpent of brass, and put it upon

a pole, and it came to pass, that if a serpent had bitten
any man, when he beheld the serpent of brass, he lived.

The typological allusion in the image works to "fit" her
virtue "unto us" and overcome the tension in comparing
a "live Serpent" with a dead girl. This allusion, certainly
intended, seems just as intentionally faint, with the emphasis of the passage on the shocking discrepancy, at first
sight, produced in the attempt to find an earthly analog
for her heavenly perfection. Analogy springs apart into
paradox. To paraphrase Donne's holy sonnet 19, contraries
here meet in one to vex the reader's understanding. By
asserting that Elizabeth Drury must be alive for her virtue
to work on us, the language harbors a thought already
poisoned, but the paradox is needed to imply the true
correspondence between heaven and earth concealed in
the terms it falsely sets in opposition: Elizabeth Drury is
alive though dead, the serpent of sin is replaced in the
scheme of salvation by the serpent of Christ, the venom of
death, rightly seen, "hurteth not" precisely because it
kills us into life with medicinal "vertue." Language must
fail in order to succeed. Like Donne's soul in "Goodfriday,
1613," his words here must submit their rusts and de-
formities to be burnt off, must be deformed in order to
be restored in their true form. The analogy of the serpent
contains, in the reader's experience of it, a tiny drama of
humiliation. Earthly speech cannot be mended into a true
accommodation of divine meaning: its logic must be
broken and made new.

Faced with Elizabeth Drury's "incomprehensiblenesse,"
language can try to "emprison her," with, however, only

one advantage over the "strict grave" that keeps her body: "Verse hath a middle nature: heaven keeps Soules,/ The Grave keepes bodies, Verse the Fame enroules" (469–74).

At the end of "The first Anniversary" the poet defends the boldness of his project—and implicitly compares himself to the divine author—by reminding us that "God did make/A last, and lasting'st peece, a song" (461–62), that is, Moses' song at the end of Deuteronomy (chapter 32). That song, like Donne's poem, is a lament for the "perverse and crooked generation" of Israel (32:5), for Moses knew that after his death "ye will utterly corrupt yourselves, and turn aside from the way which I have commanded you; and evil will befall you in the latter days" (31:29). If "The first Anniversary" is Donne's Old Testament, "The second Anniversary"—which ends on the apostolic note, "Thou art the Proclamation; and I am/The Trumpet, at whose voyce the people come" (527–28)—is his New Testament. For now the poet abandons the fierce judgments of self-reflection and urges the reader to "Forget this rotten world" (49) and join in a more joyful song, and in a different mode of speculation: "Look upward; that's towards her, whose happy state/We now lament not, but congratulate" (65–66). Now the "little gleaming light" signals the approach of heaven, and the reader must launch himself, as the poet launches the soul of the beheaded man, on the "Red seas" of death (10).

The reader must think of the deathbed in all its macabre detail—even to the putrefying of his own body—and he must "thinke these things cheerefully" (121); for as the body's ague becomes the soul's physic and death another birth, words themselves must try to pull free of earthly significance and take on the new and opposite meanings of the heavenly perspective. The reader's soul, following Elizabeth Drury's on her telescopic "long-short Progresse" to heaven (219), must grow like her "all eye" (200) and learn to see truly:

> When wilt thou shake off this Pedantery,
> Of being taught by sense, and Fantasie?
> Thou look'st through spectacles; small things seeme great
> Below; But up unto the watch-towre get,
> And see all things despoyl'd of fallacies:
> Thou shalt not peepe through lattices of eyes,
> Nor heare through Labyrinths of eares, nor learne
> By circuit, or collections to discerne.
> In heaven thou straight know'st all. . . .
>
>   [291–99]

Now we look through "spectacles," darkly—whether through eyeglasses for failing vision, or through Galilean perspective glasses, our sight is equally obscured. The new optics, Donne's quibble insinuates, has succeeded only in reinventing the Pauline mirror. Men like Bacon might welcome the telescope as an instrument for extending the domain of human knowledge into the heavens; Donne's meditation shifts our gaze from the advancement of learning ("this Pedantery") to the "Progresse of the Soule" and urges us to exchange the spectacles of mortal sight for the higher vantage of the "watch-towre"—the *specula* or summit of instantaneous, unmediated understanding such as the angels enjoy, and the *speculum* of the heavenly glass.

A language "despoyl'd of fallacies" must be a witty language simultaneously aware of the lattices and labyrinths it cannot avoid and of the heavenly meanings that turn death into life, joining the two perspectives in a flash of insight as the liberated soul "Dispatches in a minute all the way/Twixt heaven, and earth" (188–89). Such a language is at work in Donne's account of the soul's progress through the heavenly spheres:

> And as these starres were but so many beads
> Strung on one string, speed undistinguish'd leads
> Her through those Spheares, as through the beads, a string,
> Whose quick succession makes it still one thing:
> As doth the pith, which, lest our bodies slacke,
> Strings fast the little bones of necke, and backe;
> So by the Soule doth death string Heaven and Earth.
>
> [207–13]

The effect of the passage is almost impossible to paraphrase because it constructs an analogy within the paradox that life is death. Death strings heaven and earth by the soul as the spinal cord strings the vertebrae—that is the bodily analog, easily visible to the anatomist, that permits us to grasp the ecstatic event of the soul's progress. But with the perception of similarity comes the realization that what life strings, death unstrings when "our bodies slacke," but only to string it again into eternal life. So death both strings and unstrings in a "quick succession" of ideas that forces us to see the double, and paradoxical, perspectives of heaven and earth as "still one thing."

To follow Donne in these meditations the reader needs to "Double on heaven" his "thoughts on earth emploid"

(439)—not only to think on it twice as hard, but to apprehend the double significance, reflected in the poet's language, that heaven attaches to earthly events:

> Know that all lines which circles doe containe,
> For once that they the Center touch, doe touch
> Twice the circumference; and be thou such.
>
> [436–38]

The poet's geometry offers a schematic diagram for the process of perception required to read the poem. "They who did labour Babels tower to'erect," we have just been reminded, built upward from the "Center of the earth without pausing to consider "that for that effect,/All this whole solid Earth could not allow/Nor furnish forth materialls enow" (417–20). And with their crumbling tower, language also fell into a babble. Now the meditator founds his aspiring thoughts on a different center, the "new world" located in the memory of Elizabeth Drury, and builds with more durable materials: the "matter and the stuffe" is her "vertue, and the forme our practice is" (1.76–78). Our practice, formed on the model of Donne's schema, must move both upward and downward from that center. The image is of an eye looking in opposite directions at once, of a mind pulling itself apart *in extremis*— with, however, the reassurance of twice touching the circumference of the one divine circle, of unity reachieved in the end. So in the meditation on death the mind is forced to trace the lines of a double thought:

> Thinke that thy body rots, and (if so low,
> Thy soule exalted so, thy thoughts can goe,)
> Think thee a Prince. . . .
>
> [115–17]

The "labouring" with "broken breath" (90) on the deathbed, the final downward movement, is to be celebrated
cheerfully because it issues in the labor pain of a new-born
soul moving upward to its ecstasy and singing hymns in
tune with heaven's harmonies (a "broken," or part song).
This birth rewards the chaste copulation of the poet's
muse with Elizabeth Drury's soul, the two joined "to bring
forth such a child as this" (35)—this "hymn," the poem
itself—and redeems the "ominous precipitation" (1.98) of
our first birth, our fall into the flesh. Sin ("How witty's
ruine!") had "labour'd to frustrate/Even Gods purpose"
(1.99–101). Now by punningly drawing a second birth up
out of the language of death, the poet's wit labors to
frustrate ruin itself, labors to erect a watchtower of double
words out of a language that fell into ruin at Babel. The
circle with a line through it (Thomas Browne's "mortall
right-lined circle" that "must conclude and shut up all")
is the Greek letter *theta,* θ, the first letter of *thanatos*
and so an emblem of death. In Donne's language, this
baneful initial is reborn as the beginning of life.

In the end Donne must confess the ultimate failure of
human effort to approximate the "essentiall joy" reserved
for the glorified soul:

> All will not serve; Only who have enjoy'd
> The sight of God, in fulnesse, can thinke it;
> For it is both the object, and the wit.

[440–42]

He does so, however, in a double thought that transforms
the failure into at least a shadow of the divine thought:
grammatically the soul enjoys "The sight of God" as both
the "object" of its desire, what it sees, and the "wit,"

the faculty of perception. Only the "sight of God" makes possible the "sight of God": the perceiver is transformed into the divine reflection, the eye made one with the image at the far end of the perspective glass, the two no longer separated by the bodily trunk which on earth had been their only connection. In the "sight of God" language can find a phrase capable of joining the thinking mind to the object of its thought. At the moment of our fullest knowledge, as Donne would later explain in the Easter sermon, God becomes the "place," the "medium," and the "light" as distinction is absorbed into the divine "All." "The second Anniversary" enacts that moment as faithfully as it can through the perspective of witty verse.

Herbert shares Donne's search for a language of transparent perception: "Teach me, my God and King, / In all things thee to see." Herbert's prayer, in "The Elixir," voices the common theme:

> A man that looks on glasse,
>   On it may stay his eye;
> Or if he pleaseth, through it passe,
>   And then the heav'n espie.[26]

God does not reveal his mysteries "fully to us," says Herbert, "till death blow / The dust into our eyes: / For by that powder thou wilt make us see."[27] Some sights he partially conceals for our own good, representing them to us only "in perspective":

> O That I could a sinne once see!
> We paint the devil foul, yet he
> Hath some good in him, all agree.

> Sinne is flat opposite to th' Almighty, seeing
> It wants the good of vertue, and of being.
>
> > But God more care of us hath had:
> > If apparitions make us sad,
> > By sight of sinne we should grow mad.
> Yet as in sleep we see foul death, and live:
> So devils are our sinnes in perspective.[28]

If we were to look at sin directly, "we should grow mad" at the sight of complete privation. But the physical world has its "perspective" glass trained on the metaphysical, through which we see distant sins revealed in the nearby images of devils; and, in the other sense of the word, we see sin indirectly—safely, therefore, as sleep is a milder form of death—in the oblique "perspective" of an anamorphic picture.

Anticipating the medicine of death that blinds and clears the vision, heaven is always nearby in Herbert's poetry to dispense balms for the eyes:

> O Dreadfull Justice, what a fright and terrour
> > > Was thou of old,
> > > > When sinne and errour
> > Did show and shape thy looks to me,
> > And through their glasse discolour thee!
> . . . .
> But now that Christs pure vail presents the sight,
> > > I see no fears. . . .[29]

As "Hope" sends the impatient speaker in that poem "an optick,"[30] God offers us temporary helps for failing sight in the Holy Scriptures, "the thankful glasse,/That mends the lookers eyes"[31] and in the preaching and sacraments of his church: man is a "brittle crazie glasse,"

> Yet in thy temple thou dost him afford
> > This glorious and transcendent place,
> > To be a window, through thy grace.[32]

Herbert, like Donne, invites the reader to see the divine perspective in his verse by doubling his thoughts on heaven, and in fact provides a model to guide our reading in "*Coloss.* 3.3 (Our life is his with Christ in God)":

> *My* words & thoughts do both express this notion,
> That *Life* hath with the sun a double motion,
> The first *Is* straight, and our diurnall friend,
> The other *Hid* and doth obliquely bend.
> One life is wrapt *In* flesh, and tends to earth:
> The other winds towards *Him,* whose happie birth
> Taught me to live here so, *That* still one eye
> Should aim and shoot at that which *Is* on high:
> Quitting with daily labour all *My* pleasure,
> To gain at harvest an eternall *Treasure.*[33]

The poet's "daily labour" under the light of "our diurnall friend" gains an "eternal treasure" visible only in Christ, our heavenly friend. Herbert elsewhere notes with special delight, "How neatly do we give one only name/To parents issue and the sunnes bright starre!"[34] As the "sun" has a double motion (that is, its daily rising and setting and the less apparent seasonal shifts in its course), so does the greater "Son," and true "Life," whose names lie hidden in it: once "wrapt in flesh" and plain to the eye, now, since the dark hour of the crucifixion, he moves in us un-

seen but by the light of grace. To find the spiritual meaning hidden in the flesh of Herbert's words, we must read,
as we should live, with a "double motion"—one eye following the "straight" progression of the verse, the other
bent on the italicized throught that winds "obliquely"
through the body of the poem. This is precisely the double
motion we must exercise visually in our experience of
J. H. Glaser's contemporary engraving *The Fall* (figure 11).
Looking "straight," we see the Fall and the Expulsion,
the consequences of which is the daily labor we all endure; but what is "hid" in the direct view is revealed
"obliquely"—an anamorphic image of Christ with the
crown of thorns. In this view, as in Milton's, Christ is the
ultimate fruit of our first disobedience.

Though Addison would later label such acrostic double-
talk as false wit, it is clear that Herbert regards it with the
seriousness due the poet's imitation of the true wit of God.
There are times when Herbert, always suspicious of his
medium, would "plainly say, My God, My King" or even,
as at the end of "The Collar," annihilate his own faulty
language at the call of a greater voice. Yet, as he declares
in praise of the "sun"/"son" quibble, "I like our language . . . Who cannot dresse it well, want wit, not
words."[35]

In "The Sacrifice," Herbert exercises that wit to redeem
language "obliquely" from the dark perspective of the
flesh:

> Behold, they spit on me in scornfull wise,
> Who by my spittle gave the blind man eies,
> Leaving his blindnesse to my enemies:
> > Was ever grief like mine?

Figure 11. J. H. Glaser, *The Fall* (1638). Courtesy Bibliothèque Nationale, Paris.

> My face they cover, though it be divine.
> As Moses face was vailed, so is mine,
> Lest on their double-dark souls either shine:
> > Was ever grief like mine?
> > > [133–40] [36]

Here the reader shares Christ's perspective as the narrator
of a litany on his own crucifixion—or, more accurately,
shares Christ's perspectives, since the divine speaker, who
sometimes uses the first person ("they spit on me") and
sometimes the third ("they buffet him"), is both of,
and beyond, the historical moment. From this detached
vantage point Christ can direct the insistent irony of a
savior sacrificed against the narrow vision of his tormen-
tors. Their souls are "double-dark" in two ways; impervi-
ous to the old law of Moses as well as blind to the new

light of Christ, and blind also to the real significance of the passion for them:

> Ah! how they scourge me! yet me tendernesse
> Doubles each lash: and yet their bitternesse
> Windes up my grief to a mysteriousnesse:
>   Was ever grief like mine?
>   [125–28]

Seeing the "tendernesse" of Christ's flesh (and perhaps of his expression), they scourge him twice as cruelly, but they fail to see the "double" meaning of each lash. Their "bitternesse" "Windes up" his mortal grief—intensifies it, ends it in death, prepares it for the winding sheet—but paradoxically "windes" it up to a "mysteriousnesse": screws it up to its highest pitch, consummates it, winds it up as the poet's other life, in "*Coloss*. 3.3," "winds toward Him . . . on high."[37] "Wind" means "suffering" in the flesh but "exaltation" of the spirit, and this double motion of the poet's language bends us toward the hidden answer to Christ's refrain: "Was ever grief like mine?" "Never was grief like mine" (252) because, we realize obliquely, Christ's "grief" means "salvation."

When the people therefore wish Christ's "bloud on them" (107) they are willing to assume the guilt for his death without seeing that it is Christ who, through his sacrifice, will assume the guilt for theirs—that in his perspective, "bloud" means "redemption," not "sin":

> These words aright
> Used, and wished, are the whole worlds light
> But hony is their gall, brightnesse their night:
> Was ever grief like mine?
> [109–12]

In "brightnesse their night" Herbert recalls the pillar of cloud (Exodus 14:20) which the commentators had taken as a *figura Christi* and which we may appropriate as an emblem of the two perspectives in the poet's language, the "night" of the dark mirror, and the "brightnesse" of the "peace that doth passe/All understanding, more then heav'n doth glasse." That pillar, hovering between the camps of Egypt and Israel, appeared to the one as "a cloud and darkness" but to the other "it gave light by night."

Compared with Fulke Greville, Donne and Herbert are poets of greater range and passion in the expression of their spiritual darkness, but for them consolations are within closer reach. Donne's faith is buttressed by the

confidence of a witty poet emulating the divine wit, by
the steady reassurances of private meditation and public
preaching, while Herbert, nourished by sacrament and
ritual, hears the comforting whisper of divine live when it
is most needed, and least expected. More than Donne and
Herbert, whose way is at least partially lit by the beacon
of the Church, Greville is obsessed with the Pauline mirror
as the reflection of fallen man's benighted condition. His
search for the promised clearer vision is uniquely urgent
and complex and offers perhaps the most ingenious display of perspective wit among the metaphysical poets. In
the verse treatises and dramas and in the later poems of his
sonnet sequence *Caelica,* the dark glass appears again and
again as the central image of Greville's unyielding religious
skepticism. His treatise *Humane Learning* and his *Inquisi-
tion upon Fame and Honour* argue the vanity of learning,
fame and honor against the confident idealism of works
like Daniel's *Musophilus*—and "vanity," in this most rigorously metaphysical poet, means utter deprivation, an
emptiness of spirit at the farthest point from the fullness
of God. The "Rewards of earth, Nobilitie and Fame," are
the "Calues of brasse" we adore because we are deceived
by the flesh, "vanities false glasse" (91.1, 18, 17).[38] Greville refuses to judge the productions of time by anything
less intense than the light of eternity. Having forsaken the
"sinlesse pure impression" of the "heauenly Image," for
"earthly Idols," the soul can only see God as the "mirrour
of transgression" (109.7) and cry out from the depths of
its own "desolation": "Lord, I haue sinn'd, and mine
iniquity,/Deserues this hell, yet Lord deliver me" (98.
5-6).

The soul's dilemma—and the poet's—become sharper as we begin to feel the "horror" of our separation from God—the "fatall absence from my Sauiours glory—implied in Greville's negations. The soul is "desolate" (*de solare*), lonely and alone; its "iniquity" is the cause of its estrangement and also the effect because, having fallen away from its original identity with God, it is now *inaequus,* unequal to the divine image, degenerate from true being and banished to its own "private" hell. If the faculties of mind and will are corrupt beyond human repair, the poet can find no words powerful enough to see into the metaphysical world, for

> . . . the word of Power a riddle is,
> And till the vayles be rent, the flesh newborne,
> Reveales no wonders of that inward bliss. . . .
>
> [103.10–12]

Yet since language is degenerate too, the poet is free, perhaps even morally obligated, to violate its laws if by doing so he can make it a truer reflection of the divine "riddle."

It is ungrammatical to say "Before Abraham was, I am," unless the subject of the sentence is God; as Sir Thomas Browne writes: with God's eternity "I confound my understanding; for who can speake of Eternities without a soloecisme, or thinke thereof without an extasie?"[39] Browne's coupling of "soloecisme"—improper speech—with "extasie" makes the crucial connection for the reader of Greville's difficult religious verse: a language that confounds the understanding by overstepping the bounds of logical speech may also succeed in transcending the flesh. Greville's method for recovering the heavenly image in the mirror of transgression extends the wit of double perspectives (as Donne does, but more audaciously) from image and metaphor to significant grammatical improprieties:

> Wrapt vp, O Lord, in mans degeneration;
> The glories of thy truth, thy ioyes eternall,
> Reflect vpon my soule darke desolation,
> And vgly prospects o're the sprites infernall.
>   Lord, I haue sinn'd, and mine iniquity,
>   Deserues this hell; yet Lord deliuer me.
>   [98.1–6]

It is certainly the speaker who is "Wrapt vp . . . in mans degeneration," his iniquity a dark reflection of heaven's glories, but from the other syntactical point of view, "Lord" may also be the subject of "Wrapt": Christ was "wrapt vp" in the flesh at the Incarnation, and Christ descended to scourge the "sprites infernall" at the harrowing of hell. Since his joys are eternal, he is also present in "this hell" of the speaker's desolate soul with the silent promise of deliverance. Through Christ's "degeneration—his coming down to our level—the speaker is "wrapt vp" in the other sense: he is *raptus*, plucked out of his dark hell and exalted in the light of grace. The poet, like Christ, reveals the word within the word; within the word for entanglement he has wrapped up the word for freedom. And by further making man and God subject to the same sentence, the poet's language enacts and overcomes the paradox of grace posed in the refrain: the human has separated itself from the divine by iniquity, and so "Deserues this hell; yet Lord deliuer me."

The late poems in *Caelica* focus Greville's double perspective on both the depths and heights of man's spiritual condition. Sonnet 100 touches bottom:

> In Night when colours all to blacke are cast,
> Distinction lost, or gone downe with the light;
> The eye a watch to inward senses plac'd,
> Not seeing, yet still hauing power of sight,
>
> Giues vaine Alarums to the inward sense,
> Where feare stirr'd up with witty tyranny,
> Confounds all powers and thorough selfe-offense,
> Doth forge and raise impossibility:
>
> Such as in thicke depriuing darknesses,
> Proper reflections of the errour be,
> And images of selfe-confusednesses,
> Which hurt imaginations onely see;
>   And from this nothing seene, tels newes of devils,
>   Which but expressions be of inward euils.

In a bravura feat of syntactical control, the poem takes shape on the framework of a single fourteen-line sentence: "The eye . . . Giues vaine Alarums . . . And tels newes of devils. . . ." The suspension of *Giues* until line 5 forces the reader to move quickly on to the second stanza in search of a verb for *eye,* while the words *Such as* in line 9 shorten the reader's pause between stanzas 2 and 3: he realizes that the thought still needs completion and is led to anticipate a clause explaining *impossibility.* But here, at the beginning of the sestet, the reader's expectations are jolted. *Impossibility* cannot be the antecedent of the plural *reflections*—and yet it must be. It is at this moment of grammatical confusion that the poem does its work on the reader. "Thorough selfe-offence" to its own syntactical integrity, it "Doth forge" an "impossibility" in language, itself creating in the mind those double "images of selfe-confusednesses" which are the subject of the poem.

The conceit in the octave builds on the Renaissance psychology of the soul as expounded in Robert Burton's *Anatomy of Melancholy* among other common sources. In the body's "majestical palace" each organ has its place in a micropolitical hierarchy ruled by the heart; so, by analogy, the same principle of subordination prevails in the anatomy of the soul. The five outward senses (themselves ranked according to nobility from sight to touch) are properly subordinate to the inward senses—common sense, phantasy or imagination, and memory. The common sense acts as the "judge or moderator" of the impressions received from the outward senses, which alone have no such power of perception, "for by mine eye I do not know that I see." It then relays its impressions through the phantasy to the rational soul—where the wit or understanding has the greater power of abstracting the essence or "intelligible species" from the "sensible species," and the will has the power of moral decision.[40]

Greville elaborates this political imagery into a conceit exploring what happens "In Night" when the proper order of the faculties turns to confusion. All "powers are confounded" as the eye's "vaine Alarums" perpetrate a kind of mutiny in the ranks of perception. A mere "watch," the eye rules when it should be ruled, and the disorder it causes is compounded by the failure of the common sense without rational guidance to distinguish outer sense "impressions" from "expressions" generated within the

memory or imagination. The "witty tyranny" that results
is a tyranny of the eye over the inward senses and of the
inward senses over the wit—that is, a "selfe-offense," a
disorder in the soul where the lower faculties overthrow
the government of the higher.

The sestet thrusts the reader into a hall of dark mirrors where language engenders puns and unexpected
plurals. A singular "impossibility" resolves itself into
double "reflections": the imagination and its object become two "depriuing darknesses" in which "images of
selfe-confusednesses" are mutually reflected. Technically
the soul mistakes as real the false impressions stirred up
from within by fear and the vain (that is, empty) alarms
of the eye. But these images are "proper reflections" not
only of the error in perception, but also of that first great
error in the garden—which like the tyranny of the eye
over the inward senses was a "selfe-offense," an interior
rebellion of the appetite over the rational soul. The pun
on *errour* in line 10 makes the point that the soul reenacts the primal error in the errors of its daily operation;
the two errors mirror each other in fact as the two meanings are contained in a single word.

The "nothing seene" of line 13 is then both an inner and
an outer deprivation: the inner scene, "this depth of sinne,
this hellish grave" (98.13) reflects the outward scene that
man "Doth forge" (fabricate, in both senses) on the pattern of his own disordered soul—as he does that "sensuall
unsatiable vaste wombe" of the "seene Church" which
"thy vnseene Church disgraceth" (109.16). Outer "devils"
reflect inner "euils": to see nothing is both to *see* nothing

truly (because, in Donne's appropriate double phrase, the "sight of God" is denied to sinful man) and truly to see *nothing,* the nothing of spiritual deprivation. The paradox of the final couplet—that what is seen is nothing—recharges the imagery of light and dark in the first stanza. What would otherwise be a straightforward psychological treatise making the point (as Burton does) that "In time of sleep" the phantasy "conceives strange, stupend, absurd shapes"[41] takes on a spiritual meaning as well. It makes no difference whether the subject is asleep or awake, for "Night" is the condition of the sinful soul at every hour since that hour in Genesis 3:7—when the "eyes of them both were opened" after eating of the fruit, Adam and Eve became blind.

The "infernall spirits" also darken Greville's "Down in the depth of mine iniquity," but that poem contains the repeated assurance, "Euen there appeares this sauing God of mine," and closes with a more luminous reflection:

> For on this sp'rituall Crosse condemned lying,
> To paines infernall by eternall doome,
> I see my Sauiour for the same sinnes dying,
> And from that hell I fear'd, to free me, come;
>> Depriu'd of humane graces, not diuine,
>> Thus hath his death rais'd up this soule of mine.
>> [99.19–24]

Contemplation ends, according to Saint Bonaventura, with the face turned toward Christ, "seeing Him hanging on the Cross." Because line 19 may modify either "I" or "Sauiour," the speaker and Christ merge at last into perfect reflections of each other: I (on this spiritual cross condemned lying) see my Savior (on this spiritual cross condemned lying) for the same sins dying.

Line 23 has the same double significance: either (both) the speaker or (and) the Savior is (are) "Depriu'd of humane graces not divine." Through the mediation of a shared phrase—the grammatical equivalent of grace—the poem asserts the identity between the human and the divine without dissipating the force of paradox in the equation, thus compressing a complex of intersecting thoughts into a single statement: the speaker is "depriv'd [by sin] of humane graces, [and is certainly] not diuine," yet he is also "not [deprived of] diuine [grace]," for though he is unlike the "diuine" Christ he is nonetheless identical with him in that Christ himself, having taken on the "humane" image, agreed to be "not diuine" and was similarly deprived by the Crucifixion of his adopted "humane graces," which deprivation was both the death he shares with the speaker and the life into which Christ's death raises the speaker up.

This conflation—as elegant as the paraphrase is clumsy—of the dark and light aspects of Pauline vision is paralleled by the merger of past and present time in the word *come*. The historical crucifixion *is* in the present ("I see my Sauior") as the present is in the past: Christ's death "hath . . . rais'd up" the speaker's soul at the moment of the passion. The final divine perspective of the poem combines and transforms distinctions of subject and object, space and time, into the one enduring image of the man on the cross.

Each of the three poets I have considered in this chapter

succeeds in discovering a divine perspective hidden in the darkness of earthly vision—Donne in the practice of double meditation, Herbert in an oblique language of the spirit, Greville in ungrammatical ectasies. Their methods are similar—call them "metaphysical," "witty," or, on the visual analogy, "perspectivist"—as are the experiences their verse offers the reader: "depriu'd" of the certainty of direct, unambiguous perception, the reader regains his vision by piercing the veil (as did Longinus's spear) through the side.

7 Marvell's Perspectives of the Mind

Of all the witty verse of the seventeenth century none makes more perplexing demands on the reader than Andrew Marvell's "Upon Appleton House, to My Lord Fairfax." Years of critical plowing in the narrow field of Marvell's verse have unearthed its fertility of allusion, its complexity of tone and attitude, and the consequent variety of "readings" it yields up. For William Empson's early cultivation of ambiguities in "The Garden" (and the reactions it provoked) as for Rosalie Colie's recent interest in "the poet's preoccupation," in "Upon Appleton House," "with a kind of half-defined trouble," the ground was prepared in 1921 by T.S. Eliot, who noted the elusiveness of Marvell's wit: "We are baffled in the attempt to translate the quality indicated by the dim and antiquated term wit into the equally unsatisfactory nomenclature of our own time." That quality implies a "constant inspection and criticism of experience" and "involves, probably, a recognition, implicit in the expression of every experience, of other kinds of experience which are possible."[1] Eliot spoke of wit's "internal equilibrium," the proper balance of humor and seriousness, detachment and passion, that lets the poet keep his poise amid the jostlings of experience. The poet, like the "modest Halcyon . . . / Flying betwixt the Day and Night" at the end of "Upon Appleton House,"[2] directs our eye to the gray midline where the light and dark hemispheres fit together.

To follow that line, the reader needs to be a rational amphibian, equipped to live simultaneously in divided and distinguished realms of the imagination—and one whose head is not shod in the canoe of any limiting interpretation. For us the poem's interest lies beyond the polemics that defined earlier critical debates: Is the tone comic or grave? Does Marvell commend or regret his patron's retirement? Is "Upon Appleton House" primarily an allegory of civil war concealed in a pastoral rumination, a witty country house poem, an essentially private philosophical poem, a *jeu d'esprit*? Is the unfortunate rail carved by the mowers a symbol of Charles I, as D.C. Allen suggested, or, as Margoliouth stoutly maintained, "just a rail"?[3] We begin by seeing that the poem does not exclude any of these interpretations or insist on any exclusively: our fullest understanding lies in the experience of multiplicity rather than the search for simpler motives.

The visual equivalent for this experience may be found in the curious perspective—in the fooling of the eye, the shifts of scale and point of view, the puzzlements and revelations that mark the painter's wit. The poet himself invites the comparison between his own "Scene" and the painter's canvas (441–44) by making us aware at every turn of the sister art. In other poems Marvell offers us a "Picture of little T.C. in a Prospect of Flowers" and an

emblematic meditation, "On a Drop of Dew," directing
us to "See how" in "its little Globes extent" the trem-
bling drop "Frames as it can its native Element." We see
the dewdrop framed in the poem, while "gazing back upon
the Skies" the drop frames that "clear Region" in itself.
Conception as an act, not of visualization alone, but of
pictorial composition, is displayed on its largest canvas in
Marvell's late satire "The Last Instructions to a Painter,"
where the poet's survey of politics and morals is given in
the form of advice to an artist completing a "Picture" of
"our Lady State." The portrait finished, the poet bids the
"Painter adieu" and notices how well "our Arts agree;/
Poetick Picture, Painted Poetry." On a smaller canvas, in
"The Gallery," the poet's mistress appears on view in his
mind, her many moods caught in an array of contrasting
portraits: "Here Thou art painted in the Dress/Of an In-
humane Murtheress" (stanza 2); "But, on the other side,
th' art drawn/Like to Aurora in the Dawn" (stanza 3).
Inspecting and ordering its own interior space, the poet's
mind characteristically partitions itself, not simply into
the "places" of the Renaissance memory arts, but into a
series of pictures fully "drawn," each framed off in the
space of the poem by its own stanza.

In "Upon Appleton House" the "sober Frame" (1) is
not only the architectural frame of Fairfax's building but
the frame on which the canvas of the poem is stretched.
The picture opens for our inspection like the exhibition
hall of the poet's mind in "The Gallery"—no outmoded
"Arras hangings" here, but "a Collection choicer far/Then
or White-hall's, or Mantua's were" (The Gallery," 47–48)—
and closes again with the fading light, "when the Shadows

laid asleep/From underneath these Banks do creep,/And on the River as it flows/With Eben Shuts begin to close" (665–68). These "Eben Shuts" are, in one of their several senses, the "shutting dore(s) of Ebbone" that covered Renaissance picture frames;[4] in another they are the sliding, painted panels (the *machina ductilis*) of the masquing hall, and thus a reminder of the revolving "scene that turns with Engines strange" (the *machina versatilis,* 385) and the "Traverse" (419) or painted curtain, earlier in the poem. Since they are also the shutters of a house closing up in the evening, the metaphor joins the Appleton estate with the natural order, and both to the poet's art. Throughout the poem the speaker maintains a witty self-consciousness about the poem he is in the process of writing, a process of composition imagined as much visually as verbally. Through a series of self-reflexive references to painting and stagecraft he never lets us forget that we are in the presence of a work of art no less spectacular and ingenious than a painting by Lely (444), "a Landskip drawen in Looking-Glass" (458), or the feathered exoticism of "Mexique Paintings" (580).

The "painted World" (455) of "Upon Appleton House" has been explored by critics such as Kitty Scoular and Rosalie Colie, who have made us more aware (as Colie says) that "Marvell is a poet particularly alive to visual convention and technique" and that this poem is "filled with images and conceits paralleled in the visual arts." By extending the emblem studies of Praz and Freeman to Marvell, Scoular has shown that the "low roof'd Tortoises content in their narrow dwellings (14) and the figure of man as an "inverted Tree" (568) are stock images in popu-

lar emblem books like Wither's *Collection of Emblems;*
while Colie finds the playful, sometimes bizarre transformations, the flickering, topsy-turvy quality of the poem
in the illusions of Dutch landscape and still-life painting,
Arcimboldesque and other anamorphic pictures and optical amusements such as magic lantern shows.[5] That

> unfathomable Grass,
> Where Men like Grashoppers appear,
> But Grashoppers are Gyants there
>   [370-72]

may be explained as an allusion to Numbers 13:13—the
spies' report on the giant inhabitants of the promised land,
in whose sight ordinary men appeared "as grasshoppers"—
but the outsized foliage is better imagined as a version of
the magnified landscape attributed to Ruisdael, "an extra-
ordinary view of thistles and other weeds, seen from such
a perspective as to dwarf the postulated beholder with
respect to the towering plants." These huge insects, like
the "Fleas . . ./In Multiplying Glasses" (461-62), are
illustrated in Robert Hooke's *Micrographia* as they appeared to the fascinated gaze of the Renaissance through
the eyepiece of the microscope.[6]

By filling in the visual milieu of Marvell's work in this
way, such studies have made his wit seem less idiosyncratic
and privately perverse and more a temper of mind shared
by poets and painters alike. They have not, however, fully
described the effect of these witty dislocations and reversals on the reader or their reason for being in the poem.
That description can best be gained in visual terms by comparing the demanding role of Marvell's reader with the role

of the viewer of a major contemporary painting that displays the same mastery of wit in its medium as "Upon Appleton House" does in verse: Diego Velázquez's *Las Meninas* (figure 12). In both cases the experience of the witness is strikingly similar: he must accommodate his vision to a hall of mirrors whose reflections are shifting, multifaceted, and paradoxical.

When we look at *Las Meninas* our attention is first caught by the figures in the brightly-lit middle distance: the Infanta Margarita Maria—like Maria Fairfax, the luminous center of the composition—flanked by her two "meninas," or handmaidens. Our eye may move from them to the grouping in the right foreground—the Infanta's dwarfs and her pet dog—and then, perhaps, to the figure of the artist himself, posed reflectively behind his models on the left. As we fit our eye into the full depth and detail of this representation of the artist's studio, we realize that the background and foreground are each dominated by an intriguing object.

On the center of the back wall hangs an image of the Infanta's parents and Velázquez's patrons, King Philip IV and his queen: a painting perhaps, but more likely a mirror since it is much brighter than the pictures that decorate the wall around it. Above the mirror on either side hang two large dim canvases which—with the aid of some historical testimony by Palomino—can be identified; they are copies (by Velázquez's son-in-law Mazo) of Rubens's *Pallas and Arachne* and Jordaens's *Apollo and Marsyas,* copies exhibited at the time in this very chamber of the Alcázar Palace which Velázquez has so carefully reproduced.[7] Velázquez, who had earlier painted his own *Fable of*

Figure 12. Diego Velázquez, *Las Meninas* (1656). Courtesy Museo del Prado, Madrid.

Arachne,[8] surely knew the symbolic meaning of these paintings-within-the-painting, the challenge of human art to the divine, and perhaps intended their presence here as a muted commentary on his own achievement, like the red cross of the Order of Santiago pinned to his painter's doublet. For this back wall establishes three overlapping levels of reality, three points of contact between the real and painted world, that obliterate the neat distinction we are accustomed to draw between the viewer and the painting. The mirror image (itself, of course, painted) is set off against both the paintings above it and the figure just to the right, a man imagined as occupying the real space of the painting but perfectly framed, like a painting, by the doorway in which he stands. Like the viewer in front of the scene, this spectator behind it perches on the threshold (entering or leaving?) between the space of the painting and another space beyond. Each of these two points of view—before and behind the central grouping—has its advantages and liabilities. We can see the Infanta's face, hidden from him, but he can see the face of the painting on the artist's easel, hidden from us. He is in that sense our reflection, a viewer within the frame mirroring the one without. If the image of the royal couple next to him is really (the word seems shaky) a mirror, then the originals of that reflection—the real king and queen—must be standing next to us on our side of the picture plane; *they* must be what the figures in the painting are gazing at. Thus the world which the picture creates pushes through the frame and joins itself to ours, defining our space as an adjunct to its own, with, however, one paradoxical twist: we find ourselves in the company of the (invisible) royal pair

whose reflection is caught in the canvas, where our own
reflection (which should logically appear in the mirror) is
invisible.[9]

It would appear then that the focus of the painting, its
real subjects, are the two figures who do not really appear
in it; perhaps it is they who are painted on that large canvas at the front left intriguingly concealed from us. If so,
then our own expected relationship to the painting is precisely reversed: instead of standing, as it were, in the
artist's studio looking at the subject of a painting, we are
standing with the subjects looking with them into the
artist's studio. A second possibility, that it is the Infanta
who appears on the hidden canvas, is even more problematic. For in that case (since the model would be posed on
the wrong side of the easel, with her back to the painter)
the entire surface of *Las Meninas* would have to be imagined as a mirror on which the real artist—that is, Diego
Velázquez—looks as he captures both his own image and
the Infanta's on canvas. To add to the confusion, some
critics have suggested that the mirror in the background
may reflect not a real king and queen outside the frame,
but a portion of a hypothetical royal portrait depicted on
the hidden canvas—in which case we confront yet another
level of reality, a reflection at the third remove, of a
painting within a painting. As a record of the various ways
in which the painting has been seen, it is interesting to
note the several titles (none of them Velázquez's) and
brief descriptions under which it has been listed: *The
Royal Family, The Maids of Honor,* a self-portrait by the
master, a portrait of the Infanta "when Velázquez portrayed her" or "being portrayed by Velázquez"—and even

this inspired interpretation: "In 1690, the Count of Monterrey bought a picture, not attributed to any particular painter, which apparently was a copy of 'The Royal Family,' described as representing the Infanta Margarita and 'Velázquez painting a dog lying on the floor.'"[10]

The point, of course, is less to decide which of these possibilities is the correct one than to recognize that the artist poses all of them for us simultaneously; and that our own bewilderment, the jolting of our comfortable assumptions that we can discover and judge the truth of things unequivocally, or settle on a single interpretation in a world of doubles, is surely a part of the meaning of Velázquez's masterpiece. We can suppose that the artist would appreciate the gesture of the curators of the Museo del Prado, who invite the visitor to look at *Las Meninas* not directly but as it is reflected in a mirror fixed to the side wall of the gallery.

It would be possible to find thematic implications in this esthetic strategy, perhaps even a visual working out of the line by Quevedo about the court of Philip IV: "There are many things here that seem to exist and have their being, and yet they are nothing more than a name and an appearance." But such a statement would be too easy for Velázquez, who presents the problem of seeming and being as a question rather than a conclusion. The painting is a puzzle with various solutions; our enjoyment lies in the figuring out. Yet as we shuffle the pieces we realize that this game is serious business, for it invites us to test (as Arachne and Marsyas did, to their regret) the limits of the lesser world of human art against the larger world it would rival. We may even call this union of the playful with the serious the *tone* of painting, in the same sense as we speak of tone in literature, as the relationship established between the artist and his audience. That tone is captured perfectly in the figure of the painter in *Las Meninas*: somber but bemused, at once part of the scene and detached from it in a stance of unassertive but complete authority, with one eye on his canvas and one eye on us. Our obligation in this relationship, if we are to meet it fully, is to share the artist's vision rather than his opinions.

Las Meninas plays on—nearly parodies—the conventions of realistic perspectival representation perfected in the earlier Renaissance. Those conventions conferred the power, as we have seen, to specify with mathematical precision the location and relative size of objects in an image of three-dimensional space, to recreate the real within a frame that should serve (in Alberti's phrase) as an "open window" onto the world. That world is "open" to immediate understanding, to visual mastery by an observer at a definite vantage point. The complication of Velázquez's style from an early, stark realism based on Caravaggio and Sanchez Coton to the subtle manipulation of the curious perspective in his mature work may be traced to the sequence of paintings from *Christ in the House of Mary and Martha* (c. 1618) through *Venus at her Mirror* (c. 1648) and *The Fable of Arachne* (c. 1644–48) to *Las Meninas* (1656).* *Las Meninas* retains and depends

---

*Christ in the House of Mary and Martha places its brightly-lit sacred vignette in the corner of an everyday kitchen scene—a tradition which originated with the Flemish painter Pieter Aertsen in the previous century—but here the smaller image may be read as either a mirror or a window, and the figure looking apprehensively toward

upon the power of the earlier work to create a fully realized, richly detailed image of a particular room in the
Alcazár filled with careful renderings of recognizable people. But that solid world (and by implication our purport-
edly more solid one) is a flickering, precarious image that
the viewer cannot comprehend under a single visual ratio-
nale. In the mirror images, puzzles, and confusions in point
of view of *Las Meninas* Velázquez achieves the same
effect—though in a less somber mood—as Holbein does
with the anamorphic skull in *The Ambassadors*. Velázquez
creates illusory representations of reality which call attention to their own double nature. He erects a frame which
should clearly establish that open window, the boundary
between the viewer and the work—except that the work
systematically violates its own boundaries and the viewer's
preconceptions about looking at a painting. The viewer
finds that he is no longer safely separated from that
painted world, no longer able to see it unequivocally—with
the eye of cool reason—from a secure point of view. The
painting pulls him through the window and reveals a shifting, tricky world in whose uncertainties the beholder is
now a participant rather than a privileged observer.

Marvell's reader, like Velázquez's viewer, is denied a fix
on the artist's world, or at least a single-minded inter-

---

us may therefore be looking toward (the reflected) Christ or away
from Christ (in the next room over her shoulder). In *Venus at her
Mirror,* we see the goddess from behind, her portrait captured in
the mirror held up to her face by Cupid. *The Fable of Arachne* exploits the spatial ambiguities between the scene of Athena and her
human rival spinning in the foreground and a brighter scene in a
shallow alcove at the rear: Arachne displaying (and nearly merging
with) her finished product—which turns out to be a tapestry of
Titian's *Rape of Europa.*

pretation: both artists are stubbornly double-minded. Throughout our guided tour of Appleton House and its grounds, the poet's imagination transforms the quiet country scene into a spectacle full of rapid shifts of perspective and optical special effects. "Young Fairfax" rises magically "through the wall" of the Nunnery (258). The giant grasshoppers "in there squeking Laugh contemn/Us as we walk more low then them" (373–74). Cattle grazing in the meadow appear first shrunken like fleas or "Spots . . . on Faces"—our faces, since in this poem where "ev'ry Figure equal[s] Man" (48) they seem "a Landskip drawen in Looking-Glass"—then magnified (along with the fleas under the "Multiplying Glasses") to the size of stars, which nevertheless retain something of their miniature quality because they seem so distant: "They feed so wide, so slowly move,/As Constellations do above." Our own reflection in the "polisht Grass" is lost somewhere between the microscopic and the immense (457–64). In the imagery of the poem the expected order of things is everywhere subverted, and these reversals are reflected in other details of the composition—for example in the narrative reversal of stanza 51, where Thestylis, referring to the speaker, "cryes, he call'd us Israelites" (406), and so momentarily transforms him into a character in his own poem. We can appreciate their effect on our reading, if, after following one major theme through the ruined cloister, the garden, and the meadow, we pause at the woods—a passage that most clearly presents the poem's central strategy: by examining all of its subjects from several points of view and depriving the reader of the assurance of certain choice, it creates a larger ironic frame in which the contradictions of the monocular, prose world of cool reason are held together by the binocular vision of poetry's shaping fantasies.

The major theme implicit in every section of the poem is the value of General Fairfax's decision to retire from public life and cultivate a paradise "Within this sober Frame" happier far than the fallen, war-torn world without. The "Suttle Nunns" who once held the estate had tried to tempt the general's ancestress, the "blooming Virgin Thwates," to a similar retirement:

> "Within this holy leisure we
> "Live innocently as you see.
> "These Walls restrain the World without,
> "But hedge our Liberty about
> "These bars inclose that wider Den
> "Of those wild Creatures, called Men.
>
> [97–102]

Though the nuns would convince the poor virgin that they have excluded the corrupt larger world from the innocent freedom "within" their walls, their "holy leisure" is disingenuously luxurious and self-indulgent, unlike the "holy Mathematicks" that design Fairfax's house according to the rule of "Humility" (41–48). Fairfax is content to stoop for a low roof, for "Height with a certain Grace does bend" (59), but the nuns lack that very grace (or Grace):

> "And if our Rule seem strictly pend,
> "The Rule itself to you shall bend.
>
> [155–56]

Like their suspicious chastity, their cloistered arts, "'still

handling Natures finest Parts" (178), distil the fecundity
of nature into perfumed sterility:

> "Flowr's dress the Altars; for the Clothes,
> "The Sea-born Amber we compose.
>
> [179–80]

The possibility of an innocent retreat, tested and found
wanting in the nunnery, reappears in Fairfax's garden,
which, being "laid . . . out in sport / In the just Figure of a
Fort" (285-86), becomes a fragrant, playful replica of
the violent world without. So the poet suggests, in an echo
of John of Gaunt's famous speech in *Richard II,* that this
Edenic enclosure is to England what England was once to
the outside world. Fairfax's garden reflects *in parvo* the
paradise now lost to the larger world which surrounds it:

> O Thou, that dear and happy Isle
> The Garden of the World ere while,
> Thou *Paradise* of four Seas,
> Which *Heaven* planted us to please,
> But, to exclude the World, did guard
> With watry if not flaming Sword;
> What luckless Apple did we tast,
> To make us Mortal, and The Wast?
>
> [321–28]

Aided by the poet's wit, Fairfax's horticultural art has
turned war into a fertile ordering of nature; but the fragile
perfection of the private garden, we are reminded, stands
in ironic counterpoint to the ruined public garden, choked
by the arts of war—"We ord'nance plant and Powder sow"
(344)—which Fairfax has declined to tend:

> And yet there walks one on the Sod
> Who, had it pleased him and *God,*
> Might once have made our Gardens spring
> Fresh as his own and flourishing.
>
> [345–48]

Having eaten the luckless apple, can man exclude the world without from a refuge within?

In the meadow the rail learns how precarious such a refuge can be when she suffers the mower's bloody stroke. Her death comments obliquely on the low life Fairfax has chosen:

> Unhappy Birds! What does it boot
> To build below the Grasses Root;
> When Lowness is unsafe as Hight,
> And chance o'retakes what scapeth spight?
>
> [409–12]

The mower drawing his scythe "all bloody" (397) from the rail's breast creates a moment of *frisson* that disturbs our emotional expectations in this section as much as the giant grasshoppers dislocate our sense of proportion, for what seems like a conventionally placed pastoral becomes a metaphor for war in all its horror. The "green Sea" runs red as the mowers "Massacre the Grass along" (394), and "bloody Thestylis" (401) pounces on the rail like a scavenging camp follower, while the call of the bird's orphan parents creaks like "Death-Trumpets" (416). The mowers' "traverse" across the field turns into a pun on the stage "Traverse"—the painted curtain—in which

> seemeth wrought
> A Camp of Battail newly fought:

> Where, as the Meads with Hay, the Plain
> Lyes quilted ore with Bodies slain:
> The Women that with forks it fling,
> Do represent the Pillaging.
>
> [419–24]

After the harvesting the "careless Victors" (425) dance the "Triumphs of the Hay," their "Females fragrant as the Mead" and their kisses sweet as the "new-made Hay"; but these light festivities fade into a darker mood as the shape of the haycocks reminds the speaker of ancient burial tumuli: "And such the Roman Camps do rise/In Hills for Soldiers Obsequies" (439-40). We are left with a double "Landskip"—meadow and battlefield—where piles of silent dead lie entombed just beneath a surface of celebration. As cattle are telescoped with fleas and stars—the mundane conflated with the trivial and the cosmic—the Appleton meadows appear in the perspective of metaphor as inseparable from the larger, and more disorderly, world without. What is inside the sober frame of Appleton reflects what is outside in a continuum of space stretching from these meadows to the "Desert Memphis Sand," and of time from the present moment to the Roman camps.

We have noted how the meadow, with its turning "Engines strange" and "pleasant Acts" (465), its shifting scenes and traverses, is transformed in the speaker's imagination into a masque.[11] This is itself a strange turn of genre, for instead of powerful men (who make wars) representing simple swains, here harvest women with pitchforks "Do represent the Pillaging." The stage strewn with bodies, pastoral idyll turns into the tragedy of blood—as, in the biblical motif running through these lines, the Israelite-mowers' safe passage through the "green Sea"

(387–92) ends not at the promised land, but with the flood (456–80).

But—the word is inevitable in talking about the poem as it is in the poem itself, where it occurs fifty times as a guidepost to the adversative conjunctions of experience— but these are also "pleasant Acts" akin to the act of divine creation. "This Scene" of pyramids and burial mounds

> withdrawing brings
> A new and empty Face of things;
> A levell'd space, as smooth and plain,
> As Clothes for *Lilly* strecht to stain.
> The World when first created sure
> Was such a Table rase and pure.
>
> [441–46]

The "Table rase and pure"—the mowed field conflated with the painter's blank canvas—suggests the recreative potential of both nature and art, and implicitly of Fairfax's design for living by the art of nature (a potential subtly qualified by our knowledge of what usually happens in the "Toril" once the bulls have entered). Even when "Denton sets ope its Cataracts" (466) and floods the meadow, the speaker doubles our emotional response by comically exaggerating the effect of this miniature deluge, which is calamitous on the figurative level but literally restorative to the land.

The flood leads to the speaker's own retirement to the wood (481–648), a private "sanctuary" within a scene of public disorder and a figure of redemption that once again recalls Fairfax's choice:

> But I, retiring from the Flood,
> Take Sanctuary in the Wood;

> And, while it lasts, my self imbark
> In this yet green, yet growing Ark:
>
> [481–84]

But the speaker's self-satisfied exclamation later in the scene

> How safe, methinks, and strong behind
> These trees have I encamp'd my mind
>
> [601–02]

has the ring of a question: "how safe" indeed? It is a question already addressed from several points of view in the case of the general whose talents lay encamped within his garden-fort, and now posed again in a more philosophical context.

The literary frame established in this section is that of the *beatus ille* poem, a minor but well-defined genre practiced by Denham, Benlowes, and others.[12] The "happy man" poem revived the Horatian theme of simple happiness in rural retirement, and added the neoplatonic doctrine of nature as a divine hieroglyph to be interpreted by the blessed man whose mind has been exalted by solitary contemplation. But for this poem the conventions are less important than the special uses to which Marvell puts them. The *beatus ille* motif sets a context and an expected tone. Marvell's meanings reside partly in his deviations from the norm, in significant differences which always qualify and sometimes undermine the conventions at hand. Marvell will have us see things both ways: the "Wood" section is at once a presentation and a criticism of the *beatus ille* philosophy.

The philosophy is presented clearly enough. The speaker discovers that the wood is transformed for him into a "Temple green" (510); he finds his music in the singing of the "winged Quires" (511) and can understand the meaning of the moralized landscape before him. The hewel who "walks still upright" (539) becomes a figure of natural justice searching for the "Traitor-worm" within the tree, "While the Oake seems to fall content, Viewing the Treason's Punishment" (559-60). The speaker moves in this world "Like some great Prelate of the Grove" (592), achieving both the stoic invulnerability (601-08) and the rapturous unity with nature (609-16) that is characteristic of such poems.

But the meanings here are more complicated, for this is a "double Wood" (489) and the poetry speaks a double language. To "imbark" (483) means to go—like the "first Carpenter" (484)—into the ark of the woods as a refuge, but suggests also "to be barked up," imprisoned in wood. Just as here one word means salvation and confinement, the phrase "ancient stocks" (489) in the next stanza recalls the strength of the trees but suggests as well the stocks into which prisoners are put, and rhymes with "locks" in the following line. Similarly, the observation that the order of the trees is "loose" (507) means "passable and thin" but suggests lax and unproportioned, like the "Corinthian Porticoes" (too ornate, perhaps, for the simplicity of Appleton's moral architecture) to which the trees are compared—this "loose Nature" will "recollect" itself only later at the sight of Maria Fairfax (557-78).

Related to this kind of punning, where meanings look in opposite directions at once, is the double vision required by the poet's syntax and imagery. In lines 481–84, quoted above, the uncertainty of the phrase "while it lasts" may apply either to the "Flood" or the "Sanctuary." In stanza 63 the "Eye" first sees the forest, from the outside, as "one great Trunk" that "stretches still so closely wedg'd/ As if the Night within were hedg'd (503–04). But at the next two lines, "Dark all without it knits; within/It opens passable and thin," there is a sudden shift in the point of reference; we are now apparently "within" and the darkness "without." There is a semantic blur in the line "Dark all without it knits," which leaves us feeling uncertain about where the darkness is—a feeling that is crucial to our experience of the whole section. This passage echoes the themes of "within" and "without" everywhere "within this sober Frame"; the echo will return at the end of the woods section, in the image of the stream as a "Chrystal Mirrour," "Where all things gaze themselves, and doubt If they be in it or without" (636–38). Furthermore, the language of the poem consistently questions its own ability to pin down the experience it contains. Throughout, the lines are qualified by such phrases as "it seems," "as if," "as meant," "for some cause unknown," "who not mistook." The speaker's perceptions are always offered tentatively, focusing attention on the slender thread that connects fact and interpretation.

All of which makes it a very difficult matter to define the poet's tone, to say with assurance what is the poet's attitude toward the events he describes, how much distance we must place between ourselves as readers and the speaker, how much assent we should give to the speaker's assertions and emotions. At times we are invited to see more than the speaker does, for as he grows increasingly

rapturous about the safety and strength of the forest, more
caught up in the *beatus ille* mood, we become uncom-
fortably suspicious that the whole philosophy is under
attack—that this great prelate of the grove cuts a pompous,
half-ridiculous figure hardly in keeping with Appleton
humility, and that, as the puns on "stocks" and "locks"
have earlier hinted, his sanctuary may also be his prison:

> Bind me ye *Woodbines* in your 'twines,
> Curle me about ye gadding *Vines,*
> And Oh so close your Circles lace,
> That I may never leave this Place:
> But, lest your Fetters prove too weak,
> Ere I your Silken Bondage break,
> Do you, O *Brambles,* chain me too,
> And courteous *Briars* nail me through.
>
> [609–16]

These briars are "courteous"; if they allude to the crucifixion, as Empson believes, they do so with a gently
oblique irony—this is a welcome confinement of the flesh
that liberates the spirit. But neither can they be "entirely
innocent of religious implications" (Pierre Legouis).[13] The
speaker's words—*fetters, bondage, chain, nail*—offer
momentary glimpses of the "night within" even as the
speaker's delight rises to an ecstatic pitch. May this not be
the "Silken Bondage" of a mind unwittingly chained to its
own constructions? At the end of the section the speaker
expands again on his "Pleasure":

> Oh what a Pleasure 'tis to hedge
> My Temples here with heavy sedge;
> Abandoning my lazy Side

> Stretcht as a Bank unto the Tide;
> Or to suspend my sliding foot
> On the Osiers undermined Root,
> And in its Branches tough to hang,
> While at my Lines the Fishes twang!
>
> [641–48]

Unlike the natural bird who "Walks still upright from the Root" (539), the artful philosopher slides downward on an "undermined Root"; he is (to a less enraptured eye than his own) hooked, just as the fish are snared in his "Lines." He is in danger of falling out of his element, as the fish are rising out of theirs. Reflecting each other in an image of allurement and potential danger, both the fisher and the fish have taken a deceptive bait. Can these "Lines" be the "admirable Lines" designed by humility (41–42)?

The passage is preceded by an extended conceit (625–40) which becomes an appropriate emblem for the speaker's predicament: through the meadow winds a river, which might be mistaken for a snake whose muddy back is slick enough that, in the paradoxical reversal we have come to expect, "for his shade which therein shines, Narcissus like, the Sun too pines" (639–40). We have a perfect double image, the mutual reflection of "within" and "without"; but as Narcissus was the first to discover, the attempt to merge the two into one without knowing where you are leads to disaster. The speaker believes for the moment that he has created a private paradise within and excluded the world without, that he has "incamp'd" his mind "where the World no certain Shot/Can make" (605–06). But we know that the "tallest Oak" can fall by

a "feeble Strok" (551–52) because it breeds "within" itself
a "Traitor-worm" (554)—as our "Flesh corrupt within,"
whatever protective enclosures we set up around it,
"Tempts innocent and bashful Sin" (555–56).

And that is just the point: only in a state of innocence—
of Edenic *integritas*—is an unequivocal unity with nature
possible. Marvell speaks of that innocence in "The Garden," where

> . . . the Mind, from pleasure less,
> Withdraws into its happiness:
> The Mind, that Ocean where each kind
> Does streight its own resemblance find.
>
> [41–44]

Though the mind's effortless reflection in nature and of
nature ("annihilating" the distinction between outer and
inner) may be recoverable at special moments of contem-
plative perfection, the poet finally puts it in the past
tense—"Such *was* that happy Garden-state" ("The Garden," 57)—as he does also in "The Mower's Song":

> My Mind was once the true survey
> Of all these Medows fresh and gay;
> And in the greeness of the Grass
> Did see its Hopes as in a Glass;
> When *Juliana* came, and She
> What I do to the Grass, does to my Thoughts and Me.
>
> [1–6]

In view of the perceptual versatility required of us
throughout the poem, perhaps we should take more seriously than he intends the "easie Philosopher's" suggestion

that we "turn" him into the venerable emblem of the
arbor inversa:

> . . . little now to make me, wants
> Or of the Fowles, or of the Plants.
> . . . .
> Or turn me but, and you shall see
> I was but an inverted tree.
>
> [563-68]

A little turn, and he is inverted into a plant more verdant
than ordinary trees since his roots (that is, his hair) point
toward heaven. But so turned, he may also seem absurdly
topsy-turvy, with his head in the ground. We "turn" and
"turn" this philosophical angler as we do the "Salmon-
Fishers" in the poem's final stanza, who have "shod their
Heads in their Canoos" (772). Before the fall man "*was
but an inverted Tree.*" Since then he may appear erect,
but—what the mower does to the grass—his roots are
cut; he is turned again, fallen out of nature. He is forced
to peer through a darker "Glass"—in Donne's phrase,
"through lattices of eyes"—at a world that will no longer
yield up its meaning directly. Just as Narcissus mistakes
his own shadow for reality—"pines" for it without recog-
nizing its duplicity—the speaker falls victim to his own
fancy, to his desire to see the wood "as if" it fit the
interpretations of his "easy" philosophy. The result in
both cases is an entrapment within the self. But Marvell's
reader has been taught by the poem how to avoid falling
into precisely that trap.

Like Velázquez's viewer, he has learned that the "face of
things" (442) can conceal contradictions. The reader is

given a paradoxical vision of the simultaneous possibility and impossibility of becoming a happy man through mystic solitude, just as elsewhere in the poem we are left with the sense that Fairfax was both right *and* wrong to retire to his garden—"A natural perspective," cries Orsino, "that is and is not." On a field of overlapping contexts, a "light Mosaick" (582) of the biblical, philosophical, historical, architectural, theatrical, and more, the poem plays with such alternatives: nature and art, war and peace, innocence and sin, action and contemplation, out and in. It offers them all tentatively, qualified by ironies, grave tones broken by moments of humor, light tones deepened by suggestions of darker meanings—each state of mind visible in multiple facets, but none receiving the poet's endorsement, none complete in itself.

Marvell's reader, located "within" the shifting perspectives of the Appleton landscape, relinquishes the detached and commanding vantage point he enjoys in other topographical poems such as Denham's "Cooper's Hill." There the eye, perched on a high hill, conducts a "proud survey" of the realm spread below and "swift as thought" comes to see its unifying moral order. Our secure vantage in "Upon Appleton House" is undermined like the philosopher's foot: we have fallen once, and to be unequivocally convinced that the mind can artfully recreate secure and innocent enclosures for itself, whether in poems or in estates, is to risk a repetition of that catastrophe. Our Appleton tour guide marks off and then questions such boundaries. He leads us in and out of a series of frames, all of which reflect the others, the greater world which frames them, and our own frame of mind—that "double

. . . Mind" which has been the condition of our knowledge since we came out of Eden ("The Mower against Gardens," 9). He speaks to us both as a proponent of new gardens and a mower against gardens. Appleton House and its reflection in language, "Upon Appleton House," are lesser worlds than the domain of action and public commitment in a nation at war with itself. Still, "your lesser World contains the same" disorder and uncertainty, "but in more decent Order tame" (765–66); it provides the leisure and spiritual sustenance for meditations in an emergency. In it we find "Paradice's only Map" (768), drawn with "Those short but admirable Lines,/By which, ungirt and unconstrain'd,/Things greater are in less contained" (42–44).

That map spreads out not so much before us but, as in the case of *Las Meninas,* around us. At its exact center (stanza 49) we find ourselves walking "like Israelites" through a "green Sea" whose "Grassy Deeps divide,/And crowd a lane to either side." We stand in the "polisht Grass," as in a "Looking-Glass" (457–58), looking to either side of us to two halves of the poem which are, structurally, carefully ordered reflections of each other. On one side, the "blooming Virgin" Isabel Thwates must be rescued from her hothouse cloister by an earlier Fairfax, with whom her proper destiny is to plant the family tree now growing in Appleton. On the other side, the virgin Maria, growing "like a sprig of Misleto,/On the Fairfacian Oak" (739–40) must be cut loose, out of Appleton and into marriage, by the present Fairfax—as the heron in the woods "the eldest of its young lets drop" (534). We are in the midst of a rhythm of taking hold and letting go, moving in and out, pulsing in a sea of generations in time. The way to the promised land lies not in the determined march straight ahead, blindered against the "Deeps" on either side—that way lies the bloody rail, carved by the "whistling Sithe" of "one, unknowing" (391–93). It lies in the slower pace of a more reflective mind knowingly exploring the poem's many mansions.

Since it is beyond human art, in the design of those mansions, "t'immure/The Circle in the Quadrature," the poet is willing to let "others"—ambitious Palladian architects, perhaps—"vainly strive" to do it (45–46). Yet has he not succeeded in "immuring" a perfectly circular artistic and moral journey—from the house, around the grounds, and back again—within the quadrature of ninety-seven eight-syllable by eight-line stanzas? By the rules of his own "holy Mathematicks" he has built a frame both humble and ingenious. The experience offered by the poem, like that of Velázquez's *Las Meninas,* lies in our measuring ourselves against a set of rules too complex for us to comprehend as we would like, though available for us to apprehend imaginatively if we can. Both works refuse to make choices between the alternatives of a double world, but include the problematics of choice within the artist's frame.

Conclusion: The Witness
as Rational Amphibian

In this study I have applied the term *curious perspective* to a wide variety of visual styles over more than a century of European art from Holbein to Velázquez. I am conscious of having omitted the rubrics "Northern Renaissance" and "Spanish Baroque," under which these painters ordinarily appear in textbooks of art history, and of having included in my own category popular objects like woodcuts and perspective boxes without regard to levels of taste. Yet I think the loss is offset by an advantage of some consequence for literary study: the curious perspective isolates a strain of visual wit analogous to poetic wit, embodied in the techniques of perspective manipulation and available to artists working in different countries and different styles.

I have kept my description of the technique emotionally neutral to leave room for the several expressive functions it could serve—from Holbein's morbid shudder, to the disquieting and unexplained shifts in point of view in a Mannerist painting like Parmigianino's *The Madonna with the Long Neck,* to Velázquez's more playful visual intrigues.

Witty English verse in the first half of the seventeenth century displays the same range of expressive possibilities, as I have tried to show in my analogies. That variety, however, grows out of a common sensibility shared by painters and poets, an urge to go beyond what they perceived as the limitations of their media.

Although the curious perspective would have been impossible without the achievement of a systematic linear perspective in the earlier Renaissance, its effect was to parody, question, and even undermine the central cognitive assumption behind perspective representation. As in the larger world newly revealed through the perspective glass, the viewer no longer enjoyed the ideal vantage point on a painted world that had once defined itself fully and precisely to his rational understanding. Instead he now found it necessary to accommodate his vision to the double perspectives of anamorphic distortion, mirror reflections, hidden images, spatial ambiguities, and shifts of scale, all of which dislocate him from his privileged position, guaranteed in the Albertian scheme, as *misura del mondo*. The curious perspective violates the ordered perfection of pictorial space as verbal wit violates the expository clarity of language. Both exploit the witness's uncertainty in the presence of duplicitous images but repay his puzzlement with what Tesauro would call an *imparamente veloce,* a sudden apprehension of meanings beyond the geometer's grasp.

In the eye of God, the only perfect vantage point, the world in all its contrariety is still one thing, *omnis in unum.* Man perceives, and recreates in his own arts, a world (as Marvell says) "as double as his Mind,"[1] inevita-

bly split into the antimonies of human experience that pre-
occupy the writers I have considered: the body natural and
the body politic, reason and imagination, the dark glass
and the clear glass, action and contemplation, art and
nature, nature and grace. Witty art forces us to confront
the double nature of our own mind, to realize (as Sir
Thomas Browne tells us) that

> we are onely that amphibious piece betweene a cor-
> porall and spirituall essence, that middle forme that
> linkes those two together, and makes good the
> method of God and nature, that jumps not from ex-
> treames, but unites the incompatible distances by
> some middle and participating natures. . . . thus is man
> that great and true Amphibium, whose nature is dis-
> posed to live not onely like other creatures in divers
> elements, but in divided and distinguished worlds. . . .[2]

The recognition that men are "rational Amphibii" does
not lead the witty artist to despair, trapped though he may
be inside the defective apparatus of earthly perception.
By wedging opposing perspectives into a single image he
is partially able to repair the split suffered in the Fall—to
approximate the unity of the divine mind.

There are several benefits of reading witty verse, where
appropriate, in the context of the curious perspective, the
least of which is that we come to understand more fully
what seventeenth-century poets had in mind when they
wrote that griefs are "like perspectives," that devils, seen
obliquely, are our sins "in perspective," or that the
"Scene" presented by a quiet country estate to an unquiet
mind is somehow like a shifting visual spectacle. That

poets would choose to talk about the dubieties of human perception in such terms—would indeed construct a witty language that itself must be read "like perspectives"—suggests a deeper connection. The double vision required of the viewer of a curious perspective provides the concrete model of a relationship between the witness and the work of art that obtains as well in the poetry of wit.

That relationship was soon to be refashioned along the more regular lines of neoclassical taste, for the reaction against "metaphysical" indecorum and the dark conceit runs parallel to a demand for visual propriety and correct perspective codified in the dicta of the Academies. To "imitate nature" according to the Rules—whether in words or pictures—it was first necessary to curb one's fancy to the sober restraints of judgment and then to create images that would be above all clear and immediately understood. "True Wit" cannot be an enigma says Pope, but "Something, whose Truth convinc'd at Sight we find/That gives us back the Image of our Mind."[3] The "Image of our Mind" may be found earlier in "An Essay on Criticism" in Pope's admiration for the unity of a "well-proportion'd Dome":

> No single Parts unequally surprize;
> All comes united to th'admiring Eyes;
> No monstrous Height, or Breadth, or Length appear;
> The Whole at once is Bold, and Regular.[4]

The well-proportioned mind takes pleasure in the experience of objects which, like itself, are free of distortions and idiosyncratic "single Parts" marring the harmonious order of the "Whole." This mind searches for its true reflection in art and nature and immediately recognizes that reflection by its congruence with the mind's own interior shape.

Such a view of the mind leaves little room for puzzlement as a help to the understanding, and less patience for the mental gynmastics of the curious perspective. Once thought a respectable and intriguing study by men like Niceron in the 1630s, the curious perspective became a parlor curiosity in the eighteenth century—and remained so until the eventual demolition of linear perspective cleared the field for the perceptual experiments of modernism. The best piece of curious perspective in eighteenth-century English art must certainly be Hogarth's *Method of Perspective* (figure 13), which creates massive ambiguities of near and far distance by a perverse misapplication of every rule of perspective composition. But the engraving has a cautionary intent: prefixed to *Dr. Brook Taylor's Method of Perspective made easy both in Theory and Practice* (written by John Kirby in 1754), it warns in a caption: "Whoever makes a Design without the knowledge of Perspective will be liable to such absurdities as are shown in this Frontispiece."

What a later age would regard as "absurdities," as affronts to the reason, often struck the seventeenth century as mysteries. *Certum est quia impossible est* is the "odde resolution" Sir Thomas Browne learned of Tertullian, and it was Browne's "solitary recreation" to "pose" his "apprehension with those involved aenigma's and riddles of the Trinity, with Incarnation, and Resurrection."[5] Browne's recreation was also the experience of the witness to witty art.

Figure 13. William Hogarth, *Method of Perspective* (1754). Frontispiece to
Dr. Brook Taylor's Method of Perspective made easy both in Theory and Practice
(written by John Kirby).

Shakespeare's *Richard II* casts the viewer in the role of playgoer historian and forces him to see the difficulties of historical interpretation reproduced in the conflicting perspectives of dramatic interpretation. An attentive audience finds itself divided between the corporal and spiritual essence of kingship—a necessarily amphibious stance which, in a different mood, it must also assume to balance the Thesean and Hippolytan perspectives of Shakespearean comedy. In the deposition scene Richard's mirror no longer shows the divine image of a king, but, fallen and cracked into a hundred slivers, only reflects the "shadow" of a broken man. Donne, Herbert, and Greville try where Richard failed to recover that original image; and if their wit cannot piece together the broken letters of a fallen language, it can at least reveal to the reader a glimpse of hidden things shining, perspectively, in the dark fragments. The double perspectives of Marvell's poetry offer the reader a view, like that watery "Chrystal Mirrour slick" in the Appleton meadow, "Where all things gaze themselves, and doubt/If they be in it or without (636-37). The "doubt" is necessary to the reader's mental health; it is a prophylactic against narcissism. If the reader thinks he can make certain choices in art or life, he does not know his own mind when he sees it reflected in a shifting, unstable world of doubles, and, having forgotten that he fell once, is in danger of losing his mental balance a second time. But a true amphibian cannot drown.

Notes

INTRODUCTION

1 The saying attributed to Simonides of Ceos is found in Plutarch and introduced into English by Sir Thomas Hoby, whose version is quoted here. *Elizabethan Critical Essays,* ed. G. Gregory Smith (Oxford, 1904), 1: 342.

2 All quotations from Shakespeare are taken from the Pelican text, *William Shakespeare: The Complete Works,* gen. ed. Alfred Harbage (Baltimore: Penguin Books, 1969).

3 *Laocöon: An Essay on the Limits of Painting and Poetry,* trans. Edward A. McCormick, Library of the Liberal Arts (New York: Bobbs Merrill, 1962), p. 78.

4 "Method in the Study of Literature in its Relation to the Other Fine Arts," *Journal of Aesthetics and Art Criticism* 7 (March 1950): 190. For other cautionary essays, see the issue of *New Literary History* 3:3 (1972) devoted to literary and art history.

5 *The Sister Arts* (Chicago: University of Chicago Press, 1958), p. xxi.

6 Hagstrum, *The Sister Arts,* p. 117.

7 *The Art of Ecstasy: Teresa, Bernini, and Crashaw* (New York: Atheneum, 1970), p. xi.

8 Petersson, *The Art of Ecstasy,* p. 99; but on the practical question of a comparative method, Petersson retreats to the narrower position that "the best basis has proved to be subject matter" (p. x). He studies St. Teresa's ecstasy as presented in Bernini

and Crashaw—with, however, more to say about the poetry and sculpture separately than about any intrinsic relationship between them, and the most to say on the subject of St. Teresa herself. Limiting the link to subject matter, though an obvious convenience in a study like Petersson's, begs the more interesting question: how can comparisons be made in cases where the subject matter is not identical?

9 John Steadman, "Iconography and Renaissance Drama: Ethical and Mythological Themes," *Research Opportunities in Renaissance Drama* 13–14 (1970–71):75. For the literary basis of artistic theory in the Renaissance, see Rensselaer W. Lee, *Ut Pictura Poesis: The Humanistic Theory of Painting* (New York: Norton, 1967).

10 *The Flaming Heart* (1958; rpt. Gloucester, Mass.: Peter Smith, 1966), p. 247.

11 *Mnemosyne,* Bollingen Series 25.16 (Princeton: Princeton University Press, 1970), p. 31.

12 Ibid., p. 54.

13 Ibid., p. 129.

14 Ibid., pp. 82–83.

15 Ibid., pp. 92, 97.

16 *Anatomy of Criticism* (New York: Atheneum, 1966), pp. 77–79, 365.

17 I am indebted to the work of Stanley Fish for an example of criticism that addresses itself to the experience of the reader, though I am not wedded to his implication that every book worth experiencing consumes itself in the process: *Self-consuming Artifacts: The Experience of Seventeenth-Century Literature* (Berkeley: University of California Press, 1972).

18 Norman N. Holland, "Unity Identity Text Self," *PMLA* 90 (1975): 813–22.

19 "A Theory of Terminology," in S. R. Hopper and D. L. Miller, eds., *Interpretation: The Poetry of Meaning* (New York: Harcourt, Brace and World, 1967), pp. 98–101.

20 *Art and Illusion: A Study in the Psychology of Pictorial Representation,* Bollingen Series 35.5 (Princeton: Princeton University Press, 1961), p. 271.

21 *Feeling and Form* (New York: Scribners, 1953), pp. 395–96.

22 See Joseph Frank's "Spatial Form in Modern Literature" (1945),

reprinted in his collection, *The Widening Gyre* (New Brunswick: Rutgers University Press, 1963), pp. 3–62. William V. Spanos replies to Frank in "Modern Literary Criticism and the Spatialization of Time: An Existential Critique," *Journal of Aesthetics and Art Criticism* 29, no. 1 (Fall 1970): 87–104.

CHAPTER 1

1 This chapter is indebted to the following studies of perspective from different points of view: Miriam S. Bunim, *Space in Medieval Painting* (New York: Columbia University Press, 1940); Joan Gadol, *Leon Battista Alberti* (Chicago: University of Chicago Press, 1969); E. H. Gombrich, *Art and Illusion;* Claudio Guillén, "On the Concept and Metaphor of Perspective," in *Comparatists at Work,* ed. Stephen G. Nichols, Jr., and Richard B. Vowles (Waltham, Mass.: Blaisdell Pub. Co., 1968), pp. 28–90; William M. Ivins, Jr., *On the Rationalization of Sight* (New York: DaCapo Press, 1973); Erwin Panofsky, *Life and Art of Albrecht Dürer,* 2 vols. (Princeton: Princeton University Press, 1955) and "Die Perspective als Symbolische Form," *Vorträge der Bibliothek Warburg* (1924–25). See also the recent, valuable work by Samuel Y. Edgerton, Jr., *The Renaissance Rediscovery of Linear Perspective* (New York: Basic Books, 1975), and the discussion in Richard Krautheimer, *Lorenzo Ghiberti,* 2 vols., (Princeton: Princeton University Press, 1970), chap. 16.

2 Cenino Cennini, *Il libro dell'arte,* quoted and translated in John White, *The Birth and Rebirth of Pictorial Space* (Boston: Boston Book and Art Shop, 1967), p. 108.

3 Leon Battista Alberti, *On Painting,* ed. and trans. John R. Spencer, rev. ed. (New Haven and London: Yale University Press, 1966), pp. 56–57.

4 According to Vasari (see Gadol, *Alberti,* p. 22), Albert's friend and fellow architect Brunelleschi was said to have discovered the method, and perhaps to have taught it to Masaccio, whose fresco of the Trinity in Sta. Maria Novella in Florence (1425) is one of the earliest paintings to include an architectural background in correct perspective. Later treatises tend to be more mathematically rigorous than Alberti's, proceeding from axioms and definitions to increasingly complex theorems and problems. In the

later fifteenth century Piero della Francesca developed a construction slightly different from Alberti's to arrive at the same
results. This is known as the *tiers points* method, after Jean
Pelerin (Viator), whose *De artificiali p,spectiva,* published in
Toul (1505), describes it. Both methods were taught in Italy in
the first half of the sixteenth century. The logical identity of
the *costruzione legittima* and the *tiers points* methods was
demonstrated in Jacomo Vignola's posthumously published
Le due regole della prospettiva pratica (ed. Egnatio Dante,
Rome, 1583). Alberti composed a Latin original and an Italian
version of his treatise, both probably 1435–36. Neither was
printed until the Latin *De pictura* appeared in Basel in 1540,
followed by Lodovico Domenichi's Italian translation (Venice,
1547). Piero's *De prospectiva pingendi* was not published until
the nineteenth century. But the work of both writers was widely
known during their lifetimes and throughout the Renaissance—a
testament to a lively tradition of workshop instruction and
personal interchange among artists. Dürer, in a letter to his
friend Pirckheimer (13 October 1506), says he is about to go to
Bologna "um der Kunst in geheimer Perspective willen, die mir
lehren will." He revealed these secrets of perspective to the German world in his *Unterweysung der Messung* (1525; facsimile ed.
by Dietikon-Zurich, J. Stocker-Schmid, 1966, which gives
Dürer's letter in an appendix, p. 187). Cellini claims in his *Discourse* to have bought a book on perspective by Leonardo. This
has not survived, but Leonardo's notebooks give some idea of
what it must have contained: Leonardo reproduces the *costruzione legittima* and, characteristically for him, discusses its short-
comings (see White, *Birth and Rebirth,* pp. 307–15). Alberti's
construction, with some variation, was taught in Filarete's
Trattato dell'architettura (1464), Guarico's *De sculptura* (1504),
and finally incorporated in a general theory of conic projections
in Desargues's *Pratique de la perspective* (1636).

5 Alberti, *On Painting,* p. 98.

6 Ibid., pp. 56, 51. On the "open window," compare Leonardo:
"Perspective is nothing else than seeing a place (or objects)
behind a pane of glass, quite transparent, on the surface of
which the objects behind the glass are drawn" (*Works,* trans.
Jean Paul Richter, 5.1.150).

7 Alberti, *On Painting,* p. 58.

8 The details of the *costruzione* appear on pp. 57–59 of the Spencer edition. Spencer's notes are invaluable for the technical meaning of Alberti's often oblique instructions. The lines quoted in the instructions are from these pages.

9 Alberti, *On Painting*, p. 98.

10 Ibid., p. 90.

11 Ibid., p. 55.

12 See Siegfried Giedion, *Space, Time and Architecture,* 4th rev. ed. (Cambridge: Harvard University Press, 1963), p. 31.

13 *Art and Illusion,* pp. 138–39.

14 Alberti, *On Painting,* pp. 51, 57, 55.

15 Ibid., pp. 64, 68–69.

16 John Donne, "The second Anniversary," ll. 295–96, in *The Poems of John Donne,* ed. Herbert J. E. Grierson (London: Oxford University Press, 1912, rpt. 1968), 1: 259. Hereafter cited as Grierson.

17 Walter J. Ong, S.J., "System, Space, and Intellect in Renaissance Symbolism," *The Barbarian Within and Other Fugitive Essays and Studies* (New York: Macmillan, 1962), pp. 75–76.

18 Panofsky, *Life and Art of Albrecht Dürer,* 1: 261.

19 See Giedion, *Space, Time,* p. 44.

20 See White, *Birth and Rebirth,* pp. 207–15.

21 Trans. H. P. D. Lee (Baltimore: Penguin, 1955, rpt. 1972), p. 374.

22 Antonio di Piero Averlino (il Filarete), *Trattato dell'architettura* (1464); trans. John R. Spencer, *Filarete's Treatise on Architecture,* 2 vols. (New Haven and London: Yale University Press, 1965), 1: 305.

23 *Oeuvres* (Paris, 1824), 5: 39; the English version is from *Descartes: Philosophical Writings,* trans. and ed. Elizabeth Anscombe and Peter Geach (London: Nelson, 1966), p. 244.

24 Alberti, *On Painting,* pp. 43, 64.

25 Johann Faulhaber, *Newe geometrische und perspectivische inventiones* . . . (Frankfurt, 1610); "Newe geometrische und perspectivische inventiones/ Elticher sonderbahrer Instrument die zum Perspectivischen Grundreissen der Pasteyen und Vestungen wie auch zum Planimetrischen Grundlegen der Statt/ Feldlagen und Landtschaafften." All translations are mine, unless otherwise indicated.

26 Vignola, *Le due regole,* pp. 95, 96.

27 Cited in Arthur Fairchild, *Shakespeare and the Arts of Design,*
    University of Missouri Studies 12, no. 1 (Columbia, Mo., 1937),
    p. 128, along with examples from two other Chapman plays.

28 *Ben Jonson,* ed. C. H. Herford and P. Simpson (Oxford: Claren-
    don Press, 1927), 3: 538.

29 See, for example, Hendrick Hondius, *Onderswijsinge in de per-
    spective conste* (The Hague, 1623), p. 24 and Alberti (Albrecht)
    Andreae, *Zwei Bücher . . . Perspectiva* (Nuremberg, 1671), pp.
    92–96. The more sophisticated anamorphic figure is made by
    radically lengthening the distance between the centric point and
    the baseline of the *costruzione legittima,* while radically short-
    ening the distance between the distance point and the picture.

30 Haydocke translates the first five books of Lomazzo's treatise,
    but though he lists them in his table, he does not translate the
    final two books. These last are "practical" books, which he feels
    can be postponed for a later edition (never brought out) since he
    has given us the "contemplative" part. Thus the anamorphic
    figures in Lomazzo's sixth book, chapter nineteen, are in the
    English version only promised, not delivered: "How to make in-
    verted Perspective which shall seem true being viewed through a
    small hole." The first work in English to explain a method for
    drawing anamorphic pictures is H. Van Etten, *Mathematicall
    Recreations* (London, 1633); problem 106, for example, shows
    "How to disguise or disfigure an Image, as a head, an arme, a
    whole body; &c. so that it hath no proportion . . . yet the eye
    placed a a certain point will be scene in a direct and exact pro-
    portion." Other English sources that deal with perspective in its
    "manifold deceptions" though not with tricks of perspective
    per se are Solomon de Caus, *La perspective,* written in French
    but published in London, 1612; and Henry Peacham's *Art of
    Drawing* (London, 1606), a pedestrian primer for gentlemen who
    wish to dabble, enlarged and reissued in 1612 as *The Gentle-
    man's Exercise,* and reprinted with this title together with *The
    Compleat Gentleman* (1634, 1661). Also Edward Norgate's
    Miniatura, or the Art of Limning, written about 1625, revised
    1649, and extant in a number of manuscripts though not pub-
    lished by the author. Norgate, one of the agents commissioned
    by the Earl of Arundel to buy paintings on the continent, refers
    the reader to Marolois and other continental authors for the

rules of perspective, though he cautions sensibly enough: "The only inconvenience incident to Perspective, and whereof I have heard Mr. Steinwicke complaine with indignation, was that so many were the lines perpendicular, parallel and the rest, that another Painter could complete a peece, and get his money, before he could draw his lines" (in 1649 MS, ed. Martin Hardie [Oxford: Clarendon Press, 1919], p. 82). One manuscript of the *Miniatura*, signed "Daniel King," but clearly Norgate's work, is dedicated to Mary Fairfax: King was Mary's tutor in painting around 1650, while Andrew Marvell was at Appleton House (Hardie, p. xix).

31 Haydocke, *A Tracte*, pp. 108–09.

32 Ibid., pp. 188–9.

33 Accolti, *Lo inganno de gl'occhi*, pp. 48–49: "Dalle cose dette de sopra pare, che ci si vadia aprenda la strada per un'altra strana, ma dilettosa operatione de Prospettiva, median te, la quale siamo maravigliosamente ingannati, poiche propostaci si fatta operazione in disegno, ò Pittura, non sapiamo ben discernere ciò che il Pittore, ne suoi dintorni, e colori habbia volsuto rappresentarci, se non ne viene sciolto lo enigma da una specchio si fattamente situato, entro il quale volgendo il sguardo (altro cosa apparendoci quanto all'occhio) subito ravvisiamo con stupore tal pittura essere il ritratto di Persone li più volte, e notissime, e carissime, a noi stessi, tanta e la forza, tanto il valore, e potere della Prospettiva, nella quale tutta interamente s'appoggia cosi fatta apparenza: Onde bisogna dire, e credere, che anche il Disegno, e la Pittura ha la sua cifra, & contracifra, per celarsi anche ad Argo...."

34 Niceron's treatise was published in French editions of 1638 and 1652 (the one used here), and in a posthumous Latin version, the *Thaumaturgus opticus*, 1646, 1663. Dubreuil had a second edition in 1651 and a later one in 1679, and several English translations, both published and in manuscript: see Henry and Margaret Ogden, "A Bibliography of Seventeenth Century Writings on the Pictorial Arts in English," *Art Bulletin* 29 (1947): 197–201.

35 Niceron, *Perspective curieuse*, p. 6.

36 Ibid., p. 90: "suivant la diversité de leur aspect, representent deux ou trois choses toutes differentes, de forte qu'estant veuës

de front, elles representent un face humaine; de coste droit une teste de mort, & du gauche quelqu'autre chose differente." An invaluable guide to Niceron and the French circle of "perspecteurs" in the seventeenth century is Jurgis Baltrušaitis, *Anamorphoses ou magie artificielle des effets merveilleux* (Olivier Perrin, 1969), esp. pp. 39–78.

37 *Diary of John Evelyn,* ed. E. S. de Beer, 6 vols. (Oxford: Clarendon Press, 1955), 2: 373 and 373*n*5; the St. John is reproduced in Niceron's *Thaumaturgus opticus* (1646), pp. 176–78 and plate 33. The lines from Crashaw are from "The Weeper," 11. 89–90, in *The Poems English, Latin, and Greek of Richard Crashaw,* ed. L. C. Martin (London: Oxford University Press, 1927, 2d ed., 1957).

38 Dubreuil, *Perspective pratique,* 5: introduction: "pour veu qu'il soit regardé par une petite ouverture, ou poinct determiné."

39 Ibid., 3:92: "Par example, si pour premier chassis arresté, on fait la Perspective d'une grand arcade qui paroisse de relief, & espaisse de quatre ou cinq pieds en apparence & qu'au travers de cette arcade, l'on voye une Perspective de beaux Bastiments, peints sur trois ou quatre triangles: Ces deux Perspectives destachées l'une de l'autre, d'autant d'espace qu'on voudra, feront paroistre un Palais, ou quelque logis magnifique. Mais si on prend le temps qu'il faut a couler un rideau derriere ce premier chassis, pendent lequel on tournera les triangles, on ne verra plus ces bastiments au travers de l'arcade, mais un paysage à perte de veuë, ou un beau jardin de plaisir avec des fontaines ou jets d'eaux, des allées, des pallissades des bois & c."

40 Niceron, *Perspective curieuse,* pp. 147–49: "la maniere de construire des figures qui rapportent & representent par reflexion tout autre chose qu ce qu'elles pariossent estans veuës directment."

41 Dubreuil, *Perspective pratique,* 6: introduction: "Ces pièces sont extremement divertissantes en ce que d'un meslange de couleurs que semblent estre jetties sans ordre sur le plan, on void au Cylindre une belle image."

42 Ibid., 6:124–25: "en telle sorte, que pour cinq, ou six petites figures, on voye une armée; pour deux ou trois arbres, de grandes forests; pour deux ou trois maisons, des ville entieres."

43 Ibid., 6:143: "peindre sur un plan, une image separée en diverse

pièces, laquelle estant veuë sur un prisme speculaire, ou Miroir de plusieurs faces, paroistra semblable a son Prototype."

44 *The New Atlantis* in *The Works of Francis Bacon,* ed. James Spedding, Robert L. Ellis, and Douglas D. Heath (London, 1859), 3: 162.

45 Niceron, *Perspective curieuse,* p. 173: "sur le plan d'un table où seront descrites plusieurs figures ou portraicts dans leurs justes proportions, on en peut faire voir une autre differente de toutes celles qui sont au tableau, bien proportionnée, semblable à quelque objet ou pourtraict donné." The diagram is from Dubreuil, *Perspective pratique,* 7: 156.

46 "The Answer of Mr. Hobbs to Sir William D'Avenant's Preface before Gondibert," in *Literary Criticism of Seventeenth Century England,* ed. Edward W. Tayler (New York: Knopf, 1967), p. 290.

47 It was in fact a later English writer, Joseph Moxon, the "Hydrographer" to Charles II, who summed up the entire tradition in his handbook, *Practical Perspective* (London, 1670). There anyone interested in "speculatory ingenuity" could, according to the running title, learn "by the opticks, how to delineate all bodies. . . . By the catoptricks, how to delineate confused appearances, so as when seen in a mirror or pollisht body of any intended shape, the reflection shall shew a design, [and] By the dioptircks [*sic*] how to draw parts of many figures into one, when seen through a glass or christal cut into many faces."

CHAPTER 2

1 Two recent exhibitions collected a number of Renaissance examples from American and European museums: "By Design: Curious Deceptions in Art and Play" (Xerox Corp., 1975) and "Anamorphosis: Games of Perception and Illusion in Art" (Michael Schuyt and Joost Elffers, 1976). For the English catalogue of the latter exhibition, see: Fred Leeman, *Hidden Images* (New York: Harry N. Abrams, Inc., 1976). Other examples are in private hands.

2 See Ellis K. Waterhouse, *Painting in Britain* (Baltimore: Penguin, 1953) for a survey of the arts in England.

3 Fairchild, *Shakespeare and The Arts of Design,* p. 109.

4 Donne's will bequeaths sixteen paintings specifically and refers to a number of others which are to be inventoried as part of his general estate: see R. C. Bald, *John Donne: A Life* (New York and Oxford: Oxford University Press, 1970), pp. 563–67.

5 Praz, *The Flaming Heart,* p. 207.

6 Quoted and translated in James B. Shaw, "The Perspective Picture: A Freak of German Sixteenth-Century Art," *Apollo* 6 (1927):213 "Eduardi VI Angliae regis effigies, primo intuitu monstrosum quid repraesentens, sed si quis per foramen operculi ver tabellae, qua pictura tegitur, effigiem recta intueatur, tum vera depraehenditur; ingeniosum Artificis inventum."

7 See *Abraham van der Doort's Catalogs of the Collections of Charles I,* ed. Oliver Millar, Walpole Society vol. 37 (Glasgow, 1960): one painting listed "in a black ebbone turn'd box wth a christall over it," and another "in a white Ivory tourn'd box" (p. 107); another "in an Ebbone frame, wth a shuting dore of Ebbone" (p. 123); another in "a black shutting box" (p. 161), etc.

8 Shaw, "The Perspective Picture," p. 211.

9 The Edward VI portrait is listed in the *Inventories and Valuations of the King's Goods, 1649–1651,* ed. Oliver Millar, Walpole Society vol. 43 (Glasgow, 1972), p. 197, as "Edward ye 6th lookeing through a hoole," then hanging in Hampton Court.

10 See Baltrušaitis, *Anamorphoses,* p. 23.

11 Lionel Cust, "Notes on the Collections Formed by Thomas Howard, Earl of Arundel and Surrey, K. G.," *Burlington Magazine* 20 (1911–12): 235.

12 Rosalie Colie, *"My Ecchoing Song": Andrew Marvell's Poetry of Criticism* (Princeton: Princeton University Press, 1970), p. 211.

13 Though the invention of the device is ascribed to Giambattista della Porta in the sixteenth century, Alberti had put one on display as early as 1437. Barbaro discusses the camera in *La pratica della perspectiva* (Venice, 1568), p. 192, Kepler in *Ad vitellionem paralipomena* (1604), and Niceron in *Thaumaturgus opticus,* plate 2, figure 28. Henry Wotton describes the device (in a letter to Bacon, 8 December 1620) he saw on a visit to Kepler (*Life and Letters of Henry Wotton,* ed. Logan P. Smith, [Oxford, 1907], 2: 205–06). See Marjorie Hope Nicholson, *Newton Demands the Muse* (Princeton: Princeton University

Press, 1946), pp. 77–78, and Heinrich Schwarz, "Vermeer and the Camera Obscura," *Pantheon* 24, no. 3 (1966):176–77.

14 Written from London, 13 April 1622, cited in Schwarz, "Vermeer and the Camera Obscura," p. 177: "J'ay chez moy l'autre instrument de Drebbel, qui certes fait des effets admirables en peinture de reflexion dans une chambre obscure; il ne m'est possible de vous declarer la beauté en paroles; toute peinture est morte au prix, car c'est icy la vie mesme, ou quelque chose de plus relevé, si la parole n'y manquoit. Car et la figure et la contour et les mouvements s'y rencontrent naturellement et d'une facon grandement plaisante."

15 Thomas Coryate, *Coryate's Crudities* (Glasgow, 1905), 1: 294. Coryate's book was originally published in 1612.

16 Coryate, *Crudities,* 1: 393.

17 William Drummond of Hawthornden, "A Letter to Sir George Keith," in the *History of Scotland* (1655), pp. 249–52; cited in Rosemary Freeman, *English Emblem Books* (London: Chatto and Windus, 1948), p. 16.

18 Evelyn, *Diary,* 2: 254 (1644); 2: 112 (1645); 2: 449 (1645); 3: 165 (1656).

19 Hoogstraeten worked in London (1662–66) as a portraitist but made a name for himself with his perspective devices, one of which was admired by Pepys (19 January 1663) in Mr. Pavy's closet: see Waterhouse, *Painting in Britain,* p. 77, and Clotilde Misme, "Deux 'boites-à-perspective' hollandais du XVIIᵉ siècle," *Gazette des Beaux-arts* 5 (1925): 155–66.

20 Lily B. Campbell, *Scenes and Machines on the English Stage* (1923: rpt. New York: Barnes and Noble, 1960), pp. 22–24 and passim. Daniello Barbaro, the translator of Vitruvius's *De architectura,* was Venetian ambassador in London, 1548–49.

21 In five books, written between 1536 and 1547; book 2 published in Paris, 1545. The English translation, used here, is *The First [-fift] Booke of Architecture, made by Sebastian Serly . . . translated out of Italian, and out of Dutch into English* (London, 1611).

22 Serlio, *Book of Architecture,* 2: 3, 24.

23 Finished in 1584, designed by Barbaro and Palladio; seen by Coryate (*Crudities,* 2: 86–87) and Inigo Jones (see Campbell, *Scenes and Machines,* p. 55).

24 Serlio, *Book of Architecture,* 2: 3, 24.

25 Stephen Orgel and Roy Strong, *Inigo Jones: The Theatre of the Stuart Court,* 2 vols. (Berkeley: Sotheby Parke Bernet and the University of California Press, 1973), 1: 9.

26 Orgel and Strong, *Inigo Jones,* 1: 7.

27 *Ben Jonson: The Complete Masques,* ed. Stephen Orgel (New Haven and London: Yale University Press, 1969), p. 192.

28 *Ben Jonson,* ed. Herford and Simpson, 8: 93, 404.

29 Dubreuil, *Perspective pratique,* 7: 155.

CHAPTER 3

1 On "wit" and the galaxy of shifting terms around it see George Williamson, "Strong Lines," *English Studies* 18 (1936): 152–59, and *The Proper Wit of Poetry* (London: Faber and Faber, 1961), pp. 11–21 and passim; Richard E. Hughes, "'Wit'": The Genealogy of a Theory," *College Language Association Journal* 5 (1961):142–144; Tayler, ed., *Literary Criticism of Seventeenth-Century England,* pp. 3–32; and K. K. Ruthven, *The Conceit,* The Critical Idiom Series, gen. ed. John D. Jump (London: Methuen, 1969), pp. 17–52.

2 See Joseph A. Mazzeo, *Renaissance and Seventeenth-Century Studies* (New York: Columbia University Press, 1964), the second and third chapters especially, and S. L. Bethell, "Gracián, Tesauro, and the Nature of Metaphysical Wit," *The Northern Miscellany of Literary Criticism* 1 (1953): 19–40.

3 *Poetics* 1457b, 1459a; *Rhetoric,* 3 in the Loeb Classical Library edition, trans. J. H. Freese (London and New York, 1926), pp. 405–09.

4 Emmanuele Tesauro, *Il Cannocchiale Aristotelico* (Torino, 1670). Cited hereafter as Tesauro. All citations refer to this edition; the translations are my own. P. 61: "metaphoriche Argutezze di Dio," p. 63: "fisica attione . . . in se contien molte symboliche, & concettosi Argutezze."

5 Baldessare Castiglione, *Book of the Courtier* (1: 35), trans. Charles S. Singleton (Garden City: Doubleday Anchor Books, 1959), p. 58; George Puttenham, *The Arte of English Poesie* (1589), Scolar Press Facsimile Edition (Menston, England, 1968), pp. 128, 148–49.

6 Tesauro, p. 491: "l'unica loda delle Argutezze, consistere nel saper ben mentire," and p. 447: "il Concetto altro non è, che un Entimema Urbanamente fallace."

7 "The Good-morrow," ll. 19–21.

8 Robert E. Proctor, Emmanuele Tesauro's *Il Cannocchiale Aristotelico:* A Study of the Lie in the Arts (Ph.D. diss. Johns Hopkins, 1971), pp. 155 et passim. For another dissent from the "correspondence" theory of wit, see Eugenio Donato, "Tesauro's Poetics: Through the Looking Glass," *Modern Language Notes* 78 (1963): 15–30.

9 Tesauro, pp. 82–83: ". . . l'Ingegno e piu perspicace; la Prudenza è più sensata: quello è più veloce; questa è più salda: quello considera le apparenze; questra la verità: & dove questa hà per fine la propria utilità; quello ambisce l'ammiratione & l'applauso de' populari. Quinci, non senza qualche ragione gli Huomini ingegnosi fur chiamati Divini. Peroche, secome Iddio di quel che non è, produce quel che è: cosi l'ingegno, de non Ente, fà Ente: fà che il Leone divenga un Huomo; & l'Aquila un Città. Inesta una Femina sopra un Pesce; & fabrica una Sirena per Simbolo dell'Adultore. Accoppia un busto de Capra al deretano di un Serpe; & forma la Chimera per Hieroglifico della Pazzia. Onde fra gli antiqui Filosofi, alcuni chiamorono l'Ingegno, Particella della Mente Divina: & altri un regalo mandato de Iddio à suoi più cari."

10 Tesauro, p. 73: "formidabili Argutie & Simboliche Opere della Natura, mute insieme & vocale; havendo la Saetta per corpo, e il Tuono per motto."

11 I am here indebted to the introduction to an unpublished translation of selections of the *Cannocchiale* by David Gullette of Simmons College.

12 Tesauro, p. 82: "La Perspicacia penetra le più lontane & minute Circonstanze di ogni suggetto; come Sostanza, Materia, Forma, Accidente, Proprietà, Cagioni, Effetti, Fini, Simpatie, il Simile, il Contrario, l'Uguale, il Superiore, l'Inferiore, le Insegne, i Nomi propri, & gli Equivochi: lequali cose giacciono in qualunque suggetto aggomitolate & ascose. . . . La VERSABILITÀ, velocemente raffronta tutte queste Circonstanza infra loro, ò col Suggetto: le annoda ò divide; le cresce ò minuisce; deduce l'una dall'altra; accenna l'una per l'altra; & con maravigliosa destrezza

pon l'una in luogo dell'altra, come i Giocolieri i lor calcoli. Et questa è la Metafora, Madre delle Poesie, de Simboli, e delle Imprese."

13 Tesauro, p. 107.

14 Tesauro, p. 89: "Argutissime finale sono le OPTICHE; lequali per certe proportioni de prospettiva, con istrane & ingegnose apparenza ti fan vedere ciò che non vedi."

15 Tesauro, pp. 89–90: " . . . con due ale di vetro, portò la vista humana per una forata canna la dove ucello non giunge. Con essi tragitta il mar senza vele: ti fà veder di presso le pupilla: anzi volando al Cielo in un lampo; osserva le macchie nel sole; scopre le Corna de Vulcano in Fronte a Venere: misura I Monti ei Mari nel globo della luna: numera i pargoletti di Giove: & ciò che Iddio ci nascose, un piccol vetro ti revela."

16 Tesauro, p. 301: " . . . la Metafora, tutti à stretta li rinzeppa in un Vocabolo: & quali in miraculoso modo gli ti fà travedere l'un dentro all'altro. Onde maggiore è il tuo diletto: nella maniera, che più curiosa & piacevol cosa è mirar molti obietti per un' istràfóro di perspettiva, che se gli originali medesimi successivamente ti venisser passando dinanzi ogli occhi. Opera (come dice il nostro Autore) non di stupido, ma di acutissime ingegno." See Mario Praz, *The Flaming Heart,* p. 207 and note.

17 "Veste le parole medesime de Concetti": see Bethell, "Gracian, Tesauro," pp. 28–29, and Proctor, "Tesauro's *Il Cannocchiale,*" p. 84.

18 *The Poems and Letters of Andrew Marvell,* ed. H. M. Margoliouth, 3rd ed. (Oxford: Clarendon Press, 1971), 1: 21, ll. 1–4. Cited hereafter as Margoliouth. Ruth Wallerstein notes that these lines would immediately have invoked such popular emblems as that in Herman Hugo's *Pia Desideria* (Antwerp, 1645), of a child's soul imprisoned in a skeleton: see her *Seventeenth-Century Poetic* (Madison: University of Wisconsin Press, 1950), p. 154.

19 *The Metaphysical Poets,* ed. Helen Gardner (Baltimore: Penguin Books, 1966), pp. 110–11.

20 *The Flaming Heart,* p. 207n.

21 The motto is slightly changed from Horace's "egregio inspersos reprehendas corpore naevos" (*Satires,* 1: 6, 67), "[even as] you might reprove blemishes on a perfect body."

CHAPTER 4

1 William S. Heckscher, "Shakespeare and his Relationship to the Visual Arts," *Research Opportunities in Renaissance Drama* 13–14 (1970–71); John M. Steadman, "Falstaff as Acteon: A Dramatic Emblem," *SQ* 14 (1963); and Ann Haacker, *"Non Sine Causa*: The Use of Emblematic Method and Iconology in the Thematic Structure of *Titus Andronicus," RORD* 13–14 (1970–71).

2 E.g., Arnold Hauser's case for a Mannerist Shakespeare in *Mannerism: The Crisis of the Renaissance and the Origin of Modern Art,* 2 vols. (London: Routledge and Kegan Paul, 1965), 1: 342. On staging, see Mark Rose, *Shakespearean Design* (Cambridge: Harvard University Press, 1972), W. Moelwyn Merchant, *Shakespeare and the Artist* (London: Oxford University Press, 1959), and Robert Speaight, *Shakespeare on the Stage* (Boston: Little, Brown, 1973).

3 The fullest treatment of "perspectives" in Richard II is in Claudio Guillén, "On the Concept and Metaphor of Perspective," pp. 42–47; Guillén is mainly concerned with the metaphor as a means of visualizing grief.

4 In Mark Van Doren's phrase: *Shakespeare* (New York: Doubleday, 1953), p. 68. The Pelican editor glosses line 201: "'yes, no; no, yes, but also 'I, no; no, I'" (p. 659*n.*). The line is also *heard* as "I know no I."

5 2.2.19 is variously punctuated in different editions of the play— a detail which reflects the difficulty of the conceit. See *Richard II*, ed. Matthew Black, The Variorum Shakespeare, vol. 27 (Philadelphia: Lippincott, 1955), p. 137.

6 Variorum *Richard II,* pp. 137–38, note on l. 22.

7 *Self-consuming Artifacts,* p. 188. The lines from Herbert are: "And yet since these thy contradictions/are properly a crosse felt by thy Sonne,/With but foure words, my words, *Thy will be done.*"

8 *Cypress Grove* (1623), cited in Guillén, "On the Concept and Metaphor of Perspective," p. 42, Cf. Bacon: "It hath been an opinion that the French are wiser than they seem, and the Spaniards seem wiser than they are. . . . It is a ridiculous thing . . . to see what shifts these formalists have, and what pro-

spectives to make superficies to seem body that hath depth and bulk." *Essays* (1625), quoted in Guillén, p. 43. For the same sense, see Face's description of a "perspective" for cozening in Jonson's *The Alchemist* (3.2).

9 *The Advancement of Learning*, 2.8.1, cited in the OED under "Perspective."

10 *Monadologie*, no. 57 in *Oeuvres Philosophiques de Leibniz*, ed. P. Janet (Paris, 1900), 1: 716 (cited in Guillén, "On the Concept and Metaphor of Perspective," p. 53).

11 Cited in Guillén, "On the Concept and Metaphor of Perspective," pp. 55–56 (my translation): "C'est comme dans les inventions de perspective, où certain beaux dessins ne paraissent que confusion, jusqu'à ce qu'on rapporte à leur vrai point de vue, ou qu'on les regarde par le moyen d'un certain verre ou miroir. . . . Ainsi les déformités apparentes de nos petits mondes se réunissent en beautes dans le grand, et n'ont rien qui si'oppose à l'unité d'un principe universellement parfait."

12 *Shakespeare and the Common Understanding* (New York: Free Press, 1967), p. 12.

13 Chambers in 1891 suggested Holbein as a possible source of Shakespeare's lines (Variorum *Richard II*, p. 137*n*.). William Heckscher also mentions Holbein in connection with the metaphor in *Richard II* ("Shakespeare and his Relationship," pp. 10, 21). Hentzner saw the anamorphic *Edward VI* in Whitehall in 1598 (see p. 55 above); it is possible that *The Ambassadors*, of which the Edward portrait is a kind of technical imitation, also was displayed for a time in Whitehall. The "ambassador" Dinteville took his portrait back to France. It remained there until 1787, when Lebrun bought it and resold it in England. The National Gallery acquired it in 1890. Henry VIII employed Holbein in the reconstruction of Whitehall, which is known to have housed other works by the artist including the great fresco of Henry with his parents and Jane Seymour that was destroyed in the fire of 1698: see James B. Shaw, "The Perspective Picture," p. 213. My discussion of Holbein is indebted to G. H. Villiers, *Hans Holbein: The Ambassadors*, Gallery Books, no. 18 (London: Humphries, n.d.).

14 *Unterweysung der Messung* (1525), reproduced in H. W. Janson,

History of Art (Englewood Cliffs, N.J.: Prentice-Hall, 1967), p. 392.

15 See Fabrizio Clerici, "The Grand Illusion: Some Considerations of Perspective, Illusionism, and Trompe-l'oeil," *Art News Annual* 23 (1954): 98–180, esp. pp. 135–41, 152–57.

16 See Alciatus, *Emblemata* (1531).

17 Reproduced in Baltrušaitis, *Anamorphoses,* fig. 69, p. 101.

18 From the title of Cornelius Agrippa's *Declamatio* (1530).

19 Agrippa had included perspective as one of the deceptions of the arts and sciences because it deals with false appearances.

20 Edward Hall, *Union of the two Noble and Illustrate Families of Lancastre & Yorke* (1548), quoted in Geoffrey Bullough, *Narrative and Dramatic Sources of Shakespeare* (London: Routledge and Kegan Paul, 1960), 3: 16–17.

21 Hall, *Union,* quoted in Bullough, *Narrative and Dramatic Sources,* p. 68; Raphaell Holinshed, *The Chronicles of England* (1587), vol. 3, quoted in Bullough, pp. 402, 409.

22 Lily Campbell, *Shakespeare's "Histories"* (San Marino: The Huntington Library, 1947), p. 206.

23 *Anglican Homily* 23 (1573), quoted in Bullough, *Narrative and Dramatic Sources,* p. 378. See Alfred Hart, *Shakespeare and the Homilies* (Melbourne: Melbourne University Press, 1934).

24 *The King's Two Bodies: A Study in Medieval Political Theology* (Princeton: Princeton University Press, 1957).

25 Edmund Plowden's *Reports,* quoted in Kantorowicz, *The King's Two Bodies,* p. 7.

26 Kantorowicz, *The King's Two Bodies,* p. 40.

27 R. F. Hill, "Dramatic Techniques and Interpretation in 'Richard the Second,'" in J. R. Brown and B. Harris, eds., *Early Shakespeare* (London: Edward Arnold, 1961, reprinted New York: Schocken, 1966), p. 121.

28 Reproduced in Kantorowicz, *The King's Two Bodies,* figures 28, 30, 31.

29 *Shakespeare and the Energies of Drama* (Princeton: Princeton University Press, 1972).

30 E. M. W. Tillyard, *Shakespeare's History Plays* (1944; rpt. New York: Barnes and Noble, 1964).

31 Bullough, *Narrative and Dramatic Sources,* pp. 409–10.

CHAPTER 5

1 Nicholas Hilliard, "The Arte of Limning," ed. Philip Norman in the *First Annual Volume of the Walpole Society,* 1911–12 (Oxford: Clarendon Press, 1912), p. 20.

2 These illusions, though only a fanciful adornment to the power of the royal audience, could claim an important authority in their own right: the power to make the ideal virtues celebrated in the masque more palpable, more concretely perceptible, than they can ever be off the platform. Even as it fictionalizes its audience by transforming their most illustrious members into Venus or Oberon, the masque reciprocally realizes its own artifice: see the introduction to Orgel and Strong, *Inigo Jones.*

3 Sebastiano Serlio's influential *Architettura* was available in England in several versions before an English translation came out in 1611. Richard Haydocke's translation of Lomazzo's *Trattato* was published in London in 1598. See Sven Sandström, *Levels of Unreality* (Uppsala: Almquist and Wiksell, 1963) p. 102.

4 *La perspective, avec la raison des ombres et miroirs . . .* (London, 1612), n.p.

5 Haydocke, *A Tracte,* pp. 188–89; Henry Peacham, *The Gentleman's Exercise,* p. 336 of the 1661 edition; Edward Norgate, *Miniatura,* p. 51.

6 For the illustionistic trickery of Bernini's theatrical spectacles, see Filippo Baldinucci's *Life of Bernini* (1682), trans. Catherine Enggass (University Park, Pa.: Penn State University Press, 1966), pp. 83–84. See also Peter Schwenger, "Crashaw's Perspectivist Metaphor," *Comparative Literature* 28, no. 1 (1976): 65–74.

7 *The Painting of the Ancients* (London, 1638), pp. 54–55.

8 *Scot's discoverie of Witchcraft* (1584), quoted in *Twelfe Night,* ed. H. H. Furness, The Variorum Shakespeare, vol. 13 (Philadelphia, 1901), p. 299.

9 Scot, quoted in Variorum *Twelfe Night,* p. 300.

10 John Harington's 1591 translation of *Orlando Furioso* has 46 plates. About these illustrations, says the translator, "one thing is to be noted, which every one (haply) will not observe, namely the perspective in every figure. For the personages of the men, the shapes of horses, and such like, are made large at the bot-

tome, and lesser upward, as if you were to behold all the same in a plaine, that which is nearest seems greatest, and the fardest shewes smallest, which is the chief art in picture." Quoted in T. S. R. Boase, "Illustrations of Shakespeare's Plays," *Journal of the Warburg and Courtauld Institutes* 10 (1947): 84. The boast, the felt need for a definition, and the awkwardness of that definition suggest that perspective was another continental refinement Englishmen were learning to appreciate in the 1590s. Orgel and Strong believe that, a generation later, some members of Inigo Jones's audience who were bored or put off by the masque were in fact not seeing the perspective sets correctly (*Inigo Jones*, pp. 11–12).

11 *News from the New World Discovered on the Moon*, in *Ben Jonson: The Complete Masques*, p. 295.

12 Scot, quoted in the Variorum *Twelfe Night*, p. 300.

13 Thomas Nashe, *The Unfortunate Traveller and other Works*, ed. J. B. Steane (Baltimore, 1972), pp. 297–98.

14 *Friar Bacon and Friar Bungay*, ed. J. A. Lavin, The New Mermaids (London, 1969), scene 13, ll. 27–28. All citations are from this edition.

15 *Ben Jonson*, ed. Herford and Simpson, 8: 93, 403.

16 *Friar Bacon* was written c. 1589–90. For the question of influence, see Norman Sanders, "The Comedy of Greene and Shakespeare," in Brown and Harris, eds., *Early Shakespeare*, pp. 35–54. See also William Empson, *Some Versions of Pastoral* (1935; reprinted Norfolk, Conn.: New Directions, 1960), pp. 29–31.

17 *The Arte of English Poesie*, p. 128.

18 Frank Kermode, "The Mature Comedies," in Brown and Harris, *Early Shakespeare*, p. 219.

19 Barber, *Shakespeare's Festive Comedy* (Princeton: Princeton University Press, 1967); Rabkin, *Shakespeare and the Common Understanding;* Terrence Hawkes, *Shakespeare and the Reason* (New York: Humanities Press, 1965).

20 Ernest Schanzer, "The Central Theme of *A Midsummer Night's Dream*," *University of Toronto Quarterly* 20, no. 3 (April 1951): 233–38.

21 Paul A. Olson, "*A Midsummer Night's Dream* and the Meaning of Court Marriage," *English Literary History* 24 (1957): 98–119.

22 D. P. Young, *Something of Great Constancy* (New Haven and London: Yale University Press, 1966).

23 Oscar J. Campbell, ed., *Reader's Encyclopedia of Shakespeare* (New York: Crowell, 1966), pp. 545–48.

24 Kermode, "The Mature Comedies," p. 216; Rabkin, *Shakespeare and the Common Understanding*, p. 205.

25 "The Marriage of Theseus and Hippolyta," *Kenyon Review* 18 (1956): 633–41.

26 Michael McCanles offers an incisive discussion of the play that parallels my own here and at other points, within a more general treatment: "The Literal and the Metaphorical: Dialetic and Interchange," *PMLA* 91 (1976): 281–84.

27 Grierson, 1: 15.

28 See Robert Egan, *Drama Within Drama* (New York: Columbia University Press, 1975).

CHAPTER 6

1 So, for example, in Cesare Ripa's *Iconologia* (1603): see Edward A. Maser, ed., *Cesare Ripa: Baroque and Rococo Pictorial Imagery* (New York: Dover, 1971), p. 110. In the French Unicorn tapestries (c. 1480–90) "sight" is represented by a lady holding a hand mirror which reflects the face of the unicorn, the symbol of Christ.

2 Heinrich Schwartz, "The Mirror of the Artist and the Mirror of the Devout," in *Studies in the History of Art Dedicated to William E. Suida on his Eightieth Birthday* (London: Phaidon, 1959), pp. 90–105.

3 G. P. Lomazzo, *L'idea del tiempo della pittura* (1590), trans. E. G. Holt, in *A Documentary History of Art* (Garden City, New York: Doubleday, 1958), 2: 82. The passage is a literal borrowing from Ficino's commentary on the *Symposium*.

4 For Ripa, Prudence (see Maser, ed., *Cesare Ripa*, p. 179) as well as knowledge (p. 188) are both personified as female figures holding hand mirrors. For the Narcissus motif and the iconology of the mirror see G. F. Hartlaub, *Zauber des Spiegels* (Munich: Piper Verlag, 1951), pp. 86–102, and Frederick Goldin, *The Mirror of Narcissus in the Courtly Love Lyric* (Ithaca: Cornell University Press, 1967).

5 *The Sermons of John Donne,* ed. Evelyn M. Simpson and George R. Potter (Berkeley: University of California Press, 1956), 8: 219.

6 Ibid., p. 220.

7 Ibid., p. 230.

8 Ibid., p. 226.

9 Ibid., p. 219.

10 *Paradiso,* 33: 121–22, 55–66, in *The Divine Comedy of Dante Alighieri: Paradiso,* trans. John D. Sinclair (1939; rpt., New York: Oxford University Press, 1969).

11 *Paradiso,* 33: 133–36.

12 *Confessions,* 10: 1, trans. R. S. Pine-Coffin (1961; rpt. Baltimore: Penguin, 1964).

13 Ibid., 10: 5.

14 Ibid., 10: 8.

15 John Calvin, *Institutions,* 2: 7, trans. Thomas Norton (1634): cited by Geoffrey Bullough in his edition *Poems and Dramas of Fulke Greville, First Lord Brooke* (New York: Oxford University Press, 1945), 1: 279.

16 "Vanity of Spirit," ll. 19–34, in *The Complete Poetry of Henry Vaughan,* ed. French Fogle (1964: rpt. New York: Norton, 1969), p. 168. Cited hereafter as Fogle.

17 *Religio Medici,* 1: 49; 1: 13 in *The Prose of Sir Thomas Browne,* ed. Norman J. Endicott, Anchor Seventeenth-Century Series (New York: Doubleday, 1967), pp. 57, 18.

18 "Resurrection and Immortality," ll. 51–55, p. 146, in Fogle; "They are all gone into the world of light!" ll. 37–40, p. 271.

19 *The Complete Poems of Sir John Davies,* ed. Reverend Alexander B. Grosart (London: Chatto and Windus, 1876), p. 83.

20 John Davies of Hereford, "Sonet 1" ("If in a three-square glasse, as thick as cleare"), in *Select Poetry, Chiefly Devotional of the Reign of Queen Elizabeth,* ed. Edward Farr (Cambridge: Parker Society, n.d.). Cf. William Alabaster's distinction between beholding the Passion through "the common eye" and "through tears": "Like as in optick works, one thing appears / In open gaze, in closer otherwise. / Then since tears see the best I ask in tears. . . ." (*The Sonnets of William Alabaster* ed. G. M. Story and Helen Gardner [London: Oxford University Press, 1959], p. 39).

21 The poem is in Grierson, 1: 271–79.

22 Grierson, 1: 352, ll. 43, 45–48.

23 Grierson, 1: 14–15, ll. 45, 40, 42–43.

24 Grierson reports Jonson's remark to Drummond, 2: 187. "An Anatomy of the World, The first Anniversary" appears in Grierson, 1: 231–45, and "Of the Progresse of the Soule. The Second Anniversarie" in 1: 251–66.

25 See Louis J. Martz, *The Poetry of Meditation,* rev. ed. (New Haven and London: Yale University Press, 1962), esp. chapter 6, pp. 211–48.

26 All quotations from Herbert's poetry are taken from *The Works of George Herbert,* ed. F. E. Hutchinson (London: Oxford University Press, 1941), cited hereafter as Hutchinson. "The Elixir," ll. 1–2, 9–12; p. 184.

27 "Ungratefulnesse," ll. 16–18, Hutchinson, p. 82.

28 "Sinne II," Hutchinson, p. 63.

29 "Justice (II)," ll. 1–5, 13–14, Hutchinson, p. 141.

30 "Hope," l. 4, Hutchinson, p. 121.

31 "The H. Scriptures (I)" ll. 8–9, Hutchinson, p. 58.

32 "The Windows," ll. 2–5, Hutchinson, p. 67.

33 Hutchinson, pp. 84–85.

34 "The Sonne," ll. 5–6, Hutchinson, p. 168.

35 Ibid., ll. 3–4.

36 "The Sacrifice," Hutchinson, pp. 26–34; cited by line numbers in the text.

37 *OED,* s.v. "Wind."

38 All quotations from Greville's *Caelica* are taken from the edition by Bullough, cited above, and are noted in the text by the number of the poem in that sequence, and the line.

39 *Religio Medici,* 1: 11, in Endicott, ed., *Prose of Sir Thomas Browne,* p. 16.

40 *The Anatomy of Melancholy,* ed. Floyd Dell and Paul Jordan-Smith (New York: Tudor, 1927), pp. 131–39.

41 *Anatomy,* p. 139.

CHAPTER 7

1 Empson, "Marvell's Garden," in *Some Versions of Pastoral;* Colie, *"My Ecchoing Song,"* p. 262; T. S. Eliot, "Andrew Mar-

vell," *Selected Essays,* new ed. (New York: Harcourt, Brace and World, 1950; London: Faber & Faber, 1950), rpt. in *Andrew Marvell: A Collection of Critical Essays,* ed. George deF. Lord (Englewood Cliffs, N.J.: Prentice-Hall, 1968), p. 27.

2 Ll. 668–69. All quotations from "Upon Appleton House" are from Margoliouth, 1: 62–86.

3 See Margoliouth, p. 285, notes on ll. 395–96.

4 Van der Doort's *Catalogs* (pp. 107, 123). See chapter 2, note 7.

5 Kitty Scoular, *Natural Magic: Studies in the Presentation of Nature in English Poetry from Spenser to Marvell* (New York and London: Oxford University Press, 1965), pp. 121–90, esp. pp. 188–90; Rosalie Colie, *Paradoxia Epidemica: The Renaissance Tradition of Paradox* (Princeton: Princeton University Press, 1966), pp. 273–304; *"My Ecchoing Song,"* esp. pp. 188–214, 278.

6 Colie, *"My Ecchoing Song,"* pp. 205–06. The Ruisdael landscape and the illustration from Hooke are reproduced in her figures 42 and 44.

7 *El museo pictorico* (1724); see Enrique La Fuente, ed., *Velásquez: Complete Edition* (London: Phaidon; New York: Oxford University Press, 1943), p. 31.

8 *Las Hilanderas* or *The Spinners* (c. 1644–48) in the Prado.

9 The motif of a mirror reflecting figures in front of the picture plane and not otherwise represented in the painting appears most notably, before Velázquez, in Jan Van Eyck's *Giovanni Arnolfini and his Bride* (1434, The National Gallery). Here a convex mirror on the rear wall shows the back of the bridal pair and two men entering the room at the opposite end; but the masterful image is unobtrusive and unproblematic—except that, even more than the mirror in *Las Meninas,* it defines a closed space, a chamber with all four walls visible, and therefore with no room for the viewer or the artist. The picture could well have been a model for *Las Meninas,* since it was in the Spanish Royal Collections during Velázquez's lifetime. See Jose Lopez-Rey, *Velázquez' Work and World* (Greenwich, Ct.: New York Graphic Society, 1969), p. 137.

10 Lopez-Rey, *Velázquez' Work,* pp. 135–36n. For the differing interpretations and puzzlements generated by this remarkable painting, see for example: Dale Brown, *World of Velásquez,*

1599–1660 (New York: Time-Life Books, 1969), pp. 105 f.; Jon E. White, *Diego Velázquez: Painter and Courtier* (London: Hamilton, 1969), pp. 140–47; and the brilliant and difficult essay by Michel Foucault, "Las Meninas," the first chapter of his *The Order of Things* (New York: Random House, 1970), pp. 3–16. The Chinese-box effect of the painter painting a painter painting may be found in Vermeer's *The Artist in his Atelier*. Colie describes it in a suitably paradoxical vein: "Vermeer has painted a picture of an artist painting a picture . . . of the allegory of fame; or Vermeer has painted a painter painting his own fame, or of a painter imitating what in fact, Vermeer was doing when he painted the picture." See *Paradoxia Epidemica,* p. 358.

11 Marvell's lines 441–42 (This Scene again withdrawing brings/A new and empty Face of things") may be compared with the typical scenic directions of the masque—for example, with Carew's "The Scaene againe is varied into a new and pleasant prospect, cleane differing from all the other. . . ." (*Coelum Britannicum,* ll. 1011–13, in *Poems of Thomas Carew,* ed. Rhodes Dunlop [Oxford: Clarendon Press, 1949], p. 181).

12 See Maren-Sofie Røstvig, *The Happy Man: Studies in the Metamorphoses of a Classical Ideal* (Oxford: Blackwell, 1954), 1: 243–66.

13 Margoliouth, p. 290, note on line 616.

CONCLUSION

1 "The Mower against Gardens" l. 9, in Margoliouth, p. 41.

2 *Religio Medici,* 1: 34, in Endicott, ed., *Prose of Sir Thomas Browne,* pp. 41–42.

3 "An Essay on Criticism," ll. 297, 299–300, in *The Poems of Alexander Pope,* ed. John Butt (New Haven and London: Yale University Press, 1966), p. 153.

4 Ll. 247, 249–52, *Poems,* pp. 151–52.

5 *Religio Medici,* 1: 9, in Endicott, ed., *Prose of Sir Thomas Browne,* p. 14.

Index